Andrew Buckoke was born in 1955 in Havant, England. He was educated at Malvern College, Worcestershire, and Fitzwilliam College, Cambridge. He started to travel as a freelance foreign correspondent in 1979, writing first from Sri Lanka. In 1980 he went to Zimbabwe for a year. In 1983 he moved to Tanzania, where he represented the *Guardian*, *Economist*, and *Observer* for three years. Subsequently he moved to Nairobi where he reported for the *Financial Times* and later he worked as East Africa correspondent for *The Times*. *Fishing in Africa* is his first book.

Andrew Buckoke

Fishing in Africa

A guide to war and corruption

A Picador original

First published 1991 by Pan Books Ltd
This revised paperback edition first published
with a new epilogue 1992 by
Pan Books Ltd, Cavaye Place, London SW10 9PG

9 8 7 6 5 4

© Andrew Buckoke 1991, 1992
© Maps Alan Mais 1991

ISBN 0 330 31896 9

Phototypeset by Input Typesetting Ltd, London
Printed in England by Cox & Wyman Ltd, Reading, Berkshire

To my parents,

for tolerating my long and
unexplained absences

Contents

List of maps

There are peoples that have lost the power of astonishment at their own actions. When they give birth to a fantastic passion or foolish law, they do not start or stare at the monster they have brought forth . . . These nations are really in danger of going off their heads *en masse*, of becoming one vast vision of imbecility, with toppling cities and crazy countrysides, all dotted with industrious lunatics.

G. K. Chesterton, *The Mad Official*

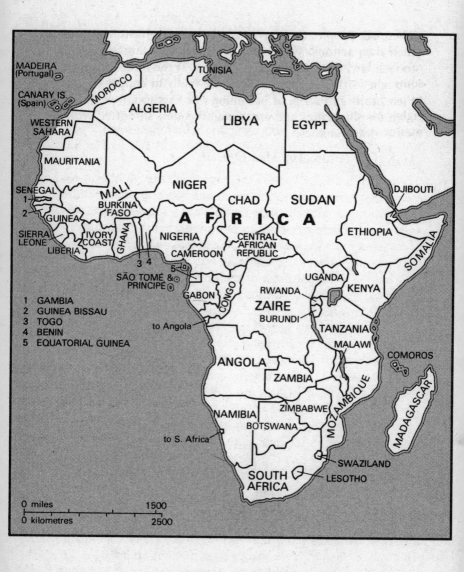

MADEIRA
(Portugal)

CANARY IS.
(Spain)

WESTERN
SAHARA

MAURITANIA

SENEGAL
1
2
GUINEA

SIERRA
LEONE
LIBERIA

MOROCCO

ALGERIA

MALI
BURKINA
FASO
IVORY
COAST
GHANA

TUNISIA

LIBYA

NIGER

A F R I C A

NIGERIA

CAMEROON

EGYPT

CHAD

SUDAN

CENTRAL
AFRICAN
REPUBLIC

DJIBOUTI

ETHIOPIA

SOMALIA

3 4
5
SÃO TOMÉ &
PRINCIPE

GABON

1   GAMBIA
2   GUINEA BISSAU
3   TOGO
4   BENIN
5   EQUATORIAL GUINEA

to Angola

CONGO

ZAIRE

UGANDA
RWANDA
BURUNDI

KENYA

TANZANIA

MALAWI

COMOROS

ANGOLA

ZAMBIA

ZIMBABWE

MOZAMBIQUE

MADAGASCAR

to S. Africa

NAMIBIA

BOTSWANA

SWAZILAND

SOUTH
AFRICA

LESOTHO

0 miles   1500
0 kilometres   2500

Introduction

I was probably the first and may be the last person to carry a fly-rod around the mountains of northern Eritrea. The secessionist rebels, who controlled the area, were curious as to its purpose, some suspecting it was a radio antenna. Explaining what it was to people suffering the deprivations and savagery of a twenty-eight-year-old war for independence, which I had come to cover, was embarrassing. My colleague and fellow fisherman Philip Williams, who had the more concealable reel and flies in his bag, relished my discomfiture.

We both felt like fools by the end of the trip. Whoever told us there were trout in the northern mountains apparently had them sadly confused with the Bale mountains in southern Ethiopia, where magnificent trout are to be caught, but you have to beware of falling cows. A senior relief official was injured by one that fell from the bank above while he was fishing there.

In Eritrea we spent most of the time driving in darkness along the rivers we thought we might have fished. We travelled at night to avoid the Ethiopian MiGs, whose accuracy if they came across an errant vehicle during the day was legendary. We drove in the rivers because the dry beds are the easiest places to build roads in the precipitous landscape. Sheer rockfaces often come straight down to the sides. Most only have water in them during extremely brief flash floods, of which you have to be wary as there may be no sign of rain when one arrives.

We were aware of the possibility one rainy afternoon, driving along a riverbed in daylight with the MiGs grounded by the weather. We came round a corner to see a tongue of brown water streaking towards us. The driver just had time to swing up on to a patch of higher ground. We sat for an hour watching the torrent go by, and listening to the boulders grumbling along on the bottom. As soon as it stopped the rebels were out clearing the larger boulders from the track to make it passable again. This was a regular chore throughout the mountains.

We did see one rise in Eritrea. I noticed a dimple in a tiny permanent pool in a riverbed road as we waited for darkness to allow us to travel again. Crawling up to investigate, I found the little pool full of tadpoles, which would occasionally wriggle up to the surface to take a tiny insect. I called Philip over, and we discovered they were easily deceived by tiny pieces of grass. We were discussing the possibility of using miniature rods and flies on them when Goytom, our guide, came up to tell us we could set off again. An Ethiopian bomber dropped napalm at a car ahead of us on the road that evening. Fortunately it missed, as the Norwegians on board gave us a lift two days later across the desert between the sea and the Red Sea Hills that leads back into Sudan.

It is fortunate that the Eritreans have a sense of humour. Our follies about fishing and other things were greeted with tolerant amusement. Some were themselves interested. A member of the central committee of the rebel movement, the Eritrean People's Liberation Front, mentioned his hopes for deep sea fishing along Eritrea's Red Sea coast. If the war ever comes to an end, the possibilities should be great. The Ethiopians have declared the coast a free fire zone, so Eritrean coastal waters are virtually a marine reserve.

It may seem unfeeling to mention fishing in areas of Africa devastated by war or famine, but for eight years as a journalist in Africa fishing has been a refuge from the horrors of a continent liable to make one callous as well as a window into its humanities. It should also be noted that the potential of sport fishing as a source of income is great in many parts of Africa, and that I have sat on the banks of rivers full of fish in the midst of famines.

An interest in fishing has also helped me to get closer to people preoccupied with other things, usually unpleasant. A man with a fishing rod is much less suspect than a man with a camera. Even on trips where a rod would have been completely out of place it seemed that asking about the local fishing reminded people of the simpler, more reflective side of life. Sometimes, for instance in Khartoum when everybody was screaming that the city was about to be washed away, such a question provided the key to understanding what was really happening. If the fishermen were happy, it seemed unlikely that Armageddon was around the corner. I could not convince my editors of that, but tales of impending doom sell more newspapers, and it is embarrassing to print an article saying that actually the story that we made such a fuss of over the last few days was greatly exaggerated. This is one of the reasons I decided to write this book. Fishing brought me closer to Africa than a relentless pursuit of sensationalism would allow. I developed an affection for the basket-case continent, and that affection made me want to put the wars and famines and disasters in context.

To start with there are a lot of people in Africa. I considered making this point by writing this book without mentioning the animals – apart from an occasional fish – at all. I decided this was too subtle a way of illustrating the disregard for Africans displayed, at its most extreme, by those obsessed with the continent's wildlife. It is from such disregard for Africa's people that acceptance and even foreign support for its dictatorships arises. And it is from these dictatorships that the threat to the animals and traditional tribes, as well as to the bulk of semi-educated, semi-urbanized Africans, arises.

Following the events in Eastern Europe there has been talk of democracy in many of the sub-Saharan black African countries which are the subject of this book, talk of allowing more than the sole ruling party that has remained the norm. There has been little more than talk. There have been a few demonstrations, a few dubious promises, even a couple of dubious polls, but until Africa is accepted as part of the real world any reforms are likely to be cosmetic. They are likely to be just sufficient to allow governments, aid donors, relief agency staff and others who benefit from the *status quo* to continue following their own ends.

Some of the supposed reformers of the late eighties were particularly absurd. Could we really imagine President Mengistu of Ethiopia – who was reputed to have solved cabinet arguments by shooting dissenting ministers – bowing to the dictates of a democratic constitution, even after he exchanged the coarse cotton of his Marxist days for a free-market pinstripe as Soviet support dried up? Could we really take ex-President Julius Nyerere of Tanzania seriously when he suggested a multi-party system might be desirable – as long as all the parties were socialist? Probably Dr Nyerere, the retired but still charismatic socialist despot, and his cronies in the sole ruling party just wanted to keep the aid rolling in and hoped yet again to pull the wool over the donors' eyes.

The blood and tears resulting from the lack of genuine reform will continue to give the foreign media the material to cater for their consumers' tendency to voyeurism, supplying occasional visions of violence and suffering in some safely distant and amusingly primitive Africa. Western governments and aid organizations can push for more significant reform, but are unlikely to do so as long as Africa remains peripheral to their constituents' concerns, a place of spectacular wildlife and tragedy, and most of all of myth. The aim of this book is to dispel myth.

Lack of space and interest combines with a short attention span to prevent most newspapers from putting stories about Africa in context. Television has an even more limited capacity to explain, tempted as it is by the continent's extravagant sights and starved of time for words. The result is that Africa is still somehow closed off from the minds of those outside. People still think of Conrad's *Heart of Darkness* and, a hundred years after the scramble to colonize the continent, refer to darkest Africa only half in jest.

I must thank the newspapers, however, for paying for most of my travels in Africa. This is not a normal travel book. There is no single route I could mark with a dotted line on a map. I have made homes in Zimbabwe, Tanzania and Kenya but most of the experiences I describe are the product of a series of haphazard journeys both within and outside these countries. The routes of these would look like the web of a crazed spider. Occasionally they were the result of an event that demanded coverage, like the floods in Khartoum or the massacres in Burundi, but more often stemmed from such accidents as the granting of a visa or travel permit applied for weeks or months before. Sometimes they were the result of a personal desire to go somewhere, backed by a request to an editor saying that "Nobody has written about it for years." They did not always reply "That's because nobody is interested." Sometimes, of course, I travelled simply to fish.

The haphazard nature of my travels reflects the haphazard

nature of the continent. There is a definite risk of hubris in claiming to demystify a place as big as Africa. In many ways I prefer to think of my fishing there in the metaphorical sense. But this haphazard travel, the fishing if you will, has exposed some of Africa's complexities, and exposing complexities is a large part of demystification.

Four Star Rebels

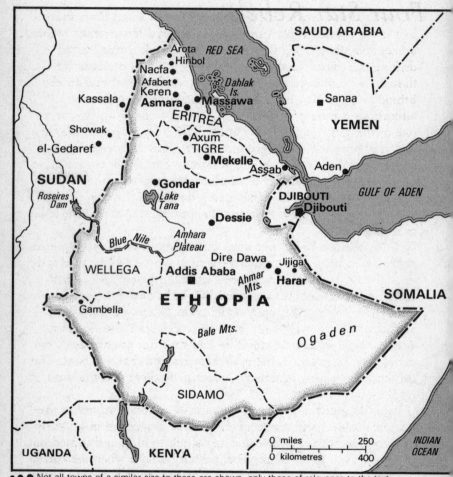

Not all towns of a similar size to these are shown, only those of relevance to the text. The same is true for all the maps throughout the book.

Ethiopia

As we came back from the front to Afabet, a small town that had fallen to the Eritrean secessionist rebels a few months before, a parachute flare lit up the road. Brilliant pink tracer started drifting up, deceptively slowly, towards it. For a moment we thought we had been caught in a rare nocturnal air raid by the Ethiopians, but Goytom, our guide, explained that the anti-aircraft guns were only practising. Cheers went up in the car as one of the guns managed to cut the flare from its parachute, so that it plummeted to the ground. More flares followed, but the shooting grew wilder. A moment later one of the heavy machine-guns started blazing away at random, the tracer flying in a crazy vortex into the night sky, like a very dangerous Roman Candle. Some of the shots skidded along the ground, one across the road in front of us.

That night we found out why. Fifty-seven couples, young men and women from the front, were getting married in a courtyard in Afabet. Trays of a special brew of *sua*, a pale brown, thick and potent beer served in captured Coke bottles, followed trays laden with *injera*, the staple whole grain pancakes, and a spicy goat stew. There was plenty of meat to celebrate the occasion. After a while somebody stood up and read out the names of the people getting married, there were cheers and that was that. The drinking and eating resumed. Occasionally there was the thud of artillery from the front.

I was sitting with a charming graduate of a law school in the USA, a bearded veteran of the nationalist movement in his early forties. One of the brides came up to talk to him, and turned out to have been a pupil at the rebel primary school where he had taught ten years before. Another slightly older man turned out to be a member of the movement's central committee. The handsome young people mingled happily, nobody taking much notice of these elders. It was odd to think that you were looking at probably the most effective footsoldiers in Africa.

The veterans joined us when we drove on back to Nacfa, along with an equally informal girl with an AK47. We wondered why she wasn't getting married too, and she laughed. Nobody good enough yet. On the five-hour drive along the rocky road through the mountains, we were led in song by the law school graduate. His time in the USA had coincided with a great era of musicals, so the songs were mostly from *The King and I*, *Oklahoma* and *The Sound of Music*, with a smattering of Italian opera.

"A female deer" may sound a strange accompaniment to the burnt-out Ethiopian tanks and trucks lit up by the headlights north of Afabet, caught in a murderous ambush a few days before the town fell. The law school graduate paused his singing to shout; "I was here, I was here, up on the hill up there." Life in the Eritrean People's Liberation Front is austere, but when its members are celebrating the informality, simplicity and cheerfulness are infectious. Every so often someone would yell "Drink! Drink!" and the driver would stop to allow the jerry can of sua we had been given at the wedding to be passed around.

The seriousness never entirely disappeared, however. The law school graduate had shouted at us at the wedding "Look at the files, look at the files," emphasizing the perfidy of the British when they encouraged the federation of Eritrea with Ethiopia in 1952. Eritrea was an Italian colony until 1941, when the British took over its administration. The Soviet Union's assistance to the Ethiopian army since 1977 seemed more easily forgiven than the British role after the Second World War.

The Americans also supported the UN-imposed federation, though most of the territory included by the Italians when they formed the colony of Eritrea in the 1880s had never been under the regular control of Ethiopia. It was a thank you to Haile Sellassie, the Ethiopian Emperor, for his allegiance that has cost nearly thirty years of war and, as the famines in northern Ethiopia and Eritrea owe much to the disruptions of war, millions of lives. It was a thank you made possible by a blithe lack of concern for the opinions of the population.

The determination of the Eritrean fighters is the major factor that has prevented Ethiopia, with a population of forty million, from making a reality of the annexation of Eritrea, with a population of three and a half million, that was announced in

1962. When Philip Williams of UPI and I went in with the rebels in November 1988 they had recently begun a series of offensives that would leave them in control of Massawa, the main port, and surrounding Asmara, the capital, by mid 1990. The fall of Asmara would mean a *de facto* independent Eritrea, but there was a major obstacle. If the rebels started shelling the airport, upon which the city depended for its supplies, the civilians would starve long before the Ethiopian garrison.

The rebels had controlled nearly all of Eritrea except Asmara and Massawa before, in 1977, but internal faction fighting, combined with the beginning of massive Soviet military assistance to the Ethiopians, drove them back into their northern mountain strongholds by late 1978. Since then the EPLF had absorbed or eliminated its rivals, and become the only significant nationalist movement.

The Soviet Union originally objected to the federation and subsequent annexation, but provided millions to ensure the continuation of the war the annexation spawned once a Marxist Ethiopian government led by President Mengistu and his friends had emerged from the chaos that followed the overthrow of Haile Selassie in 1974. Eritrea remains a rare case of a former colony that has failed to achieve independence, but at the time of writing nobody had raised this at the UN, which was supposed to guarantee at least Eritrea's autonomy, or at the Organization of African Unity.

The OAU's headquarters are in Addis Ababa and most of the despots who attend its summits are deeply nervous of discussions about borders. I had attended the twenty-fifth anniversary of the founding summit earlier in the year. The city was lit up with coloured lights in celebration, despite the heavy fighting a few hundred miles to the north. One in five of the organization's members were still involved in wars or border disputes, none of which it has ever managed to solve.

The OAU is held together by ritual condemnations of South Africa, about the only thing on which its members can agree, and the opportunities for duty free shopping. Duty free shopping may soon be the only thing left. A constant stream of cases of whisky was wheeled from the shop in the Africa Hall out to

waiting Mercedes, passing under a plaque which said that the
building was dedicated to the service of the African peoples by
Haile Sellassie in 1962. The presidential and ministerial jets
returned home laden with their delegations' goodies.

There was little hope for an early end to the fighting in Eritrea.
The Ethiopians had only offered regional autonomy to the
northern part of Eritrea, separating off the southern Danakil area
and the port of Assab for inclusion in another region. The EPLF,
suspicious of the reality of the autonomy offered, said nothing
short of total independence for the whole of Eritrea would do.
No Ethiopian government was likely to sign away its access to
the Red Sea to people it had been fighting for nearly thirty years.

On the other hand the Ethiopian government's position was
becoming increasingly desperate by mid 1990. The rebels in Tigre
had taken advantage of the Ethiopians' preoccupation with the
Eritrean rebels to capture most of the province, and move south
towards Addis Ababa. The Tigre People's Liberation Front
(TPLF), which seeks reforms rather than secession, does not offer
much hope for the future, however. In late 1989 one of its
commissars described Gorbachev as a bourgeois liberal and said
Albania was the only genuinely socialist country left.

Meanwhile the Soviet Union's bases on the Dahlak islands off
Massawa remained largely neutral in the battles for the port,
and Soviet officials made no secret of their increasing weariness
of the wasteful, ineffective support of an unpopular regime. This
was due to be sharply cut back by the end of 1990, and there
was open encouragement for Mengistu to find a peaceful
solution. Many had hoped the coup attempt of May 1989,
involving most of the armed forces' senior generals, would speed
the process towards peace, but Mengistu's East German trained
security services and loyal troops proved up to the challenge.
Too many people relied on his survival for their own, but
thousands of Ethiopians still want his blood in revenge for that
of their relatives.

A veteran Africa correspondent, familiar with many of the
continent's murderous or megalomaniac leaders, described
Mengistu as the most evil presence he had ever met, perhaps
because of his apparent reserve. But despite the deadly tentacles

of the state that spread from him, there were some relaxed places in Addis Ababa. One was Castelli's, the restaurant that served superb Italian food on white tablecloths, accompanied by very drinkable Ethiopian wine. The tables in a row of dining rooms were nearly always booked by aid workers, diplomats or journalists, on the rare occasions the Ethiopians would give us visas. I remember walking back one night to the Ras Hotel, affectionately known as the Rats, singing a scurrilous song that began "Old Mengistu had a farm". We stopped when we realized that it was close to the midnight curfew and two militiamen were following us.

Another, rather different place, was the Buffet de la Gare. On Sunday nights a curious collection of Russians, East Germans, Western European and American aid workers, Ethiopians and Armenians, Greeks and Italians long resident in the capital gathered to listen to music, dance and, if they were brave, eat. I went with a journalist from the Christian Science Monitor and his photographer wife. He commented on the beautiful Ethiopian girls hanging around: "I'm sure they're not prostitutes, they look like nice girls." He returned to the table shortly afterwards to tell his wife "I think its time to go now, dear." I had not warned him about the sanitary arrangements. Outside the back door was a ditch with a path running along it to a single cubicle apparently reserved for the girls. The men simply peed into the ditch as the girls passed or chatted behind them. Addis Ababa seemed a long way from the war.

The rebel couples in Afabet seemed more concerned with the history of their conflict than the realities of its present. They faced major offensives and counter-offensives, and even if they were confident of victory they knew lives would be lost and ghastly injuries sustained. They were all leaving for a month's honeymoon and perhaps a more traditional religious celebration of their nuptials with their families if these were not in areas still held by the Ethiopian army. They might be called back early in case of emergency. They all said they were happy with this, but the dedication was not entirely pure. When I asked one of the brides what she would do if the war was over, she replied "whatever I am assigned to do". The peer pressure was intense.

According to one EPLF slogan "one who does not volunteer is a living dead".

The newly weds might have said these were the best times of their lives, with the adrenalin and camaraderie of what they saw as a heroic struggle. I was told many of these marriages did not last, however, and owed a lot to the coldness and boredom of those nights at the front. It was not boring all the time at the front of course, and many of them may since have died. One of the biggest problems faced by the rebels was how to defend themselves against the Soviet supplied MiGs, which could attack virtually any target they could see by day with impunity.

A few days after the wedding we were near Hinbol, a rebel administrative centre, staying at the headquarters of the Eritrea Relief Association. A dull roar came over the rocky ridges and I went outside to look. The cook, a wounded veteran, yelled at me to get back under cover. As I did so the first of the two Ethiopian MiGs hurtled over the valley. As they began circling she threw two brightly coloured chairs and a big pot that might have flashed into the bunkered guesthouse. I looked at the malevolent darts through the camouflage netting draped over the brushwood that concealed the building, too fascinated to feel the terror clearly experienced by the cook. With good reason. One of the pilots had obviously seen some movement around the guesthouse or the three tiny, camouflaged offices which shared the valley. Though they were a few hundred yards apart and carefully concealed she knew that if the MiGs could pick out a target, little in the vicinity would survive. There might be napalm, which would incinerate everything for several hundred square yards.

Goytom knew too and had grabbed my short-wave radio. Apparently at this range you could hear the pilots talking even without knowing the exact frequency, and so be warned when one told the other he was going in to attack. He was listening intently, crouched in the corner Philip and I had also decided would be the safest. After three passes the pilots gave up. Nobody said anything for a while after the shattering noise had faded. Perhaps we were all thinking about the washing that had been hanging on some bushes a little earlier. The pilots could hardly have missed that.

When we first got to Eritrea, Philip and I had wanted to see all the action, and perhaps some unfished river high in the mountains, though we did not say much about the latter. Goytom had reproved us. "Don't ask for a MiG," he had said. Having been circled by one, it was hard to disagree. It was a long time before I thought about fishing again.

Our trip into Eritrea had begun two weeks before at Port Sudan. The first place of any interest we saw there was the Red Sea Hotel, once the haunt of colonials travelling on the imperial routes to East Africa and the Far East. It is now a government-run hotel, like most of its kind in Africa superbly indifferent to the comfort of its guests, if any. But you could still imagine the dancing in the courtyard, in formal dress despite the stifling heat and dubious smells rising from the Red Sea in front. And a wooden plaque survived above the reception desk, listing the notable captures, mainly barracuda and shark, made by a small but obviously enthusiastic fishing club.

It is unlikely that those catches could be repeated, with the incredible pollution now released by the town. A beach a few miles from the main harbour consisted entirely of plastic flip-flops and the sheets of plastic from which they had been cut, glued together with occasional gobs of crude oil spilled from the town's oil terminal. The green slime beyond confirmed our decision not to swim, or consider casting a line.

But the catches recorded on the plaque would be considered poor in many other parts of Africa today, and are evidence of the desire of fishermen to transcend their surroundings. Port Sudan must be one of the most squalid cities in Africa, and must have been almost equally grim from the beginning. It was opened in 1909, one of the major works designed to develop Sudan sponsored by the British and Egyptian partners in the Condominium administration. The site may have been logical to the engineers, on account of the opportunities for a deep water port, but to a layman it looks like any other spot where a featureless desert coast meets the salt humidity of the Red Sea. It has no claim to the patina of age, though at night the colonnaded blocks that house the market acquire a hint of seedy romance. If you are about to leave for Eritrea you can also buy very cheap Chinese torches and batteries.

Like the lieutenants and their ladies in Port Sudan fifty years ago, we were prepared for a little bit of sport if it came our way. The multi-section fly rod protruded from my pack. Even the rebels' hospital for those crippled by the war, near our hostel in Port Sudan, failed to discourage its inclusion, though it made us rather less carefree about our journey. When the evenings' slanted sun brought some relief from the heat the men and women who would never return to the front came out for their exercise, doggedly swinging useless legs under their crutches or pushing wheelchairs. Those less fortunate would have their beds pushed out on the balconies to catch the faint breeze. As Philip said, "I would rather have seen that when we got back." Most of them were in their twenties.

It was a relief to set off down the coast towards Eritrea, the town soon being replaced by the scattered tents of camel-herding nomads. These did not appear to be any noble tribes of the desert, however. A rusty car would often be parked or blocked up next to structures likely to include bits of plastic as well as the traditional cloth in their patchwork roofs. The children playing nearby looked ill-fed.

Our immediate destination was Suakin, still for some reason a fabled port though Winston Churchill described it accurately in *The River War*, his account of the reconquest of the Sudan in 1898: "At a distance the tall buildings of white coral, often five storeys high, present an imposing appearance, and the prominent chimneys of the condensing machinery – for there is scarcely any fresh water – seem to suggest manufacturing activity. But a nearer view reveals the melancholy squalour of the scene. A large part of the town is deserted. The narrow streets wander among tumbled-down and neglected houses. The quaintly carved projecting windows of the façades are boarded up. The soil exhales an odour of stagnation and decay. The atmosphere is rank with memories of waste and failure." The old town has crumbled even further, only the mosques standing among heaps of rubble. There is no sign of any condensing machinery. The people – one suspects only those too fatalistic or unintelligent to move elsewhere are left – live in a shanty town between the rubble and a prison. The water laps more cleanly at the shore here, but the port is still a depressing relic, its function usurped by Port Sudan.

After visiting the rebels' transport depot south of Suakin, where dozens of new Mercedes trucks awaited commissioning, we set off on the dirt road along the coast that is the rebels' main supply route. We met their camouflaged bulldozers, maintaining a road that was still well inside Sudan. We would not reach Eritrea – or Ethiopia according to the government in Addis Ababa – until we had turned inland and reached the foothills of the mountains long after dark.

The rebels had not maintained the telephone line. The wires had gone, but the posts stood splendidly for mile after mile of desert. On nearly every one sat an Egyptian vulture, a ghoulish line facing out to sea, only broken every few miles by a solitary osprey. There was nowhere else to roost.

Our driver was taciturn in the extreme. He accepted our assistance wordlessly when we had a puncture and never stopped sucking on the wad of tobacco in his cheek. He spat out of the window every few minutes, little droplets occasionally spraying back on me, a cause of concern when Philip suggested his languor and yellow eyes might be the result of hepatitis. It transpired the alcohol and boredom that followed some brave deed that made him a war hero were more likely causes.

We stopped near the border at the first of the Eritreans' "service stations", which were dotted around the spectacular mountain road network they have built. Completely hidden under the umbrella-like shade of a stand of thorn trees are a few trucks, a petrol pump and a simple workshop. The focus is a cement circular seat with a thatched roof. All comers are served a communal platter of injera over which a spicy lentil or goat meat stew is poured. The injera act as edible plates, pieces of which you tear off to scoop up the stew. Glasses of strong, hot, sweet and milkless tea follow. If you are lucky there is some sua, the sorghum beer made from scraps of injera. There is no charge.

The rebel movement does not use money, issuing food and other requirements to its members and guests.

By the end of the trip we were joking that the EPLF should receive four stars in the good rebel guide. Once we had persuaded our guides that we preferred their food to tinned pilchards, pasta and packet soup, often all mixed together, we ate splendidly. Neither of us got sick and we both put on weight, an almost unheard of result of visiting rebel areas in Africa. The accommodation was also adequate. The simple guesthouses, with dry stone walls and shutters instead of windows, were half buried like bunkers into hillsides and hidden by trees or other camouflage, like all the buildings in the rebel controlled area of Eritrea. Some of them even had showers – though no hot water.

On our first night in Eritrea, however, the accommodation was a little sketchy. The driver announced he wanted to sleep a little way after the "service station", promising to wake in time to reach Arota, a major rebel centre in the mountains, before daylight brought the risk of Ethiopian air attack. It was a pleasantly cool night after the heat of the coast, and I could not understand why one of the rebels laid several *fota* – the thick cloths that the rebels wrap twisted around their bodies when not in use as blankets, capes or carrying bags – close together, indicating that we should lie in a line like sardines.

I wandered a short distance away to put my sleeping bag in the moon shadow of a pine tree, feeling the soft warm dust and the pine needles and listening to the soft trickle of the tiny stream coming down the riverbed that was our road. An English agriculturalist travelling with us came to say this was not a good idea. A hyena might take your face off if you slept alone, he said. I was just suggesting there was little likelihood of such beasts in such a barren land when we heard the distinctive high yelp from just across the valley. I do not know why anybody refers to hyenas laughing. I joined him and the rebel travelling with us on the fota, Philip and the driver deciding to sleep in the car. I fell asleep after half an hour watching the stars against the black masses of the hills, a vigil punctuated by the yelps of the hyenas and the rattle of the stones they disturbed on the river bed.

When we woke next morning it was nearly dawn, and Philip

was highly excited. The hyenas had apparently come right up to the car and to our sleeping bodies during the night. He had shouted out of the window, but failed to wake us. He dared not get out of the car, and the driver failed to respond to his most vigorous shakes.

The probable explanation for the hyenas' presence became apparent a few miles up the road, which now wound between jagged rock faces and scree slopes. Our driver had agreed to drive on to the house of the local rebel commander, where we would be more comfortable waiting out the day and we might get something to eat. We climbed up a short, zig-zag flight of rough steps from the riverbed to where it nestled under a cliff. The roof was covered with a couple of feet of earth, but to one side was a pleasantly screened veranda paved with the slaty rock that seemed to be breaking up all around. As we looked up the valley further into the mountains, a patch of what we had taken to be natural piles of boulders at the base of a scree slope suddenly erupted with tiny black figures. These were some of the twelve thousand-odd prisoners of war held by the rebels, a large proportion of whom lived in this valley. They were going down to collect water from the thin trickle at the side of the road.

The commandant of Red Star Camp – eponymous with a massive and disastrous Ethiopian offensive in 1982 – soon emerged from his bedroom, fota draped over his shoulders, to join us for a breakfast of scrambled eggs, injera and the inevitable sweet tea. The eggs came from flocks of pure white chickens we later saw wandering the valley. Since the flocks came from a European, battery variety, the donor had obviously combined his generosity to man and bird. There was little conversation before most of us were snoozing quietly to the strains of Dean Martin, the Beatles and Bob Dylan coming from a battered cassette player. The commandant even looked a bit like Bob Dylan – the same hawk nose, sketchy beard and fuzzy hair. But the complexion was darker.

People have often compared the organization, determination, longevity and effectiveness of the Eritrean rebels with the Vietcong. The music seems to have changed sides. Though the Eritrean rebels began with a Marxist ideology, and their current,

purer nationalism is imbued with a confused socialism, the
necessary austerity of their lives has not translated into
puritanism.

We had little time to ask the Commandant about his taste for
the American music of the sixties, as our driver decided to take
advantage of the massing clouds, which would discourage the
Ethiopian pilots from hurtling through the mountain tops, to
push on to Arota. He was also concerned about rain in the
mountains turning the road into a torrent. As it was we were
nearly caught in a flash flood as we arrived in Arota.

The next day we had hoped to see some of the installations at
Arota, all invisible in the bowl in the mountains overlooked by
the camouflaged guesthouse, but our driver never turned up. We
were forced to contemplate the distant red rock mountains, and
stunted thorn trees clinging to pockets of soil amongst the litter
of fissile rock around us. You could follow the movements of
the goats on the hillside above by the rattle of a series of minor
rockfalls. Our agriculturalist friend busied himself with
identifying all the different species of thorn tree around us. He
waxed indignant about my description of these northern
mountains as barren. Apart from the goats, whose contribution
to erosion was continually audible, and a few tiny, rocky fields,
the only sign of agricultural potential was an occasional camel.
Though these belonged to the pastoral nomads who shared the
mountains with the rebels, the Ethiopians bombed any
concentrated herd, as they were used for carrying ammunition
in particularly difficult terrain.

The agriculturalist was clearly one of those European converts
we nicknamed "Eritrea groupies". Passionately dedicated to the
cause of Eritrean independence, they tend to blind themselves to
the darker sides of the liberation war and to the problems that
would face an independent Eritrea. There is more fertile land in
the west and central areas, but there is little point exaggerating
the potential of the northern mountains which are the rebels'
stronghold.

The mountains have given the rebels something other than a
natural defensive position, however. Their exacting, savage
beauty may have helped purify their intentions, and accustom

them to the hostile environment they have faced for nearly thirty years. As we waited at the guesthouse, such thoughts seemed incongruous with the plastic flowers placed to welcome visitors, or the few books left to while away the hours. Apart from a traditional acupuncture manual there was a Le Carré spy novel in Finnish. Waiting for the sun to go down or be obscured by clouds made Eritrean afternoons monotonous, and made one prey to strange thoughts. One afternoon I went for a pee, and was startled by the bright red colour of my urine. It transpired this was the result of a powerful drug we had been given to protect us from an epidemic recent arrivals were feared to have brought from the Ethiopian side.

Finally our driver appeared to start the long journey to the front. We did not complain when an axle broke on the boulder-strewn road soon after we left, and we were given another car and another driver. It was also at Arota that we were assigned our guide – assistant, protector and exponent of rebel policy – who would be with us for the rest of the trip, looping his pistol and grenade belt over the headrest on his seat. Goytom Asghedom was a tall bearded veteran of over ten years at the front, but still in his thirties. A cheerful man, if slightly suspicious of western decadence, he insisted on pronouncing my name Androy.

A couple of days later we reached Nacfa, shaken and dusty from the riverbeds and rocky hairpins the rebels have carved into the cliffs, mesmerized by the dark voids over which the headlights lurched. The key point of a natural defensive line protecting their northern bases, this erstwhile administrative and trading centre was virtually flattened in ten years of near-continuous bombardment. The inhabitants and defenders had retired underground. We stayed in one of the bunkers they had built – just like a normal house, except that the window shutters opened onto ventilation shafts that rose seven or eight feet to the surface. Some previous occupant had whiled away the hours by painting curtains and other draperies on the walls. I slept on a stone couch covered with cushions in the corner of the main room, looking straight up at the stars through a ventilation shaft above my head. Pieces of sand and grit kept falling down, however, and I had to move.

The only building in the town to remain more or less intact above ground was the mosque, though its walls and minaret were scarred not just by bullets and shells, but by revolutionary slogans. A few walls were all that was left of the houses along the main street. The dusty ground was strewn with bullets, cartridge cases and fragments of shells and rockets. In a couple of places used shell cases had been hung up as alarm bells. Elsewhere I saw the fin sections of bombs being used as bases for tools. On a hill overlooking the shattered town was the shell of a house once built for the deputy governor. The Italian style was still discernible in the crumbling yellow stone, a hint of the Mediterranean under the sharp African light.

The church also still stood, a tiny building on another hill overlooking the town. Some rebels were living in it, and had set up some ammunition boxes as beehives in a bell tower like a sentry box a few yards away. Prickly pears were growing by some neglected graves. The EPLF has eschewed religion altogether in an effort to avoid rivalry between Christian and Muslim Eritreans, one of the roots of the faction-fighting of the seventies. The weekly holiday is on Thursday.

Goytom's fiancée joined us at Nacfa, filling him with pride and good humour. Like most of the young rebels we met, she had served on the front line and been wounded, shrapnel hitting her head close to an eye and at the back of her neck. The head wounds hardly showed, however, and one marvelled at the skill of the Eritrean doctors. She was now working at a hospital near Nacfa herself. She had permission to accompany us to Afabet, to see for herself the scene of the rebel victory. There was almost a holiday atmosphere about our group. Later I would take photographs of the couple standing hand-in-hand on a rock overlooking Afabet. They didn't come out.

We started before dark to enable us to see the old lines on the escarpment outside Nacfa. Goytom was also prepared to take a chance because of the low level of air activity in recent days. You could see the old Eritrean line like a thread running along and sometimes almost vertically up the steep hillsides, occasionally punctuated by a strongpoint or artillery post. The Ethiopian lines were at some points less than fifty yards away. One spot was known as the volley ball court because of the traffic in grenades.

There was evidence of the violence of the massed infantry assault that broke the Ethiopian line in December 1987. At the side of the road a tank hung precariously on the yellow grass of the hillside, its barrel pointing drunkenly at the sky, the turret blown free of its mountings. At the bottom of the slope lay other wrecked vehicles. The battle ended the ten years of stubborn resistance that followed the "strategic withdrawal" of 1978, prompted by the introduction of massive Soviet support for the Ethiopian army. In March 1988 the rebels struck again, advancing the front nearly sixty miles and virtually wiping out three Ethiopian divisions totalling about eighteen thousand men in a series of lethal ambushes set for the fleeing columns.

We saw the remains of one column, bulldozed off the road where it passed through a particularly narrow and rugged ravine. About sixty mangled tanks and trucks lay heaped and charred, armour and heavy chassis torn and twisted to improbable angles. The slaughter must have been appalling, the men trapped by their own exploding vehicles and a withering fire from the ridges above. After such losses the Ethiopian taskforce had little chance of defending its headquarters at Afabet, a few miles beyond the ravine, and the rebels pushed on twenty-five miles, to within artillery range of Keren, the third largest city in Eritrea.

President Mengistu of Ethiopia often referred to the rebels as bandits. Wadi Suhul, surveying the Ethiopian positions ten miles out of Keren with his one eye – the other was shot out, leaving an empty socket – looked a bit like a bandit. In fact he was a veteran of the last fifteen years of the Eritreans' near thirty year struggle for independence, and at thirty-three a brigade commander in the Eritrean People's Liberation Army (EPLA), as the rebel force is officially described.

As ravens and falcons cavorted around his mountain top command post, we peeped carefully over the rocks at the Eritrean lines on the slope below, and those of the Ethiopians five hundred yards beyond. A sentry had been posted at one point on the climb to warn people that that section of the route was covered by snipers. At the top Wadi Suhul was concerned that a reflection from the chrome on a camera might be spotted, and give the Ethiopian battery on a hilltop opposite us grounds for some practice. I asked why fire was not directed onto an Ethiopian jeep leaving a trail of dust on a track beyond the lines. Apparently ammunition was too precious.

Unlike most bandits Wadi Suhul had tanks and heavy artillery stationed in the valleys behind. We had seen some of the T54s and T55s the night before, captured behemoths clanking and squealing into new positions. Most of the artillery – including guns up to 130mm in calibre and Stalin Organ multiple rocket launchers – was also captured, and equally carefully concealed from Ethiopian air attack during the day.

Despite the occasional crack of an AK47 and the dull detonations of the Ethiopian artillery behind the ridge five miles away that concealed Keren from our view, the front was quiet, he said. The rifle fire was the EPLA fighters ranging their weapons and the artillery fire was the Ethiopians shooting over the heads of raw recruits being prepared for an expected counter-offensive. We had heard explosions from twenty-five miles away in Afabet the night before, but he dismissed that as a little heavy mortar fire. There had been no casualties.

As we panted up the mountain at dawn, we had been passed by groups of fighters running down with jerry cans to collect water from a tiny stream a couple of miles behind us. They then had to run back up well over a thousand feet, over the ridge and back down to the line, perhaps under fire for the last stretch. They were cheerfully shouting across the dry, rocky valleys to friends, apparently racing each other on this dangerous chore. Just below the ridge we stopped at the backward position where we met Wadi Suhul. This was little more than a series of covered ledges, but apparently a welcome respite from the line itself for the group of young men and women we joined for breakfast there. Several of them bore the scars of war wounds.

They seemed to assume visitors were hopelessly soft, and I'm sure my red face gave away the toll the rapid climb took on untrained legs. I almost had to use force to retain possession of my small bag. I had to ask them if they would let someone else carry their AK47 before they stopped trying to take it. Most of them were friendly enough, with one exception. A short distance below the mountain top, called Mohammed Drur, or Mohammed's dinner, we stopped at a battalion commander's tiny bunker, nestling on a steep, rocky slope, to have lunch. An excellent lentil stew, soaked up with injera, was followed by some sua and talk before we set off down the mountain. In our host I saw for the first time what were obviously killer's eyes, devoid of human warmth, almost of expression. Perhaps the explanation lay in his young wife, who cooked the lunch. She had only one leg.

On the other hand a friendly smile often crossed the face of the one-eyed Wadi Suhul – which means son of Suhul. With his air of calm wisdom and the obvious respect for his command it seemed hard to remember that he was the same age as me. He asked me about Europe. I asked him about the war. At least I had a little experience to fill out the answers in my mind. The main complaint of the fighters, he said, was "Why don't we attack?" Despite its recent victories, the EPLA remained wary of over-extending itself. It had established the horseshoe line around Keren in May, nearly six months before my visit. Though it hoped to squeeze the Ethiopians out, there was no hurry. There were believed to be twelve divisions in Keren at the time, or about seventy thousand men out of the one hundred and fifty thousand stationed in Eritrea. It transpired that the rebel strategy was to bypass Keren, by taking Massawa, so breaking the Ethiopians' marine supply route, and besieging Asmara, the capital.

The EPLA could probably have taken Keren if it wanted to, despite being heavily outnumbered. The Ethiopian officer corps' efficiency had been eroded by purges ever since Haile Sellassie was overthrown in 1974. The commander of the Afabet task force was reportedly called to Asmara and shot by Mengistu personally for suggesting a political solution to the war was necessary after the Ethiopian line had been broken at Nacfa. The domineering style of the imperial days was retained, so that the soldiers usually hated their commanders. Though the Ethiopian armed forces were the largest in black Africa, with over three hundred thousand men, most of the men were recent conscripts, many snatched at random from streets or schools. Training was often minimal and morale abysmal. Single rebels had captured as many as fifty men at a time.

The EPLA fighters, in contrast, were highly motivated, many of them men or women veterans of many years of frontline service, their handsome young faces belying their lethal efficiency. Usually between eighteen and thirty, they were fit, agile mountain soldiers who went into combat with an AK47, a belt with ammunition and grenades and a fota wrapped round their waist. A few fighters in each unit carried a rocket propelled grenade launcher, a mortar or a machine-gun.

We talked to some at Afabet. "I don't want a salary," said Letekidan Woldu, a twenty-seven-year-old woman with ten years' experience of the front, "I came here for my goal – liberation and peace – and that is my salary." When I asked how she and her husband, who was in the same division, felt about the war, she replied, "I will sacrifice and he will sacrifice." They seemed to feel almost guilty about the low standard of the opposing troops. "Of course, they are innocent people deceived by the system, I feel sorry for them, but they are trying to kill us," commented Stefano Tesfai, a twenty-eight-year-old male who joined the EPLF in 1977.

The EPLA had no formal ranks, seniority, insignia, decorations or uniforms. Jeans and T-shirts were most common. There were two commanders for each unit, from platoon to division, but little evidence of formal discipline. The self-discipline was extraordinary. The conventional estimate of EPLA strength was about thirty thousand regular fighters, but the fixed positions they had assaulted, the length of lines that they had held and the movement's training capacity suggested the figure was much higher. At one training camp we saw one thousand recruits undergoing a six-month training course. There were six other camps, so a total output of ten thousand a year would have been possible, especially if, as at the time, there were plenty of captured weapons with which to equip them.

A total of about sixty thousand regular fighters appeared likely, while EPLF members working in administration, road construction, transport, workshops, hospitals, schools and other departments – all of them with military training – probably offered a reserve of a similar size. The movement refused to give any details of its manpower, or of the total number of tanks and other heavy weapons it had captured. The number of operational tanks was believed to exceed two hundred. As we drove through a forest of cactus one day, I had been startled from my doze by the realization that there was a tank hidden every hundred yards, nearly invisible from the road, let alone the air. Their effective use had been demonstrated by the expulsion of the Ethiopians from the coastal plain north of Massawa since 1985. This was achieved as a result of several set-piece tank battles.

Though special teams stripped every wreck for spare parts – they were still at work around Afabet – the supply of fuel and ammunition for the tanks and heavy weapons was a continual problem. Though some was captured the bulk had to be brought by truck at night from Sudan along the twisting tracks through the mountains, as did thousands of tonnes of food for the hundreds of thousands of people who could not plant or harvest because of the war. Low rainfall also had an effect, but one which would have been of little significance if war had not also prevented people from building up stocks in the good years.

The end of the little valley where we were buzzed by the MiGs was the base of Gebremicael Menghistu, the Eritrean Relief Association (ERA) field co-ordinator. A small diffident man who was stiff and formal when we asked him to pose in front of his office – a hut under a tree – he was supervising an annual $100m relief effort and calmly reeled off the statistics of starvation in this part of Africa.

The ERA distributed about one hundred thousand tonnes of food in 1988, feeding six hundred thousand people and so averting the threat of widespread famine in Eritrea. Western relief agencies, which also provided food for nearly one million people from the government side, did not believe such an effort was possible when the harvest failed in 1987. In 1989 harvests failed again in Eritrea and Tigre, as heavy fighting combined with poor rainfall. Though the rebel movements by then controlled much larger areas and had to feed many more people, their relief wings still managed to avert widespread starvation, again surprising the Western agencies and journalists who had predicted it.

Most of the money for the ERA operation and its equivalent in Tigre came from a consortium of Western relief agencies and governments. Governmental assistance was often channelled through national non-governmental agencies, rather than given directly, to minimize difficulties on the Ethiopian side, where the governments were often directly involved in major relief programmes.

The donors accepted the feeding of the prisoners of war held by the Eritrean rebels, even at a kilogramme a day, twice the normal ration. As Gebremicael pointed out "sometimes there is some hard work". Most of the camps were along the usually dry riverbed that was the main supply route from Sudan. Every time there was a flash flood the POWs had to clear away the boulders from the track. This was one example of the crossover between ERA and EPLF operations. It was almost impossible to disentangle them. The ERA's two hundred trucks were unmarked and indistinguishable from those of the EPLF. I saw armed men and women on the backs of trucks carrying food as they bounced past in the night. Most of ERA's staff were also EPLF members. Even if EPLF members did not receive relief food, its presence reduced market prices and so made it easier for the movement to buy. Food aid decreases the incentive of farmers to plant for the same reason, and the continual need for food aid in northern Ethiopia and Eritrea is the result of this vicious circle as well as the wars.

There was little doubt the EPLF benefited from the enlarged pool of trucks and fuel in the areas it controlled, but the donors said this did not matter as long as the agreed amount of food got to the most needy people. Relief programmes benefit both sides, in this and most other African wars, by removing from the antagonists the burden of supporting civilian populations. Though the programmes undoubtedly contribute to the wars' continuation, it is unlikely that a sudden halt to relief would force the antagonists immediately to compromise, even if Western opinion would allow it. Human life is cheap in most of Africa, and such an action might take months to force serious negotiation. The donors should ask themselves whether a few months of carnage is worse than decades of misery. Do not ask the aid workers, they have careers to consider.

The Eritrean rebels have more of a cause than most, and can be expected to continue to cope with the situation in their area. They are keenly aware of the contribution equitable and prompt distribution of relief supplies has made to the strength of their movement. There are places they cannot reach, however. There were believed to be serious pockets of famine in the Danakil region, along the southern Red Sea coast, in 1988. The ERA used to get some supplies to the Afar tribespeople there by boat, but in May 1988 the Ethiopian government ordered all boats to gather at the ports of Massawa, Assab and Tio, establishing a free fire zone for 10km along the entire coast. Apart from preventing the traditional activities of fishing, trading and smuggling, the Ethiopians have bombarded coastal settlements in an effort to force the people into the major towns.

Despite the efforts of the donors, the EPLF and the ERA, the effects of war and famine can only be alleviated. At Filfil, a camp for eight thousand displaced people near Nacfa, we saw nineteen tiny stone mounds, the graves of children stillborn or unable to survive at birth because of their mothers' malnutrition. These were mostly new arrivals, however, and most of the people at the camp looked reasonably well fed. They still had to build their huts into the rocky hillsides and cover the roofs with branches to camouflage them. Refugee camps were not free from the aerial attacks that forced many of their inmates to flee their homes in the first place. Hidad Isak, a twenty-eight-year-old with a wife and two children, had recently arrived from their home near the front line at Keren. He said of the Ethiopians: "They want the land, not the people." He told us the army had given the people in his village two weeks to move, and then started mortaring it.

There were regular reports of napalm or cluster bombs being dropped on such villages to force people to move to government controlled areas. Napalm was a regular weapon of the Ethiopian air force. It was used at least three times to my personal knowledge while I was in Eritrea, once in the attack on a car driven by some Norwegian aid workers and twice near Arota.

Some camels were incinerated in these attacks, but no people. The Norwegians said a hillside burst into flames a few hundred yards away from them. They had not heard the aircraft engines above their own. Nor had we, driving a few miles behind them, but we had been flagged down and switched our lights out.

One of those raids on Arota had just ended when we returned there. There was a mild stir of excitement and admiring descriptions of the anti-aircraft tracer flying from the mountain tops – with as little effect as the bombs. None or the scattered web of buildings, all hidden along the valleys of the mountain bowl, had been hit. This was the usual effect of these Antonov raids, made as darkness descended with the apparent intention of catching early travellers or other foolhardy displayers of light. The Antonovs, designed as transport planes, lumbered high above and seemed to scatter a few bombs more or less at random. The Eritreans used to joke that you were only in danger if they were aiming at someone else. Goytom said that they could easily be persuaded to drop their bombs around decoy fires.

The Ethiopians' desire to bomb Arota was understandable, even if they did not know exactly where it was. They did know it was a centre for many of the support installations that sustained the rebels' morale and confirmed that in all but name an Eritrean state already existed for the one and a half million people living in the areas controlled by them at the time. That number has since nearly doubled.

As any military strategist could tell you, an army needs more than weapons to fight with. It needs something to put on its feet. Here in Arota was a workshop with an injection moulding machine that produced the black plastic sandals that were the nearest thing the EPLF had to a uniform. As any traditional military strategist could not tell you, an army nearly a third of whose fighters are women will have other needs. There was also a workshop with automated machines with the capacity to produce ten thousand sanitary towels an hour.

In neither case would the EPLF tell us how many were produced, "for obvious reasons" said the man in charge of the sanitary towel workshop. Philip and I had thought for a moment that here was a way to discover the strength of the movement.

But concealment of such statistics as well as all their installations had become second nature to the EPLF. After darkness fell the generators were switched on and little chinks of light appeared among the trees and rocky valleys, where nothing had disturbed the forms of nature during the day.

There was a school for four thousand students, and a hospital for one thousand patients spread along six kilometres of a tortuous valley, with operating theatres, X-ray departments, and a maxillofacial unit that could repair the most disfiguring of war wounds. At one end of the hospital valley there was a pharmaceutical unit with sophisticated machines and sterile laboratories in old containers that produced tablets, capsules and intravenous solutions that accounted for 40 per cent of the requirements of the rebel-held areas.

Elsewhere in Arota and throughout the base areas there were workshops which could repair anything from a captured tank to a wristwatch, and a network of rudimentary services to connect them. There was a telephone service, a postal service run on motorbikes, even a bus service.

All EPLF members, from the general secretary to the lowliest fighter or workshop assistant, were unpaid volunteers. Food, clothes, medical treatment and other services were all distributed to them without money changing hands. When Goytom described this as "to each according to his needs" he was apparently unaware he was quoting Marx. In many respects the EPLF was more socialist than the Soviet-backed government in Ethiopia, yet from top to bottom members of the movement denied it had a socialist ideology.

Despite the denial the movement's National Democratic Programme specified the nationalization of land, big businesses, natural resources, banking and insurance, and called for the regulation of private business in a way that mimicked the worst failures of African socialism in recent decades. The denial was bizarre, given the movement's organization, with a Politburo and Central Committee. The question I was asked most often was "What do you think of our revolution?", not our "nationalist struggle". The slogan chanted by new recruits as they practised stripping an AK47 was "Awet ne hafash" or "victory to the masses".

Yet a central committee member, Ahmed Baduri, said, "We sincerely believe in a multi-party state." The right of "nationalist parties" to contest seats in a post-independence People's Assembly was enshrined in the National Democratic Programme, even though the rest of the programme apparently predetermined what it could decide.

The EPLF's route to dominance of the nationalist movement in the late seventies does not argue for a tolerance of differing viewpoints. It fought a civil war against the original Eritrean Liberation Front and other factions. But the EPLF's policies could be as much a reflection of its isolation – in which socialism has become such a norm that it is no longer considered as such – as of an attempt to court support from the west by pretending to be more liberal than it is. Most of its members may simply be unaware of the contradictions in its programme.

The need for external support is great. An EPLF central committee member told me the war was run largely on the $20m a year it got from Eritreans living abroad, against an Ethiopian defence budget of $1.75bn. Though the EPLF has captured large quantities of Soviet supplied weapons and other *matériel* from the Ethiopians, it was obvious that the fuel, ammunition and other supplies it was importing through Sudan required considerably more support than it admitted receiving.

The sources of assistance were not clear, though it appeared a collection of European, American and Arab millionaires were involved. They were presumably reassured by declarations of support for multi-party systems and mixed economies, even if the EPLF retained the guardianship of the definition of "nationalist parties". There were none apart from the EPLF at the time of writing, but, according to Ahmed Baduri, they would have to support the "aspirations of the people" and "social justice".

The austere, self-reliant philosophy that has been so successful in the war against the Ethiopians will not necessarily transfer to the sort of nation state that is the Eritreans' goal. Even their friends concede that the selfless but cheerful idealism that characterizes the EPLF could very easily be transformed into the sort of corrupt, self-serving bureaucracy all too common in Africa. It will be very difficult for its members to be genuinely tolerant of opposing views, if, or when, it leads Eritrea to independence.

The Ethiopian raw recruits were encouraged to have a very different view of the rebels. "They will cut off your penis, they will cook you in oil or if you are lucky they will shoot you." This, according to Abate Sowinet, one of the twelve thousand Ethiopian prisoners of war held in Eritrea, was what his officers said would happen if he surrendered to the rebels.

We had stopped at Nado Camp, named after the Ethiopian Nado Command that had been routed around Afabet earlier in the year, to talk to the prisoners taken in that battle. This was one of a number of camps, including Red Star Camp, strung along the valley by which we had arrived in Eritrea and by which we were now leaving. There was little security, except the occasional post along the road where a rebel lolled with an AK47. A few other guards mingled freely with the prisoners. There were no fences.

I climbed up the ridge above in the afternoon, sweating up the hot loose rocks. At the top all you could see was other equally steep, jagged and waterless ridges, marching away into the distance. There was an almost lunar grandeur to the landscape, and anyone trying to cross it would be little more likely to survive than on the moon. The only water, and only escape route, would be along the road, where no prisoner could go far unnoticed. Few had tried, but few wanted to anyway.

What Abate told us was just one example given us by the captives of the lengths to which the Ethiopian army went to motivate its poorly trained and often underaged conscripts. Abate said he was taken forcibly from his school in Addis Ababa at the age of fifteen. He was told he was fighting Arab invaders, an astonishing delusion which President Mengistu once included in a speech to the troops from the top of a truck.

Abate had never heard anything about the Eritrean secessionist war. He had little time to find out before he was captured, seven days after arriving in the north. If Abate, a schoolboy from the capital, could be so ignorant it was unsurprising that conscripts from the distant provinces of the Ethiopian empire could be told, and believe, virtually anything their officers chose.

Ashenafi Waari was fourteen when he was taken from night school in the southern province of Sidamo. He was told he was going to fight bandits, or even invaders from Somalia, to the south of Ethiopia. He was captured on his first day in the trenches, with a bullet wound in his arm, but he was treated and, like most of the prisoners, looked well fed and healthy. Several were washing in the stream in front of us when we arrived, and smiled when we waved. The camp rose like a labyrinth up the hillside above, a mass of dry-stone shelters roofed with cloth or thatch. The main problem seemed to be boredom, which they tried to alleviate by playing games. They had made cards and board games from scraps of paper, card and wood. We saw several hundred men walking down the track to watch a football match at another camp, guarded by three Eritreans.

Another youngster told us that he had no time to change the magazine on his AK47 before his trench was overrun, on his first day at the front. The rebels are full of stories about the Ethiopian soldiers they have captured. Goytom told us about one who was walking through an EPLF area, saluting everyone he saw, when somebody asked what he was doing. He replied that he had deserted and was walking towards the sunset. It would take him four days to reach his home village in Wellega province, he thought. It had taken him four days, albeit by plane and truck, to get to the front. He assumed it would take the same to walk back to his home on Ethiopia's western border. Goytom told us about a prisoner from a particularly remote village. When asked what most surprised him after he was conscripted, he apparently replied "how they get meat into tins" and "how aeroplanes fly without touching the ground".

Another refused to hand over his weapon after he surrendered, on the grounds that he would get into terrible trouble with his corporal. A rebel who accepted the surrender of some fifty Ethiopians with a couple of colleagues told us about the difficulty of carrying all the rifles. The rebels often called on the troops to surrender, and if they were hard pressed they would ignore the propaganda.

Not all responded, however. There were many stories of soldiers who believed the propaganda, or thought it was a matter of honour, and committed suicide. The officers were not allowed to surrender. They were supposed to go down fighting or kill themselves. Though we saw several hundred who had disobeyed the instruction – Goytom said they were kept in a separate camp for their own protection – Lieutenant Mulugeta Hailu, a political officer responsible for spreading the propaganda, told us of one who did not.

Colonel Asafa Temesegu, deputy commander of the 14th Division, was attempting to organize its retreat from Afabet, but all he had left was seventy people from the headquarters. He was sitting exhausted under a tree when the EPLF started shooting over their heads and calling on them to surrender. He shot himself in the throat with his Soviet-made automatic pistol. He had a family, but believed in the officer's duty not to surrender.

Lieutenant Mulugeta, still a socialist and still displaying the skills of the propagandist, said, "Directly or indirectly this war has knocked on the door of every Ethiopian. The Derg government has to be overthrown. In fourteen years there has been no solution for the people, no solution for the army and no solution for neighbouring countries." The Derg was the name given to the ruling group of Marxist army officers which Colonel Mengistu came to dominate after Haile Sellassie was deposed.

The officers had more reason than most to hope for a change of government. They would face a firing squad or imprisonment if they returned. Two thousand of the rank and file had been returned to Ethiopia. Though most were elderly or disabled a few were conscripted again and recaptured. The Ethiopian government did not recognize the existence of the remainder. Three thousand of the long-term POWs had been freed within the area controlled by the EPLF and worked in the civil departments of the movement, such as construction. An Eritrean captured by the Ethiopians, however, was likely to be interrogated, tried by a military court and shot.

We met the Norwegians again at the camps and got into their

landcruiser to return to Port Sudan. Philip and I began to wonder if we had escaped unscathed from Eritrea to be killed in a car crash on the way back. The car hurtled over rocks and drifts of sand as the driver took the role of Scandinavian rally ace. This time the sun was setting behind the Red Sea hills, silhouetting the rocky pinnacles of the peaks. In the foreground clouds of locusts were picked out by the light like dancing snowflakes. Sated hawks tumbled in the breeze above the desert. The scene was almost Biblical, except for the trucks. Again and again we had to pull off the track as they barrelled towards us, great plumes of dust rising behind them. Our Norwegian driver scorned the risk of boulders hidden in the soft sand, and hardly slowed down. Sometimes you could see another group coming miles away, bringing more food for the hungry and more shells for the guns.

The Sudanese government's acquiescence to the use of its territory to supply the Eritrean rebels has led the Ethiopian government to support the rebels of the Sudan People's Liberation Army in retaliation. The SPLA have been fighting since 1983 against domination by the Arabized, Muslim north and for greater autonomy for the African, Christian or animist south. A previous, seventeen-year-long insurrection in southern Sudan was only ended in 1972 with the grant of regional self-government. The withdrawal of regional self-government and attempts to enforce Sharia, the Islamic legal code, throughout Sudan led to the new insurrection, which promptly received Ethiopian support.

The fact that both groups of rebels have reasonable causes is of little significance to such support. The governments simply want to twist the knives in each other's side. They occasionally suggest a mutual cessation of assistance to the rebel groups, but this would probably just expose their own ineffectiveness. The SPLA could easily arrange other routes of supply. The EPLF now has a major port, Massawa, in its hands and could build other harbours less vulnerable to Ethiopian airpower further to the north. Neither war will end without governments prepared to accept whatever degree of autonomy, including complete partition, the people of their rebellious regions want. Such governments will probably only be produced by genuine elections which give the minorities, the civilians and the soldiers and their families a voice.

Floods, Frogs
and Famine

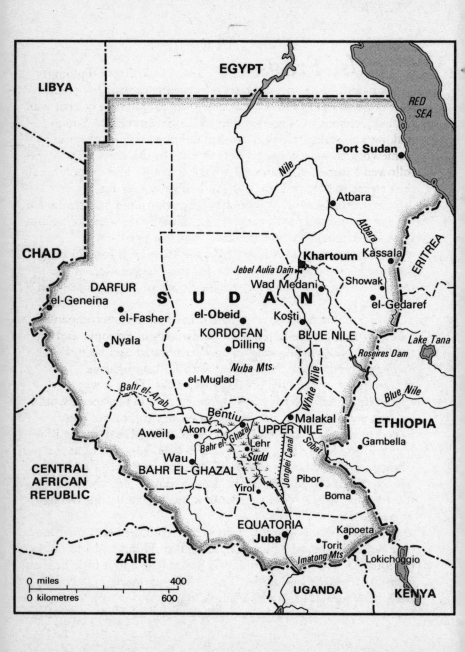

Sudan

The first time I went to Sudan, in 1986, I talked to a diplomat long resident in Khartoum, testing him with various hypotheses to explain the situation – the country's usual mixture of civil war, famine, economic collapse and unstable government. "You are making a mistake," he said "to assume that there is a logical framework to what happens here at all." In the visits that followed I came to understand what he meant. The country's hot dust seems to absorb logic and sap one's capacity for astonishment. Nobody is immune. Distortions and half-truths are the norm not only for the country's unusually devious politicians, but for the rebels, the aid agencies, mullahs, priests and unfortunate writers sent to try to make sense of it for Western readers. Most of the writers settle for the exaggeration of the romantic or sensational aspects. The floods of August 1988 were an example.

A spectacular downpour in Khartoum had been accompanied by heavy rain on the Blue Nile's headwaters in Ethiopia and on the White Nile's headwaters in southern Sudan and Uganda. The damage already done by localized flash floods might be compounded by the Nile breaking its banks. This, it was confidently predicted by many of the world's newspapers, would happen within days, if not hours, when the authorities were forced to open the sluice gates on the Roseires Dam on the Blue Nile and the Senna Dam on the White Nile. Khartoum, at the confluence of the two rivers, would disappear under a gigantic whirlpool. One report even had the city centre already under three feet of water. Whoever wrote it must have been standing in a pothole.

Tuti, a low-lying island just above the confluence on the Blue Nile opposite central Khartoum, seemed to Philip and I to be the obvious place to go. A man with a moustache and a little English appointed himself our guide. We met him on the ferry across to the island, an old boat whose single engine was the only thing between the short but laborious passage to Tuti and a swift drift

towards Egypt. We were in search of a new angle on a story
which a quiet August and good pictures had transformed into
front page news. The islanders had been advised to evacuate their
homes. Abdulla, like most of them a member of a family that
had lived there for generations, was unconcerned. Nobody was
planning to leave. He proudly showed us his house, which he
was extending, his lime groves, which he was glad to see were
getting a healthy load of Ethiopian topsoil, and his family, with
whom hospitality demanded that we spend an hour drinking tea
and eating sweet cakes. The fishing, he said, was excellent. All
you had to do was set nets between the lime trees. For the larger
Nile perch, which can grow over two hundred pounds, he advised
a large chunk of meat cast into the deeper water on a stout line.
The Blue Nile, like the White at this time, was an opaque reddish
brown, so my sort of light tackle would have been useless.

Puzzled by the islanders' nonchalance – which my editors chose
to take as heroism – I decided to go to the Department of Dams
and Irrigation, rather than rely on the two British water engineers
who had been giving alarming details of the impending
catastrophe to other journalists in the lobby of the Acropole
Hotel. The Acropole was an institution run by a Greek family
with a remarkable ability to keep telephone and telex lines open,
even when the public telexes and phones were down. The floods
were a small matter to George, the manager. As usual he urged
patience on journalists clamouring to file. Even the bombing of
the dining room by Arab terrorists earlier in the year, in which
a British family, an Army major and a waiter were killed, had
proved only a hiccup in the hotel's operation, though the
reduction of the number of rooms made it even harder to get in.
It was always a good place to go and gossip with aid workers
and other journalists while waiting for a line, however. The
rumours were no more or less wild than elsewhere in Khartoum.

The Director of Dams and Irrigation politely told me that the
sluices at the dams were open, as was normal for the time of
year, so that the first heavily silted floodwaters could pass through
the dams. They would be closed later when the water cleared
somewhat. The level in the dams was low, and the gates could
easily be closed early if there was any serious risk to Khartoum.

He did not think there was. The levels in the city had begun to drop that day. He said he knew the stories in the international media were wrong, but nobody had asked him before.

I returned to the Hilton, where most of the journalists were staying in the usual comfort despite its position overlooking the confluence, which theoretically meant it would be the first place to be cut off if the Nile burst its banks. It had its own water and generator, however. In the first few days we had amused ourselves by watching the slow encroachment of the White Nile on the tennis courts at the back, speculating on when they might be closed and joking about the importance of this event to the story. But before anyone could get a line in about the tennis courts at the Hilton being flooded, the management had installed a pump and some sandbags to ensure the guests' continued ability to play. The American-style bowling alley in the basement was also popular. The garden provided the occasion for a piece of breathtaking journalistic licence. Many of us had been struck by the almost Biblical nature of Sudan's suffering in recent years – drought, floods, war, famine, locusts and pestilence. On the basis of a few amphibians hopping about in the grass one journalist added a plague of frogs to the catalogue.

But the story was still being taken very seriously in the outside world, and I was rebuked by a telex demanding more drama and detail as a television crew set up a mobile satellite dish at the back of the Hilton. Under a hundred people died in the flash floods and the predictions of further flooding were simply wrong. Ten times as many were dying every day as a result of civil war and famine in the south. More than two hundred and fifty thousand southerners are believed to have died in 1988, though nobody will ever know the exact number. An estimated twenty thousand people died in tribal massacres in Burundi shortly after the floods. Yet the floods were the biggest story out of black Africa for the year. The British government immediately gave £1m for the relief effort and a public appeal raised over £2m.

Words like *catastrophic* and *devastating* were freely bandied about, even before any considered eyewitness reports had emerged. How did the coverage and the response of relief agencies get so distorted and imbalanced, as they so often do when Africa is involved? Well it was August, but there were other reasons. The floods were relatively easy to get to and made good television. People wading through filthy water between the mounds of mud to which their homes had been reduced made for strong pictures and graphic descriptions. But few of the TV crews or print journalists made an effort to qualify them by pointing out that apart from the few spots that provided most of the pictures most of Khartoum was in its normal, dilapidated condition.

Much was made of the cuts in water and electricity supplies and telephone and telex lines. These were worse than usual, and cuts in all services did not usually coincide, but most people in the developed parts of town were used to them. The first thing a wealthy householder bought was a generator and you rarely got through to anyone on the phone at the best of times. In the poorer parts of town none of these services existed anyway. Many of the journalists who flooded into Khartoum did not know how little changed most of the city was, never having been there before, but before they even arrived the whole story was out of control. Journalists, aid agency workers, the government and donors had been caught from the beginning in a self-sustaining spiral of exaggeration.

Initial reports made it sound like the greatest natural disaster of the decade, and made me fill my suitcase with food, water purifying tablets, medicines and batteries before I left Nairobi. I needed none of them. The Nile never did burst its banks, nor was any significant damage due to the downpour evident in central Khartoum. The government asked for food for a million people for three months, but nobody asked how the downpour could actually have destroyed that amount of food. There was a bumper harvest because of the massive increase in the rain-fed acreage that could be cultivated that year.

The images of suffering in the shanty-towns of Khartoum, whose poor construction and situation meant they bore the brunt of the damage, were in a sense not of a natural disaster at all. Most of the people living there were southerners who had fled the civil war and famine in the south. The appalling conditions even before the downpour were apparently an improvement on the south. Some of them lived at a place called Jebel Kusha, which means rubbish mountain, which is exactly what it was.

The government had ignored these people, apparently in the hope they would go away. Even when relief supplies started arriving after the floods the government tried to keep them away from them. The Army and the main political parties were entrusted with distribution. These were drawn from the northern Muslim majority and favoured their own people. Christian or pagan southerners were unwilling or unable to collect supplies handed out at mosques. After considerable acrimony the Western agencies started reaching them, but only after reinforcing the northerners' perception that the agencies' sympathy for the southerners equated with sympathy for the southern rebels.

The agencies were understandably keen to get money to help the southerners around Khartoum and the floods provided a lever. It is true they did valuable work in getting clean water and medical supplies to the worst-affected areas. But it is also true that the people who responded to the appeal were deceived by the agencies, media and Sudanese government as to the scale of the disaster and the real reason the money was needed. The agencies' and government's motives were obviously pecuniary, though they wanted to help different constituencies, but the media were simply stuck with their initial overestimation of the story and the editors' continuing demand for drama.

Reporters keen on keeping their jobs are forced to respond. One described people struggling to get on to a plane leaving a partially flooded town on the lower Nile. In a continent where planes are chronically overbooked, this is not unusual. In many places the only way to confirm your seat is to sit in it. Such deception is common. The camera can lie as well. I was once told by a cameraman filming hungry children "always shoot down on them – then the body looks thinner and the head bigger".

Another big story out of Africa in late 1987 and early 1988 was the new Ethiopian famine. It did not happen, though an American news magazine devoted a cover story to it. For several months we were told by relief workers that the mass migrations, the harrowing feeding camps and the haunting faces of the dying would be back within weeks. Eventually, and rather shamefacedly, they started asking why not. It appears the people had far more stocks than the agencies' surveys had revealed, and that the rebel movements in Eritrea and Tigre had brought in far more relief supplies than the agencies had believed possible. The donors had again been deceived.

Nobody wants to be caught unawares by something like the great Ethiopian famine of 1984/5 again. But it could be equally dangerous to go on crying wolf to people in the West who are already suffering from compassion fatigue. And once supplies are on the way they tend to be handed out whether they are needed or not. One of the reasons for the low harvest in Ethiopia in 1987, and consequent risk of famine in 1988, was that the farmers had planted less. Good harvests in the previous two years had coincided with continued distribution of "relief food" left over from the huge but somewhat tardy response to the previous famine.

The development of recipients' dependence on aid has been widely discussed: the development of aid workers' dependence on their salaries less so. The aid agency worker's aim should be to do himself out of a job. The fact that this so rarely happens may not be solely due to the incompetence of many of Africa's governments or the intractable poverty of its people.

There are other areas in which the use of donors' and tax-payers' money should be questioned. In Showak, a small town that housed the headquarters of the United Nations High Commission for Refugees' programme to assist the Eritrean and Tigrean refugees in eastern Sudan, nearly every vehicle I saw had "donated by the UNHCR" stencilled on the side. Few were on UNHCR business. In many African capitals one becomes familiar with the striking array of aid agency logos, almost always on new, fully-equipped and expensive four-wheel-drive vehicles.

In contrast to the publicity given to the Ethiopian famine that wasn't, the carnage in southern Sudan in 1988 went largely unnoticed until it was too late. Most agencies refused to work in rebel areas, for fear of jeopardizing their operations in northern Sudan, where the situation could no longer be defined as an emergency. A few agencies organized road convoys or flights to the government garrison town of Juba, the former southern capital where thousands had sought food and refuge. Only one small Norwegian agency was operating into rebel-held areas, and it was having trouble maintaining flights by a single light aircraft that could only carry ten bags of grain. The International Committee of the Red Cross (ICRC) was painfully negotiating with the government and rebels for an arrangement to supply isolated government garrisons at the same time as rebel areas on a strictly reciprocal basis. It would finally get the go-ahead at the end of the year, nine months after the programme was proposed and too late for thousands of people.

The flow of starving Dinka and other southern tribespeople into Ethiopia, most of whom reported walking for weeks on the sustenance of leaves and watching many of their fellows die, was clear evidence that something was amiss from April. But there seemed for months afterwards to be a conspiracy between agencies, the rebels and the government to conceal the extent of the tragedy. When I was covering the floods in August an Irish relief worker whispered in my ear that hundreds of people were dying daily in camps in southern Kordofan, walking skeletons from the war zone who could not be saved. He would not go on the record or help me get down there, however. He did not want to get his agency into trouble with the government. It seemed that all the agencies were waiting for another one to blow the story wide open, get kicked out and so generate the international assistance and pressure that would enable those remaining to expand their operations. I asked several times why all the agencies did not do it together, and received all sorts of answers about the need to remain independent or responsibilities to donors. The real reason seemed to be that the thousands of dollars of the salaries of the expatriate aid workers made them too timid to expose the thousands of deaths in and around the south.

As I flew down in March 1989 to el-Muglad, site of one of the death camps in southern Kordofan, I saw from the air the real reason for the war. Immediately outside Khartoum was pure desert. Then fields began to be visible, faintly etched on the pink sand. Further south there was an occasional baobab, lonely monuments to the forests that once grew there. The desert is swallowing the once fertile land, abetted by the agricultural "schemes" that allow northern businessmen to clear thousands of acres, plant millet or dura for a few years and then move on.

As we reached el-Muglad we could see trees and belts of green along riverbeds. The north needs the land of the south, with its swamps, waterways and trees, not the people. Though they are supposed to be parts of the same country, the south is essentially resisting colonization by the north. Though much is made of the religious issue, it is symbolic and secondary to the issue of land and resources. To many northerners the death of thousands of southerners is of little concern. In this area of Sudan two Arab tribes, the Rizeigat and the Messariya, have traditionally fought the Dinka and other southern, African, tribes over grazing land. The pressure of the desert and the provision of weapons has made their raids increasingly lethal, destroying the capacity of the survivors to feed themselves.

We were a year late to cover the famine. The journalists were being allowed in *en masse* – there were two plane loads of us – for the first time, but only to a place on the fringes of the south and only after the carnage had faded, some said because all the vulnerable people were dead. Though an Irish agency had taken a leading role in establishing several camps for the displaced where adequate food was available for the continuing flow of refugees, its officials were still nervous about upsetting the government.

There was a macabre comedy on the plane on the way back to Khartoum over the governor of Kordofan's invitation for us to stop and have lunch with him in el-Obeid. We knew the government had not lifted a finger the year before, and that it continued to obstruct the efforts of the agencies. We had little desire to hear one of its members try to take credit for them. Most of the journalists wanted to get back for hotels or deadlines, and did not see why they should be hijacked by a governor in search of media attention. We had packed lunches anyway. We told the pilot to radio back to the governor's plane to this effect. The same relief official who had refused to go on the record at the time of the floods, seven months before, became incensed, and told us that our refusal could jeopardize his entire programme. He was unmoved by our argument that the government was unlikely to court the embarrassment of stories saying that our refusal to go to lunch with him had persuaded a governor to starve a few thousand more southerners. He even rejected the sound excuse that a stop in el-Obeid, and the extra fuel and flying time paid for out of relief funds, would make us late for a scheduled press conference with the Prime Minister (it was of course postponed anyway, as everybody expected). Eventually he simply ordered the pilot to land at el-Obeid, where we careered through the streets in a convoy cacophanous with horns led by a jeep full of gun toting soldiers. Lunch was graced by an exhibition of dishonesty crowned by the governor's claim that far from arming the Arab militias that raided the south for young slaves and cattle and contributed to the famine by burning crops and villages as well as shooting many of the adults, the government was actively trying to arrest all those carrying weapons illegally, and that there were not any militias anyway.

After lunch the governor insisted on showing us the brimming food stores in his capital. He seemed unaware of the callousness this displayed after what we had seen in the morning. Perhaps, like many northerners, he could not conceive of southerners as people with the same level of humanity as himself. Though most of the people at the camp at el-Muglad had been reasonably fed, one child at least was dying of starvation, beyond hope, and many more were seriously malnourished. Further to the south the situation was worse. About two hundred people were arriving every day at the camp at el-Muglad alone.

Despite its vast deserts, swamps and savannahs, Sudan for a journalist was a country of camps. Well over a million southerners had fled to the north by 1989. Another three hundred thousand had fled the southern countryside for the relative security of the handful of government garrison towns. Such people are referred to as displaced. There were also about a million Eritrean and Tigrean refugees in eastern Sudan, while nearly five hundred thousand southern Sudanese had sought refuge in Ethiopia. That all these people have been forced to leave their homes is an eloquent statement of the failure of the region's governments and rebel movements to care for people they say they represent. It might be different if civil war was not the only way of expressing opposition, as it is in most of Africa.

The camps all over Africa have a depressing sameness, but you develop a keen appreciation of the subtle gradations of misery, so that you can soon tell within a few minutes of entering a camp how bad the food or health problems are. In the older camps thatched huts have replaced most of the often unbearably hot tents supplied by the agencies and the conditions are generally reasonable, as long as it is dry. The wetter it is the more likely that a series of epidemics is sweeping the camp, due to inadequate sanitation, though hot, dry conditions favour the spread of meningitis.

The medical tents or huts are the focus. If the stench of old sweat, disinfectant, vomit and excrement is overpowering before you even enter them, you know it's bad. But what seeps into you immediately and almost unconsciously is the mood of the people. At a camp in Malawi once I saw children playing and adults playing the fool as food was distributed on a sunny evening, while a spirited football game went on nearby. A sense of happy relief pervaded the scene. Next morning it had rained. Many of the people had no shelter. Worse, the news had spread that there had been several cholera cases. People stood in little groups, a blanket over their shoulders if they had one, staring into smoking fires.

The distinction of the grades of misery is a peculiarly journalistic one, however. Even the best camp would be hell for a European, though it would usually be a vast improvement on what the inmates had left behind. Any provisions governments or aid agencies can provide normally go to the camps first, where they are most easily distributed.

During the famine of 1988 there were no camps in the sprawling hinterlands of southern Sudan loosely controlled by the rebels and virtually no provision for their scattered population, estimated at about four million. From the beginning of the year I tried to get permission from the SPLA to go into the rebel areas and approval from the only agency then operating there to hitch a ride on the small plane it was using. Ground transport was out of the question because of the distance, danger and absence of passable roads. Though thousands of their own people were dying and the SPLA representatives in Nairobi kept saying how bad the situation was, that the government was operating a policy of genocide and that yes, they wanted journalists to verify this, all sorts of bureaucratic obstacles kept arising. Though the agency confirmed rumours that thousands were dying on the death marches to the north and towards Ethiopia, leaving skeletons littering the trails, and Egil Hagen, in charge of the operation out of Kenya, kept saying he would put me on the next flight, there was always a last-minute hitch. Neither the rebels nor the agency seemed completely committed to publicizing the people's plight, except when it also served their own interests.

Egil Hagen of Norwegian People's Aid was an oddity even for an aid agency worker, with a military style preserved from his days in an élite Norwegian Army unit. He still gave "briefings" using a telescopic pointer on the map, his carefully developed biceps bulging under his shirt. He was intensely proud that he had managed to establish the trust of the SPLA, and pioneer operations in their area. Some workers from other agencies said this was because most of the limited supplies he arranged to be brought in went straight to the SPLA. None of them were getting anything in at all, however, and without his groundwork and that of the ICRC the huge relief programme for 1989, announced in a blaze of publicity by the United Nations, would have got nowhere.

Operation Lifeline Sudan, which had an initial and hopelessly ambitious target to ship over one hundred thousand tonnes of food into the south in a single month, depended to a large extent on routes already established by other agencies. Its directors had to massage the figures to make it look like it was even approaching its steadily redefined targets. The operation was originally supposed to take place during a "month of tranquillity" agreed by government and rebels. They did not agree it, however, and we slipped from "bubbles of tranquillity" to the final "corridors of tranquillity". The new corridors planned by Lifeline took weeks or months to open, despite a unilateral declaration of a ceasefire by the rebels, which was sketchily observed by both sides until late 1989.

Though it cannot be denied that the operation saved a lot of lives, a series of crude publicity stunts reinforced the distaste of many people in the region for an operation pretending to be the cavalry coming to the rescue when it was a year too late and two hundred and fifty thousand people were dead. Flying in film stars to weep at the camps and flagging off trucks which were not actually going to Sudan at all did not help. Relief workers in Khartoum told me a train carrying food for the garrison town of Aweil was nearly flagged off half-full, apparently because Mr James Grant, the UNICEF Director in charge of Lifeline, was in town and some of his people thought it was a good chance to get some publicity.

There was a general impression among the Nairobi press corps that the operation leaders were fools, thought we were fools, or had totally failed to brief themselves properly on the difficulties of doing anything in southern Sudan. When the SPLA threatened to bombard Juba on one occasion, jeopardizing an airlift into the town on which nearly three hundred thousand people depended, Mr Grant telexed Nairobi to say the airport would be safe because it was on the east bank of the Nile, opposite the town on the west bank. The airport is in fact near the town on the west bank. The only place you could find it on the east bank was on a glossy, stylized map produced by Lifeline. Brightly coloured bands marked the "corridors of tranquillity", several of which were as imaginative as the placing of the airport at Juba.

Outside the towns southern Sudan can best be described as early iron age, with the exception of the rebels' weapons. A completely naked Dinka well over six foot tall with an AK47 over his shoulder is not an unusual sight. The difficulties of doing things in the south were amply demonstrated by my first visit to a rebel-controlled area, which finally took place in April 1988, three months after I started trying to get in.

Our departure was delayed for a day, as the rebel offices in Addis Ababa had failed to relay a radio report on the condition of the airstrip at Pibor, our destination. Mike Grenell, our American pilot, could not tell if it was too soft from the air and had nearly bogged down or crashed on several occasions. He would not fly without the radio report, unreliable as it could be. The SPLA commanders at various airstrips sometimes proved optimistic about their condition in their desire for supplies. Though the ten bags of grain, medicines and other items each flight carried were supposed to be entirely for the civilians, it was clear the SPLA benefited, if only by taking control of them and distributing them. Mike cheerfully described himself as a mercenary. There were inevitable rumours that he was connected with the CIA, and carried more than relief supplies.

The seven hundred and fifty-mile flight, on an aircraft with twin turbocharged engines, would take three hours from Nairobi. Once we passed Lokichoggio, a remote settlement near the Sudanese border west of Lake Turkana in Kenya's Northern Frontier District, we were less able to enjoy the view. According to our flight plan Lokichoggio was our destination. The Kenyan government's sanction for the flights was unofficial. Once we passed the border we were illegal entrants into Sudanese airspace. Though many of the rebels knew the blue striped aircraft, the only one the SPLA allowed to fly into its territory at the time, many more might be too trigger happy or nervous to look carefully before they fired. This meant we had to stay at about fifteen thousand feet, above the range of the rebels' missiles but clearly visible if one of the MiGs based in Juba happened to make one of their occasional sorties east. Mike once flew right past a Sudanese Airforce Hercules transport plane, but either the pilots did not see him or the MiGs failed to respond to their report. This time our passage over the empty grey plains of south-eastern Sudan was uneventful. As we circled down onto the airstrip all we could see was a few corrugated iron-roofed buildings damaged by shellfire and a few more, rather newer looking thatched huts. This was Pibor, a very small town in the middle of nowhere that had been captured by the SPLA about a year before.

Nobody gave the place – stranded on a seasonal riverbed on the dry plains – much thought, until Egil and his colleagues said that several hundred Dinka were arriving every day on their desperate trek to the refugee camps of south-western Ethiopia, and that most of them were starving. Many of those arriving in Ethiopia were hardly able to walk. Pibor was a staging post where many stopped for a few days to regain a little strength on the meagre rations made available from the tiny amounts of food flown in by Mike's plane. Egil had described it as a "holocaust", and Lindsay Hilsum of the BBC and I had taken two precious seats in place of further grain so that, in Egil's words, "the world will know".

After a bumpy landing, in which we broke the steering gear in the nose wheel, so that Mike had to use the engines to control our direction on the ground, we jumped out into the fierce heat. We were met by the local SPLA commander, known simply as "Commander", Clement the area administrator, Abraham the security officer and a character of mysterious responsibility called Dr Dow. Only Commander had a floppy hat to protect him from the sun, his authority also marked by a loosely slung holster round his waist. They did not apparently want the world to know, however. After they had accepted our gifts of whisky, cigarettes and magazines we were told we did not have the right papers and must leave again immediately.

We should perhaps have guessed that that great millstone around Africa's neck, bureaucracy, would have reached such a desolate spot moments after the rebels had captured it. Egil told me later that one of the first things the SPLA had asked for after he had begun flying in small quantities of supplies a month before was a filing cabinet, despite the desperate shortages of food and medicine.

We were repeatedly assured we could come back the next day, while we appealed to be allowed to stay. We pleaded that people's lives were more important than bits of paper, that the bags of grain we would displace on another flight could save several lives, that this trip had taken months to arrange and that we did not believe there would be another opportunity. The rains might close the airstrip any day, we said, to be assured it would be dry the next day. We did not say we did not relish again risking being shot down either by the Sudanese Airforce or the SPLA itself.

Mike had been shot at by the rebels before. He had heard

gunfire when he approached the airstrip at the SPLA headquarters on the Boma plateau. He had immediately started to climb, but an SPLA commander in the back – Mike said he had never seen a Dinka, normally one of the darkest skinned of Africans, look so pale – yelled: "Dive, dive. If they're firing the guns they'll fire the missile." Mike dived, fortuitously over the SPLA camp. The heat-seeking missile, apparently distracted by the camp fires, exploded there.

I thought Commander was wavering under our appeals, but his colleagues were watching him and he decided to stick to the rules. Apparently all would have been well if the SPLA office in Nairobi had remembered to pass a radio message to him via Addis Ababa warning of our arrival. He agreed we would not have got on the plane without approval. He recognized Lindsay's voice from her broadcasts and had heard of my articles. He appreciated the whisky we had brought for him. I think he knew we would be unlikely to get back soon. Rain did close the airstrip the next day, and by the time everything was sorted out Mike's plane was stranded at another airstrip in the south, having broken down while trying to take off in waterlogged mud.

Our suspicions about the SPLA were further aroused by an apparently reassuring remark made by one of its men at Pibor. "Don't worry, we'll keep the displaced people here until you come back," he said. We told him not to. Food and relative security lay two weeks' walk away in Ethiopia. The government's policy appeared to be to starve the south into submission. The result of arming and then turning a blind eye to the activities of the militias was predictable enough given the precariousness of existence in the south. But the SPLA seemed just as prepared to use food as a weapon as the government. It wanted to maximize the relief supplies on its side and so win the hearts and minds of all the southern tribes, but did not want to allow the supply of the government garrison towns, despite the presence there of hundreds of thousands of threatened southern civilians. Many of these civilians reported ill-treatment by the SPLA.

The SPLA's reports of atrocities committed by government troops or pro-government militias were not matched by an all out effort to help the victims. On several occasions the rebels demanded hundreds of dollars from journalists who wanted to visit their areas. Their intransigence delayed the implementation of relief programmes just as much as that of the government. It was only after international pressure stemming from the carnage of 1988 forced both government and rebels to allow more extensive relief efforts on both sides in the south that access became easier. By late 1989, however, a new military government had ordered a suspension of relief flights following a series of bombings and military engagements, and the SPLA appeared to be mobilizing for attacks on the remaining garrisons in the south. Sporadic relief flights were permitted to resume but the army too was preparing to go on the offensive.

I finally managed to spend a few days in the rebel areas of the south in April 1989, at the beginning of the six-month lull in the war and a year after our brief stop in Pibor. The ICRC allowed us to go in on one of its aircraft, but in line with its strict rules of neutrality insisted we had permission from both the government and rebels. So we set off from Nairobi with a Sudanese government visa specifying permission to enter a rebel area stamped in our passport, much to our amazement. After a couple of weeks of the usual bureaucratic delay, the SPLA had finally given us the correct papers as well.

Though the ICRC planes were marked with prominent red crosses and communicated with Sudanese air traffic control, I was still slightly nervous of a long flight over the south. On the way back from Pibor I had asked Mike Grenell, who had made about twenty-five flights into SPLA territory and nearly been killed at least once, why he went on when the SPLA were so obviously unreliable. He answered that he would just do a few more, to pay for his daughter's education. He did one too many.

I saw his daughter at a hotel in Nairobi at the end of 1988, being consoled by friends and relatives after he had disappeared with Gary Taylor, his co-pilot. The Kenyan papers said at first that he had been on the way to Lokichoggio, but this was based on the falset flight plan. Nobody was very surprised when the SPLA said they had found the remains of the aircraft and two bodies in the Imatong mountains in Sudan where they had apparently crashed due to bad weather. Nobody else has seen any wreckage. There are rumours that they were in fact shot down. Mike and his colleague were taking spares with the intention of recovering the aircraft he had been forced to abandon months before in Yirol.

We spent a night at the ICRC base camp at Lokichoggio before flying into Sudan. Twenty of the organization's Swiss workers, who had left the south for meetings, a few days' rest or treatment for various tropical diseases, were also staying there. The mess hut was well stocked with cold beers and good food, but the safari tents were stifling at night. Even the termites here seem to have difficulty with the heat. Instead of the normal mounds, they send narrow cooling towers up to fifteen feet above the ground. Their association with the succulent candelabra trees, or euphorbia, that have also adapted to the hot, dry environment makes for an outlandish landscape. The camp's mascot was Alice, a rescued chick which had turned into a full-grown male ostrich. He wandered peacefully around the camp, and drank soapy water over the shoulders of the undisturbed washerwomen. It was dangerous to pull his feathers. The woman running the camp told me she had seen Alice chasing one of the staff, and then sending him flying with a kick in the back. The man had attempted to snatch a plume.

Jim Malone of the *Voice of America*, Guenther Krabbe of the *Frankfurter Allgemeine Zeitung* and I climbed aboard the plane early in the morning, accompanied by some supplies for the ICRC workers at the various strips spread through the thousands of square miles of the south. There can be few places on earth where there is so little sign of human habitation. The few dirt roads built in the past have largely reverted to bush. The huts of the tribespeople are scattered in an immense landscape into which they blend. The occasional herd of cattle is the only sign of human existence.

Our first stop was Lehr, one of those places that leapt to prominence in the south because of the presence of a dirt airstrip. The only sign of an erstwhile civilization was a little row of brick and corrugated iron buildings and trees that had once had aspirations to be a main street. Vultures waddled on the ground, unafraid of people and apparently hoping for a repeat of the previous year's bonanza. The larger and more secure buildings had been taken over as food stores, while tribespeople squatted in the remainder. The traders who had once occupied them were long gone. It was a brief stop, just long enough to drop a passenger, some supplies and mail and have a quick look around. The next stage of the flight to Akon, our destination in the southern province of Bahr el Ghazal, took us over the middle of the Sudd. This mass of swamps, lakes and shifting waterways, carpeted with papyrus and other floating vegetation, ebbs and flows with the rains over most of central southern Sudan, making it one of the most impenetrable parts of the world. *Sudd* means "barrier" in Arabic.

It felt as if we were flying over some massive cell diagram. The brown, fast flowing waters of the White Nile carved a thin, snaking meander through the emerald green of the vegetation. On either side circular lakes had opened up, blue with their clearer water, though wisps of brown showed on the side nearest the main current of the river. Further patches of vegetation, almost perfectly circular, floated in the shifting lakes, gathered in groups at one end by currents or the wind. Occasional low islands or tongues of land, distinguishable by trees, protruded into the seething mass of natural production. There are rumours of pink aquatic elephants here, and other species never recorded. There is a good claim for the worst mosquitoes in the world. What is certain is that here were tonnes of fish while thousands starved, and here were millions of tonnes of water that could have fed rainless fields. A few of the agencies had only just started thinking about bringing in hooks, lines and nets. Irrigation would take the sort of development which has bypassed the south, and neither the northerners nor the Egyptians further downstream would wish it to happen without their control.

One of the major grievances of the Dinka and the SPLA was the Jonglei Canal, a two hundred-mile channel designed to bypass the Sudd, and so reduce evaporation and increase flows downstream. We could see the great line across the south for much of our eventual flight back to Lokichoggio. It must be one of the easiest of man's engineering works to see from space. It was never finished, and it is unlikely that the SPLA or its successors will ever allow it to be finished. The huge excavating machines stand idle, bombed and rusting. The bush and the traditional migrations of cattle and wild animals that it threatened are eroding the banks. Most of the great groove is dry. A friend wanted to make a collection of "development archaeology as art in Africa". Here would be the grandest folly of all, more than worthy to join the silent factories, the jetties built into dry lakes, the tractors used as one end of a washing line. A little further north is another aspirant for the collection, an oil field on which Chevron has spent over $1bn, but whose exploitation has been stopped by the war.

Water is thicker than oil for the Sudanese. The breaks on Sudanese television always show the Nile and the lush crops irrigated by it in the north, waving in the wind to what to the Sudanese are the lyrical strains of violins. Oil may run a few trucks, but in Sudan the possibility of dying due to the lack of water is built into the soul. In the north you still see the amphorae of porous earthenware in public places that allow a cool drink to passers-by.

When we landed at Akon, on the edge of the Sudd, it was obvious that here was a place that, to an even greater extent than Lehr, owed its position on a map to an airstrip. On a relief agency's map anyway. On most others it does not appear. There was never a pretence of a main street, though there were a few crumbling brick buildings, used as clinics and stores by the ICRC. One of the details unaddressed by the planners of Operation Lifeline when they proposed to ship one hundred thousand tonnes of food to the south to see people through the three rainy months that make ground transport impossible was where to put it. There are hardly any weather and pest proof buildings left in the south. It had taken the ICRC at Akon five months to get into the position where the food arriving by two or three Hercules flights a day could be carried by truck to six surrounding distribution points and stored there with reasonable safety. They had to fly in the trucks, cut through the bush that had grown on the tracks, then repair and secure storehouses. One of the two trucks was stuck in a swamp the day we arrived.

Soon after we arrived the first of the Hercules came in from

Entebbe in Uganda. In this wilderness the huge plane seemed almost as remarkable to me as to the Dinka, especially when it sent a great pall of dust into the air with its reversing engines. In parts of the south people had spontaneously started building airstrips, complete with makeshift windsocks, in the belief that the planes would magically arrive. They had little idea where they had come from. There was further evidence of a sort of cargo cult. Amongst the group of several hundred people who had filed out to the airstrip when the plane landed were two witch doctors. They had incorporated the Red Cross insignia, cut from the tins of oil provided by the organization, into their headdresses.

When the ramp was opened a group of about forty local men immediately began unloading the two-hundred-pound sacks of grain by hand, with much shouting, gesticulation and sweat. They also had to fend off the encircling crowd, all trying to pick up a few grains of spilled maize from the poorly tied sacks. As one naked Dinka boy dashed in for the third time, one of the unloaders swatted him with a stick. He still got away with a handful. The unloaders did a little better when the twelve tonnes of food had been stacked on the airstrip. They filled their pockets, if they had any, or stashed a pound or two into rag pouches from the ample pickings on the floor of the hold. Every single grain on the dirt below the ramp was pecked up by the encircling group of women and children. A bare-breasted Dinka woman tried to hide herself in the cargo hold, presumably expecting to reach some unknown paradise in Entebbe, seven hundred and fifty miles and a different world away, but was spotted and ejected.

Most of these people were not yet starving, by the definition that they still had the energy to walk to the airstrip and search for a handful of grain every time a plane arrived. The only reason the ICRC was not distributing the grain as it arrived was to save more lives later, when the rains made the airstrip and the surrounding apologies for roads impassable. A difficult decision, given the obvious hunger of many of the people, but it was one essential not only to prevent a repeat of the previous year, when twenty six thousand people are believed to have died in and around Akon, but also to prevent thousands gathering at the airstrip. The idea was to send the food out to the satellite distribution points so that when the tentacles of the Sudd left the people stranded on patches of slightly higher ground they would be less vulnerable to disease and more likely to plant.

The several hundred people who pressed around us as we walked to the store did not seem impressed by this logic. Despite continual explanation people kept asking for food. To hunger was added a natural curiosity about Europeans, and my clothes darkened with sweat as the throng prevented the slightest breeze from reaching me. The others were similarly hemmed in and stewed. Dominique Nardin, the short and attractive Swiss nurse who ran the simple clinic in Akon, occasionally disappeared from view. She was well-known among the people and several of the young girls, usually dressed only in loincloths, competed to hold her hands. We were not the only excitements. One of the witch-doctors was showing off by sticking the tip of a knife two inches into his eye socket above the eye, using his eyelid to cushion the blade.

The five months it had taken Peter, the ICRC boss in Akon, and three other ICRC staff to get to the stage where relief supplies could be properly handled in the area demonstrated the absurdity of the Lifeline bosses' plans to do the same throughout the south in weeks. It is as well they could not get the food in as fast as they hoped, or thousands of people may have concentrated at a few places, spreading disease and guaranteeing that another harvest failed and that the relief programme had to be extended for another year. At the time we visited Akon twenty-five thousand people had already gathered in Torit, a rebel-held town into which the United Nations had started flying food and other supplies.

Akon was listed as one of the places where Lifeline had established a presence by the time we went there. We found out what that presence meant. The poor man had the advantage of speaking some of the Dinka language, but if it had not been for the presence of the ICRC team he would probably have starved himself. He had virtually no equipment or supplies of his own and lived at the ICRC campsite. He spent his time writing reports and speculating on when a Lifeline relief train would finally move down to the government garrison town of Aweil, some sixty kilometres to the west of Akon, and how he could unload and distribute some of the food on board in the rebel areas as it passed with virtually no transport or staff.

The first major piece of equipment he had received arrived on the plane with us, several weeks after he had been dropped in Akon. Out of sympathy Peter and Dominique tried to keep quiet about it, or at least not to laugh. After we had had a drink in the evening the story came out. The various boxes had contained a computerized transmission system, which would enable him to make telephone, telex or fax calls anywhere in the world by satellite. There were only two problems. There was no generator to run it, and even if there had been the unique combination of heat, dust and humidity this region offers would have destroyed it in days if not hours. There were certainly no air-conditioned rooms to put it in in Akon. I had fried a portable computer of my own by using it outside in Khartoum.

The ICRC camp consisted of three safari tents under a tree, surrounded by the flimsy protection of a thin fence of dried grass. It would have to be moved soon, as the ground where it stood would be flooded when the rains came. In this place, as in much of the south, nature is unremittingly malign. In the dry season meningitis flourishes. It is endemic. When the rains come the meningitis stops, but swarms of mosquitoes carry the annual plague of malaria. The people here have to resist an environment apparently bent on their destruction, as well as the disruption and occasional violence of the war. Drought, floods or locusts had destroyed their crops for the last two years. Rinderpest was killing their cattle, which they could not sell to buy food because of the war.

Most of the people were infected with worms. Dominique was trying to provide a basic health service, but she said "there is not much point treating people for worms if they just get reinfected". She was vaccinating women against tetanus and children against tuberculosis, diptheria, measles and whooping cough, all common and lethal in combination with malnourishment. She said nobody had been vaccinated before.

Many got injected with snake venom, however, usually from puff adders or cobras.

A snake bite victim joined a man shot in the chest to be evacuated to the ICRC hospital in Lokichoggio on the morning we arrived. I had seen another snake bite case at the hospital. Necrosis of the skin and flesh had left the bones exposed, and the doctor did not know if he could save the leg. Such a wound and the associated infections would have killed a European, he said. The Dinka have an astonishing resistance to infection. Dominique told me of another case where a man walked around with a grossly infected jaw without treatment for seven years, until he turned up at the clinic at Akon. Many did succumb to the combination of starvation and disease, however, especially the previous year. Many bodies went unburied, as their relatives were too weak to dig. As a result, as in Eritrea, the hyenas acquired a taste for human flesh. Many cases of hyenas attacking people, usually boys herding cattle, had been reported. The animal's trademark is to go for the face. Dominique also had to treat someone mauled by a lion.

About the only benefit to the people in this area until the ICRC arrived in December 1988 was that it had been held by the SPLA for more than two years, in sufficient strength to discourage the Arab militias from raiding. We talked with the local commander one morning, sitting in the shade of a group of mango trees on low chairs of rough wood and untanned leather. His bodyguards took up positions around the trees, and we were all startled when a sharp crack split the air. It was a branch breaking off one of the trees, however, and some naked Dinka boys started running in to grab the unripe fruit. They were obviously nervous of the rebels, though the men started throwing fruit towards them. Commander Daniel Akot told us that further north the raiding was still going on, with the militias taking the cattle and young boys and killing the rest. The Commander said the Rizeigat sold the children to Libya. Though it will always be hard to prove, slavery appears to be alive and well in Sudan. I heard many stories of southerners being pressed into service in northern homes or farms, particularly when walking north to escape the war and famine.

After seeing and hearing about such things all day, you begin to hope for a respite. Though Guenther produced a bottle of whisky, which he offered by saying "have some disinfectant" to everyone, and amused us by appearing in black pyjamas and sandals that could have come from the Vietcong, this was not to be. As I lay on a camp-bed outside to escape the heat – eggs have a tendency to partially cook by themselves here – I could hear a continual rustle as thousands of termites devoured the fence a few feet away. Peter warned us they would eat your clothes if you left them on the ground. He also told us to watch out for scorpions in our shoes in the morning. When Jim went to bed shortly afterwards he called that there was one in his tent. A three-inch pale-brown specimen was clinging to the wall next to his bed. It was dispatched and the camp went to sleep. In the distance a woman wailed monotonously.

Southern Sudan is a trying place at the best of times. If Prime Minister Sadiq el-Mahdi's feeble northern coalitions were content to leave the southerners to rot in the bad times, with a little help from the militias, the military government led by General Omer el-Bashir that took over in June 1989 could be expected to actively encourage a return to the inferno. After the coup it pretended, in another example of Sudanese political deviousness, to be in favour of a negotiated end to the war, which many people in the north were coming to desire as much as those in the south. This was simply playing for time. Once the junta had entrenched itself it started to pursue the war more vigorously and arrest anyone who dared speak against it. It became obvious that the officers of the junta were closely allied with the Islamic fundamentalists.

It has been argued that the failure of el-Mahdi's three-year long series of governments, the result of a popular uprising against former dictator Jaafar Nimeiri, was a classic failure of multi-party democracy in Africa. It is true that el-Mahdi's Umma party, the largest, depended on the Ansar to the south-west of Khartoum, the Muslim sect that had enabled his great-grandfather to defeat General Gordon and expel the British from Sudan in the 1880s. It is true the second largest group, the Democratic Unionist Party, depended on the Khatmiya sect, living mainly in eastern Sudan. It is true that this traditional rivalry encouraged both sides to seek support from the fundamentalist National Islamic Front, which gained a disproportionate amount of influence and so blocked moves towards peace. It was at this time that a colleague's comment that "Sudan's problem is too much democracy" seemed all too apposite.

But it might have been very different if all the southern seats had been filled in the elections of 1986. A large southern block – second only to el-Mahdi's party in size – could have prevented el-Mahdi's breach of faith, his failure, wilful or otherwise, to deliver the repeal of Sharia law and negotiated settlement to the war he promised before the elections. In retrospect foreign governments could have pushed the Sudanese government and the rebels much harder to allow elections in all the southern constituencies, rather than in less than half, as well as offering assistance in transport and policing. It was a golden opportunity missed. What was needed was more democracy, not less.

Town of
the Living Dead

Juba

There were signs of the carnage to come when I first visited Juba in February 1988. The former southern capital was then beginning its long siege by the Sudan People's Liberation Army. Of all the besieged towns of the world, it would be the best for fishing. Near the town centre and past the camps for the thousands who had fled the countryside flowed a river teeming with Nile perch, tigerfish and other species. By October people were starving next to this river. They had nothing to catch the fish with.

When Nile Safaris' Boeing 707 reached the town, nestling ten thousand feet below in a bend in the White Nile, it went into a steep banked, spiralling dive onto the airport. A normal approach would have exposed us to the rebels' missiles or gunfire. Later in the year the SPLA got so close to the airport that several planes were hit despite such precautions, including this Boeing.

Flying in Africa — insecurity and deterioration of the road and rail networks makes it the only way to travel — is fraught with difficulties at the best of times. It is the continent of overbooking, delays and cancellations. This is reflected in the nicknames given to the airlines. Air Tanzania Corporation was known as Air Total Chaos, the Zairean carrier as Air Peut-être and Sudan Airways as Sudden Death. Nigeria is one of the worst places to travel by air. People fight their way to the front of queues, fearing that someone else will bribe their way into their seat or leave them last in the interminable wait to clear cumbersome formalities. When I flew from Nigeria to Ghana once there was the usual rush out of the plane as soon as the doors opened. One of the Ghanaian stewardesses shouted out, "Hey, you're not in Lagos now."

My arrival at Lagos was one of the most harrowing I encountered in Africa. Our passports disappeared into a cubicle surrounded by baying travellers, all sweating and anxious. The passports eventually returned one by one, the name of the owner yelled out, often indistinguishably, by an official. After a long wait for your baggage, and a surprisingly perfunctory customs check, you plunge into the maelstrom. Dozens of touts clamour to take your bag, get you a taxi, change money or smooth your onward booking. Several simply attach themselves to you, and a rebuff may be met with fierce determination, even if you say quite firmly that you are not paying for services you have not asked for.

I was supposed to be met, but the man had not turned up so I waited, exposed as a target. Cunning developed. A man came up, the first of three, and said "Mr Buckoke? I'm here to meet you." Relief was followed by suspicion. Why had he not paged me before? I asked him who had sent him, and whom I worked for. "Your boss," he said. "Not good enough," I replied. He had read my baggage tags. I decided to get a taxi to my hotel and walked outside. It was even worse. Apparently some system of bribery limited the number of operators inside. I was besieged. I picked the most honest looking taxi driver. As I got into the car a man I had never seen before demanded furiously why I had not paid him. We drove off after another man joined the taxi driver, increasing my suspicions I would be mugged and abandoned in some slum.

I had no idea where the car was going, and then the driver said "You pay me now." There was nothing resembling a hotel in sight and I refused. "I take you back to the airport then," he said. "Just let me out here, you get nothing unless I get to the hotel," I said, wondering what I would do on some unknown street in Lagos in the middle of the night. He drove on and a few minutes later we reached the hotel. A friend told me I would have been fleeced if I had given in.

Overbooking is not always a problem. When I arrived at Khartoum airport to fly back to Nairobi after my first trip to Juba I was surprised that so few people were about. I spread a cloth on the ground and rested my head on my bag, preparing to sleep through the inevitable delay. Soon someone tapped me on the shoulder and asked if I was flying to Nairobi. I said I was and he led me through security, where nobody was on duty, and

onto the plane, a Boeing 737. There was nobody on it except me.
Sudan Airways had only recently reopened its route to the
Kenyan capital, which passes over the south. Though the planes
went far too high to be hit, and other airlines regularly flew the
route, Sudan Airways had been nervous of doing so ever since
one of its planes was shot down leaving another isolated southern
garrison town, Malakal, killing all on board.

Airport was a grand title for the runway and rudimentary
terminal at Juba, but at least the strip was tarred. The eight
kilometres in the centre of Juba was the only tarred road in the
south. The charter company's Boeing was the only plane carrying
civilian passengers on the seven hundred kilometre run from
Khartoum, the only way, in fact, for a civilian to get to Juba
from the north. Sudan Airways cabin staff had refused the
bonuses offered to them for flying the route. The British crew
on the Nile Safaris' plane were apparently well enough paid to
ignore the repeated threats on SPLA radio to shoot it down, on
the grounds that it was carrying military supplies. It was. Behind
my seat the fuselage was filled with racks of green canisters I
was told contained artillery ammunition.

The government had denied the plane carried military supplies,
so my presence next to them was one of those absurdities you
came to expect in the Sudan. It had taken two weeks to get a
permit to go to Juba. Security refused my first application,
presumably on the grounds that I would see things like the shells
in the plane. I asked a lady in the department of information to
appeal for me. She asked why I wanted to go so badly since
everything was fine in Juba. I asked why I could not go if that
was the case. Much to my surprise Sudanese bureaucracy
capitulated and I was given the permit. About twelve visits to
five different offices was all it took to get everything properly
signed and stamped. I was the first journalist to be allowed in for
over a year. The few expatriates working for aid agencies in Juba
were amazed at my arrival.

Sudanese officials seem unaware of the absurdity or dishonesty
of their actions or statements. When I interviewed the Finance
Minister, Dr Bashir Omer, in late 1986, after waiting for a week

outside his office, he promised that a constitutional conference to end the war would be held by the end of December. He said the same thing as Information Minister in late 1988, with equal conviction and equal lack of accuracy.

Once I got into the centre of Juba, I was surprised to find that many of the things the SPLA was fighting for were already happening. The Arab-influenced turbans and jellabiyeh of Khartoum were replaced by the Western styles of black Africa. Black Africans were running the government offices. People worked, or were supposed to work, on Fridays, the Muslim weekly holiday, and not on Saturdays and Sundays. Beer and whisky, though in short supply, were on sale at bars and clubs, in open contravention of the Sharia law whose repeal was a major goal of the SPLA.

I spent the first night at the Juba Hotel, nicknamed the Juba Hilton. The pathways between the crumbling buildings were lined with empty beer bottles, mainly Zairean, pushed neck first into the ground. Some grimy red velvet curtains in the dining room hinted at grander days, but when a Japanese colleague visited a few weeks later he had to lend the manager some money to buy food. The swimming pool was long empty. The rooms had domed concrete roofs that acted like storage heaters, retaining the heat of the sun to radiate down on you all night. I was impressed when the shower worked, a welcome relief from temperatures over 40°C, and astounded when a faint tinkling sound proved to be reception calling to say I had a visitor. He told me the tap water came straight out of the Nile and could carry bilharzia, a disease caused by intestinal parasites whose larval stage enters the body through the skin. Now more than ever, with the normal population of eighty thousand swollen to two hundred thousand by the war, the water was likely to be contaminated. My astonishment that the room phones worked was tempered when reception explained it was impossible to call out of the hotel, as the town's phone system no longer functioned.

I begged a room at the United States Agency for International Development (USAID) resthouse the next day. The luxury of clean sheets, a ceiling fan and intact mosquito netting was almost overwhelming. The USAID club was next door, complete with bar, full swimming pool and tennis courts. Here the fifty-odd expatriates in Juba at the time, nearly all of them aid workers, gathered every afternoon to sip cold Kenyan beer, shipped via Uganda in the last road convoy to get through, and discuss the day's events. As we talked everybody surreptitiously kept an eye on the planes circling down or spiralling up from the airport, wondering when the first one would be hit. That would probably close it, stranding us all in Juba, but you also wondered if all the flights arriving and departing safely were going to leave you holding the short straw when your turn came.

Meanwhile a petite Frenchwoman working for OXFAM would be relentlessly swimming her laps in the pool, and the players on the tennis courts, taking advantage of the relative cool of the evening, were dressed in white.

One of the first things that I heard at the club was that the Army had commandeered seven trucks from OXFAM. These had been paid for by the British Government and were used to distribute relief food in and around Juba. Despite strong protests another three were taken a couple of days later. As an OXFAM worker wryly noted, "It doesn't make much difference, we haven't got any food to distribute anyway." The Arab traders still had food, but the prices were beyond the means of most of Juba's salaried residents, let alone the displaced in the camps. The government had promised relief flights from Khartoum, but the four or five trips each day by Nile Safaris and a Sudan Airways cargo plane were entirely devoted to military supplies or goods for the traders. It was said the army deliberately limited the number of road convoys, in collusion with the traders.

Though most of the people in Juba were from tribes other than the Dinka, from which the SPLA is mainly drawn, and feared their domination, the rapacity and indiscipline of the soldiers meant more and more sympathized with the rebel movement. Though nobody was yet starving, the danger signs were there. I visited Kadoro, a camp three miles from Juba on the east bank of the Nile, with a medical team. About ten of the sixty children we saw had the stick limbs and swollen bellies of severe malnutrition. We were told many others did not come to the clinic because their mothers were out in the bush gathering fire wood to sell for food, despite an SPLA mortar attack on an army post nearby two nights before and the mines that both sides were beginning to lay around the town.

Military objectives took priority over food for southerners. The rebels had taken Kapoeta, a small town two hundred miles east of Juba, a month before. The government had promised to recapture it. The rumble of shelling woke me at about 3 a.m. one morning. The firing continued intermittently until nearly midday. The army said it had found some rebels on a hill outside town, and had shelled and obliterated them. It later became clear that the army had attempted a breakout towards Kapoeta, but had been stopped by a strong SPLA force about ten miles out of town. When the OXFAM trucks were returned most had bullet holes or other damage. The trucks were not the only things to be commandeered. My departure from Juba was delayed when the Nile Safaris plane was dispatched to Uganda to pick up five hundred soldiers who had fled there after Kapoeta fell.

There were still some people dreaming of other things in the midst of war. One day we went out to visit Peter and Anne McClinton, conservationists who lived under a conical hill on the banks of the Nile at Rejaf, about seven miles south of Juba. This was no man's land. Their eccentricity was apparently sufficient to protect them from the attentions of rebels or army, though Peter had made their vehicles and other equipment appear inoperable to prevent them being appropriated. Two young white Zimbabweans were staying with them, keen on helping with various projects, or dreams, of the McClintons. The most immediate concerned a party of heavily armed Rizeigat who were believed to be coming down from the north via the Central African Republic with the aim of crossing back into southern Sudan's game reserves to pillage the ivory. Peter said there were plenty of southern volunteers for an opposing party he was trying to organize. As he said, "They all want to bag an Arab." But it seemed highly unrealistic to expect the army to spare the necessary transport and equipment at such a time.

So we sat on some logs at the edge of the river watching the birds and the rapids, which Peter said were a great place for tiger fish, while there was a long delay in the project at our feet: the two Zimbabweans spent most of the day in the water, disregarding the possibility of bilharzia while trying to get a water powered irrigation pump they had built to work. The device consisted of a paddle like that on a paddle steamer fixed to an oil drum pontoon. The blades were of corrugated iron. The paddle was attached via a crude series of gears to a pump which was expected to lift the water about twenty feet to the McClintons' hypothetical vegetable garden. Once in a while it would clank away merrily, only to groan to a halt after a few spurts of water came out of the end of the pipe. The Zimbabweans would swear, then struggle to adjust the rig's position in the current or bend some part back into shape. We would top up our whiskies. Anne was not drinking. Alcohol aggravated manic depression, she said.

When we got back to town that evening there was a party at a Belgian sleeping sickness expert's house. We sat looking out over the plain north of Juba, hazy under the moonlight, and attacked the whisky. An immense amount of alcohol is drunk in Sudan, as much in the north, where the majority are supposed to support Sharia, as in the south, where it is disregarded but supplies are limited by the war. Parties in Khartoum are usually distinguished by a table covered with bottles of spirits, to which the guests help themselves liberally. The problem lies in getting home. A Sudanese friend got so drunk at one such party that he was incapable of sitting up, and I had to drive his car. A policeman's attention was drawn by his head lolling out of the window, and he waved at me to stop. I accelerated past. The policeman made to unshoulder his rifle, then shrugged.

Opening the diplomatic bag had a new meaning in Khartoum. This was how the embassy staffs brought in their drink. This they consumed openly in their houses, often with the assistance of Sudanese government officials. I went to one party on the tennis court of a diplomat's house. About two hundred people, including turbaned members of the government, were drinking in full view of the street. Flogging had been suspended as the punishment at the time, but drinking was still illegal. I wondered about the implications of leaving such a party, where you were protected by diplomatic immunity, with a skinful.

But Sudanese in every walk of life were keen on an occasional tipple, or often rather more. In the poorer parts of town as well as the wealthy they were voting with their feet – or rather with their bottles or any other handy container. The feeble civilian government, faced with the threat of a military takeover which had been so long expected that it caused hardly a hiccup when it came, argued about the finer points of Sharia law. The people of Khartoum continued with their pleasures.

In a dark street near the city centre cars pulled up, and people strolled by, most clutching the tell-tale plastic bag. Those in the cars that jolted up the potholed road preferred old Coke bottles, plastic flagons and the like, to avoid spills. Those on foot, their jellabiyeh looming ghostlike in the night, were happy to carry the fluid poured off directly into the plastic bag, as if they had won a fairground goldfish. The goldfish was missing, of course, and would probably have dissolved if you had put it in. The flow of customers, only a few very respectable looking northerners in turbans apparently as nervous as myself, made it obvious that the shebeen was tolerated, with the help of bribes to the police.

Many of the pedestrians got no further than the football field across the road, surrounded by the crumbling brick wall banked up with dust that was the distinctive architectural feature of modern Khartoum. Cheerful calls played with the moonlight as ever more customers wandered up. In this secular Sudan there was no distinction between the African, animist of Christian southerner, or the Muslim northerner, whether he was an Ansar or a Khatmiya. They were unified by a taste for *aragi*, a liquor distilled from fermented dates that varies hugely in quality and strength. Even the best is an acquired taste, though there is little doubt how strong it is if you put a match anywhere near it.

When I returned to Juba in December 1988 it was on a Hercules transport plane carrying food from Nairobi. Flights from the Kenyan capital and Entebbe in Uganda had brought the town, with a population now swollen to three hundred thousand, back from the brink of an abyss. The last of the increasingly infrequent road convoys had got through from Uganda in September, and

Juba faced mass starvation until the flights began on 26 October. The people there now depended entirely on the airlift for their survival.

Desultory negotiations between the rebels and a civilian government on its last legs in Khartoum were taking place, but few people expected much to come of them. The Hercules pilots were taking no chances. The classic approach remained a tight, six-turn corkscrew over the centre of town. The SPLA had ordered its units not to fire on relief planes, but its members were not renowned for their discipline or education. One slip, and a downed plane, could have sealed the fate of thousands. The rebels were determined not to let their grip on Juba slacken. An experimental road convoy was on the way while I was there, stocked mainly with goods for the Arab traders. It eventually got through after being attacked six times. It took four days to travel one forty-mile section of road.

As a result of that tightening grip and the government's failure to do anything for the civilians, though cargo planes were coming down from Khartoum daily, the population concentrated in the city centre, society breaking down as the struggle to survive overcame all other considerations. Though the flights had rescued them, a deep pessimism remained. Father James Odok of the African Inland Church told me: "We are just waiting to die, we are like the living dead." Though many people had returned to the camps of tukuls, or thatched huts, that surrounded the few modern buildings of Juba, many others still dossed down in the schools or wherever else they could find shelter in the centre. In places the edges of the streets were covered in dried excrement. One of them was outside the Catholic Cathedral. The words high on the building – *Haec est domus dei* – seemed hard to justify.

Until the first flights arrived people considered braving the mines the rebels and army had laid round the town. We saw a victim at the hospital whose leg had been blown off. "At least there are leaves and wild fruits in the bush," said one of the people I talked to. Jane, a schoolteacher, told me she and her three children had lived on greens and salt for two weeks. One day all she could get for the children was one unripe mango each. One kilogramme of maize had reached a price of more than a tenth of her monthly salary, and she had no money left to buy any. A few days later she and some friends found a trader's store being looted, and carried off a bag of maize. They were repeatedly attacked by men trying to take it from them. Only close relatives helped each other, she said, and sometimes not even them. In the camps they were eating rats. Children were selling them, skewered and roasted on a stick, for 25p.

Despite the flights and a resumption of food distribution 20 per cent of the children at camps like Lolugo, whose sprawl of tukuls housed twenty-five thousand people, were still severely malnourished. Four thousand children at Lolugo were getting what was known as "wet feeding". This meant a grain, bean and milk porridge was cooked and served to them at a feeding centre. If the dry rations were given to their families they might never receive them.

All around the tukuls at Lolugo stood the accusing fingers of millet seed pods, waving in the hot breeze above the healthy plants. It could have been a record harvest in the south in 1988, if the war had not stopped people planting. The tiny acreage per person at Lolugo did little more than show what could have been achieved.

Places like Lolugo, about three miles out of the centre of Juba, were occasionally patrolled by soldiers during the day but belonged to the SPLA at night. Some of the rebels came right into the town under cover of darkness, making the soldiers even more nervous and trigger happy. Hardly a night passed without a burst of automatic fire. One night shots were fired right outside the aid agency compound where I was staying, the USAID guesthouse and club having finally closed down. We never found out what they were about.

Despite this chaos and collapse around them, the ministries in the centre of town continued to function. Though all they had left to administer was themselves, they went at it with a will. When an occasional visiting journalist turned up, the officials were determined to keep up to the normal standards. You still had to wait half an hour outside one idle man's office, only to be told you should in fact be seeing someone else. I was compelled to listen to a half-hour lecture on southern politics from a chaplain who doubled as a government official. Finally I was issued with a press pass and photography permit which nobody ever asked to see.

The photography permit announced: "This is to certify that the bearer of this card has been permitted to take still photographs in Equatoria Region of the Sudan with the exception of Military, Police, Prisons, Demonstrations, Government gatherings and nude persons", which covered about everything. The borrowed camera did not work anyway. The permit cost $30. I thought this was a bit steep when the Governor of Equatoria had personally encouraged us to come and publicize the woes of his capital. Though Juba was all he had left to govern, if the army let him, his government was apparently still bent on extorting money whenever it could. I met a television cameraman walking around town with all his equipment, dripping with sweat and fuming. He had been forced to pay $1,000 for a permit to film the plight of the people of Juba. They charge similar sums to film the gorillas in Rwanda. Starving people, it seemed, had become a similar revenue producer. Maybe they would have to be conserved.

The final example of neglect, both by the northern and local governments, was the hospital. Forty people had starved there in October, though a contractor, an Arab trader, was receiving money from the government to supply food. Dr Malik Abutarboush, a rare bird in such a place, was horrified by the callousness of his fellow northerners. He reckoned that the food delivered to the hospital over the previous two years was worth less than a tenth of the money allocated. Presumably the trader and the government officials who awarded the contract had split the difference. Dr Malik told me what a patient's relative had said when he was asked to bring food from home. "Dr Malik, you better discharge him because we have so little food at home we cannot divide it." Even with aid agency assistance, the hospital could still only offer its patients a bowl of porridge a day.

The hospital and the medical department of the University of Juba, which was also somehow still functioning, were led by Professor Alan Woodruff, a tall, gaunt and determined Englishman who had devoted his retirement to Juba. His contempt for governments, aid agencies and others who failed to approach his high standards was restrained with difficulty.

"The government has done damn all since I came here six years ago," the Professor said of the hospital. "There's a huge budget, but none of it comes down here." As far as he could see the only government expenditure on the hospital had been the staff salaries. He waved his long arms around at the colonial buildings, peering over his gold-rimmed glasses at torn veranda screens, cracking plaster and mouldering paint. "There's been no maintenance since the place was built in 1924," he said. With the help of the aid agencies, boreholes had been dug to replace the irregular and dangerous supplies of tap water. Dr Malik said he had found five different types of worms in the tap water at the children's hospital nearby. The agencies had also helped to repair the blocked drains at the Juba hospital, supposedly the best in the whole south, so draining the open pools of sewage that had spread out in the grounds.

"The only effective drugs come from Salisbury," said Professor Woodruff. "Many of them are out of date, but that doesn't matter, they save lives." He had arranged through the Bishop of Salisbury for time expired drugs to be collected and sent to Juba. They still had to pay import duties on them. A Sudanese doctor had hitched a ride on the Hercules I arrived on. His baggage included boxes of food. The customs men impounded them.

The Professor was incensed when he heard that millions of tablets of time expired chloroquine had been thrown away in the north. The hospital had had none of this crucial anti-malarial drug for nearly four months. Doctors had to tell patients to buy their own. "If they could not afford it," said Dr Malik, "they suffered." Untreated malaria is a killer, especially if the patient is malnourished. At times they had to ask patients scheduled for an operation to bring their own soap, spirit, gauze and bandages.

The hospital had been connected to a special electricity hotline, reserved for the army and senior government officials. They had asked for it to be switched on in the mornings, for X-rays, operations and other uses. "But they'd never do that, because they'd have no electricity in their houses in the evening," said Professor Woodruff. Despite his and his colleagues' efforts the mortality rate at the hospital was around 30 per cent of admissions. Many of the patients came from outlying villages and only braved the walk into Juba after trying the local herbal remedies for too long.

I went to dinner at Professor and Mrs Woodruff's house in Juba one night. He apologized that he had no whisky, and produced some *karkadeh*, a sweet cordial flavoured by dried hibiscus petals, and some beer made with a kit from England. The meal was tinned tuna, dried mixed vegetables and dried mashed potatoes. Welcome in the circumstances. There was some three year old HP sauce on the table. It was just like the time expired medicines, he said, reverting to medical language, "a slight drop in efficacy, but no toxicity."

Another of the Professor's hobby-horses was the behaviour of the aid agency personnel. There were only a handful of expatriates in Juba at the time. Most had left in September and October, and few had returned to back up their local staff even when the relief flights began. "Why," he asked "do they all leave when things get a bit difficult? I would have thought the whole point of being an aid worker is to be there when things get a bit tough."

The Professor's relaxation was astronomy. He had a large telescope under a sheet by the veranda. He said there was remarkable visibility here sometimes, but the lights of the army camp nearby would interfere with any attempt at observations that night. I was reminded of what Oscar Wilde said somewhere. "We are all in the gutter, but some of us are looking at the stars." Very few people in Juba were looking at the stars. My conversations with Jane, the teacher who came to share the meals at the house where I was staying and take some food back for her children, were typical. She echoed Father James's pessimism, relief flights or no relief flights. "There is nowhere for us to go. We might as well stay here and die."

Like many educated southerners, she saw little hope for the south if it remained part of a united Sudan. The Muslim north would not give up trying to dominate it and treating its inhabitants as second class citizens. On the other hand there was as little hope for the south if it was turned over to the SPLA and

Dinka domination. Had I not seen how her own people in the local government, drawn from the smaller tribes in the area, behaved? "When the British left the Arabs came and it has been terrible ever since," she concluded. The answer, it seemed, was some form of temporary recolonization of a separate south. "Somebody from outside should come and rule us for a few years," she said. It is a refrain you often hear in parts of Africa ravaged by war, famine or economic mismanagement. Where thousands are suffering and dying it makes little difference whether they face humiliation by a local despot or by a foreign power. At least the foreign power may allow them to plant, and harvest enough of what they plant to survive. This is a damning judgement on the quality of most African leaders since independence. All too often nationalism has become indistinguishable from the personal pride of the dictator. As long as there are enough Mercedes in the cavalcade and the shanty towns are screened from view all is well. Service is defined by the lip.

It almost makes Churchill's justification of colonialism, written in his account of the reconquest of the Sudan in 1898, look valid today. "What enterprise that an enlightened community may attempt is more noble and more profitable than the reclamation from barbarism of fertile regions and large populations? To give peace to warring tribes, to administer justice where all was violence, to strike the chains off the slave, to draw the richness from the soil, to plant the earliest seeds of commerce and learning, to increase in whole peoples their capacities for pleasure and diminish their chances of pain – what more beautiful ideal or more valuable reward can inspire human effort? The act is virtuous, the exercise invigorating and the result often extremely profitable." The appeal to profitability detracts from the argument, with its modern connotations of wealth extracted at the expense of a land's inhabitants, and modern ethnologists will no doubt bridle at the suggestion that parts of Africa are barbaric.

Newspaper editors frequently refer to "small wars in Africa", more concerned by the latest political scandal or exchange rate movement at home. It was estimated that there were six million

people in southern Sudan at the outbreak of the current round
of fighting in 1983. By late 1989 nearly two million had fled to
the north and to Ethiopia. Though nobody knew for sure, it
appeared probable that one million, or one in six, had died. With
the intensification of the war in late 1989 the toll was bound to
rise. These figures do not include the deaths in the seventeen years
of fighting that followed independence. That phase ended when
the south was granted limited autonomy, but the underlying
causes and callousness remained, ready to flare up into war
again.

This is barbarism. In proportion to the population it is a
barbarism far worse than anything that happened in Europe in
the Second World War. Yet are we to ignore it on the basis of
some inverted racist notion that says we should not interfere
because this is a sovereign African state? Or are we to ignore it,
as the newspapers do, on the basis of the straightforward racist
notion that since these are Africans, the numbers don't really
mean anything? The answer seems to be "choose whichever you
prefer". If you are really upset get a job with an aid agency where
you can salve your conscience at the same time as having an
adventure and earning a lot of money. But beware of the
contributions you are making to the war, if you have a real
conscience.

The real answer is for Western governments to ignore the
inevitable cries of neo-colonialism, and lean extremely hard on
governments such as Sudan's and rebels such as the SPLA. Most
governments in Africa would fall if aid was cut off. Khartoum's
riot prone population long depended on American wheat to meet
its acquired taste for bread, for example. Colonel Garang, the
SPLA leader, has said he is opposed to partition, but it is the only
long term solution for Sudan. Garang probably knows this, but
is unwilling to say so in public because of the alarm it would
cause in Ethiopia and other countries that support his movement.
The long years of attrition have already led a number of
northerners to support the idea of separation. Most southerners
know they will never be accepted as equals by the north, that
southern ministers will never be privy to the innermost councils
of a government in Khartoum. It is time that sacred cow, the

colonial map of Africa, is amended. Several countries contain groups too disparate ever to form a genuine nation state. Sudan is the most obvious example. African leaders should accept that this is so, rather than be swayed by selfish fears about the consequences for their own fiefs.

Ambassadors, Sharks
and a Princess

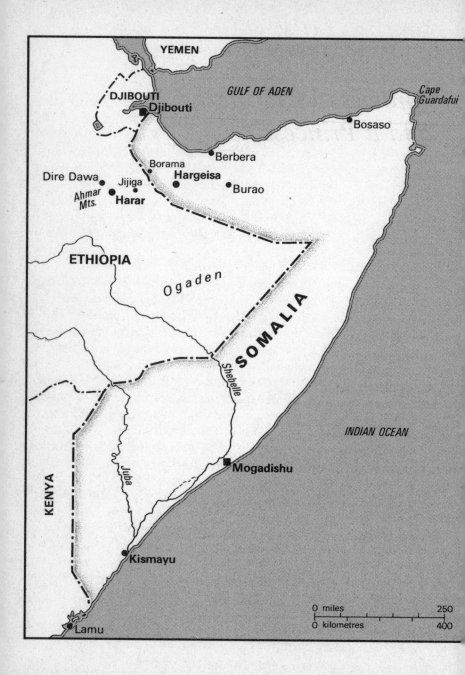

Somalia

The tragedies of Somalia have not been as great as those of Sudan and Ethiopia, if only because it's much smaller and the predominantly nomadic population has proved more able to look after itself. But as the third major country in the Horn region it is inevitably involved in the same merry-go-round of rebel movements, refugees and relief agencies. The dictatorship of one group over others has led to the same sort of civil war and the consequent greatly increased risk of famine. Foreign support of that dictatorship has, as usual, guaranteed the longevity of the suffering it spawns.

The end of the cold war has removed Somalia's strategic attractions, however. Having helped reduce the country to a state of anarchic collapse, the last patron of Mohammed Siad Barre's dictatorship, the USA, was already withdrawing from the role by March 1988, when I finally got into the country. The military bases taken over from the Soviet Union were too uncomfortable, hot and, it was becoming increasingly apparent, useless.

Mogadishu airport was like a museum of aviation. All around the runway lay crumbling civilian and military aircraft of various vintages. Somalia has rarely had enough money to maintain the planes it bought or was given by the various powers who have sought influence there. I was met by officials from two embassies, the American and British. Both sought to take me under their wing. I chose the American, because he was a friend I had met in Nairobi, and also because the Americans were still the biggest donors and so probably the best informed of the diplomats. He had offered to meet me and give me a room at his house.

The Briton seemed rather concerned that I should defect on arrival, though I had not requested or expected any help from the embassy. I was surprised by his presence and concern. I soon found out the reason for it. The British ambassador had appointed himself an assistant to the Somali government, one of the most repressive in the world, in an attempt to prevent any adverse coverage during Princess Anne's visit. She was coming for five days, primarily to look at the activities of Save the Children Fund, the UK version of which she headed. I had taken advantage of the visit to get a visa, very rarely granted to journalists in normal circumstances.

The British ambassador asked to see me the morning after my arrival. After a few formalities he said, "We expect you'll only be covering the visit, of course."

"No," I replied, "Why do you think I came a week early?"

"But your visa application specifies coverage of the visit."

"No. I put general reporting as well and I plan to report on the general situation in the country."

I was astounded that one of the first times I spoke to a British ambassador – they were usually considerably less co-operative to journalists than those of other nations, palming you off with junior officials who knew little and would say less about the country they had been posted to – he should suggest I ignore the evils of a vicious dictatorship.

Later, after angry complaints from the Somali government about my coverage, I sympathized with his position, though I would have written what I did whatever the details of my visa and whatever he had suggested. Few people in the Somali government – or indeed any African government – would recognize the relative independence of British newspapers from the British government, and he must have been hauled over the coals by the Foreign Ministry. When I saw an official from the British embassy at Mogadishu a few weeks later in Nairobi he told me, "Things weren't quite the same after your visit." I can only assume the only British journalist the ambassador had regularly dealt with previously was one who gained access to the country because he was virtually in the pocket of the government.

When the heated beginning of our conversation was over he gave me a very useful briefing on the state of affairs in Somalia. He ended with an appeal not to concentrate on such things as the sharks in Mogadishu harbour and the menageries kept by senior members of the regime, apparently in an effort to boost their egos. Take the government and its problems more seriously, he suggested. By mid 1990, two years later, it was hard to find a government to take seriously. President Siad Barre's control had shrunk to little more than Mogadishu itself and he was finding it difficult to find any Somalis willing to take posts in a regime fighting a losing battle with several rebel groups. The alienation of the people had been completed by massacres of protesters against his government. Since many were shot on a beach, the sharks may have been well fed.

The sharks at Mogadishu exert an unusual fascination. There are dozens of attacks every year. When another party of journalists were in Mogadishu a year before a boy had been taken in knee deep water collecting a football. The Russian-built abattoir, which dumped its waste straight into the sea, was widely blamed for encouraging the sharks. Though the discharge was supposed to have been cleaned up, the sharks' predilection for attacking people, even in very shallow water, appeared to remain.

The Russians were expelled in late 1977, having shifted their allegiance to Ethiopia's Marxist government and led the Ethiopians' resistance to Somalia's attempt to annex the Ogaden region, which is mainly populated by ethnic Somalis. Russian and Cuban support allowed the Ethiopians to regain control of the Ogaden by March 1978. Despite this betrayal – in Somali eyes – and the arrival of the Americans in 1980 the Somali Revolutionary Socialist Party remained the sole ruling party ten years later. Though there had been some liberalization the economy was still run on planned, socialist lines, meaning that there had been little progress or development. Export earnings of about $100m a year came mainly from camels, bananas and incense. Imports of around $400m a year had to be supported by foreign aid. Barre could count on getting the necessary money despite the human rights abuses as long as he could play the card of the strategic importance of the Horn of Africa. For nearly twenty years from the time he took power in a military coup in 1969 the strategy worked, but by 1990 the trump was turning into a club.

Not many countries have combined a Revolutionary Socialist Party with a US Military Co-operation Office. Somalia was a land of strange combinations. In central Mogadishu the state-owned Commercial and Savings Bank – which often ran out of money because the black market had siphoned off so much currency – overlooked a neo-classical triumphal arch dedicated to King Umberto when Mussolini's Italy was the colonial power. To the left stood the yellow ochre palace once occupied by the governor appointed by the Sultan of Oman, to the right a whitewashed mosque.

Apart from the architecture of the towns and loose adherence to Islam of most of the population, however, the Italian, British and Arab colonial influences are hard to detect. Somalia is unusual in Africa for the ethnic unity and fierce nationalism of its six million people, 60 per cent of whom are still pastoral nomads herding their flocks through semi-desert, even if this is often obscured by the fierce rivalry of the Somali clans.

A Somali leader must balance the interests of the different clans like a juggler. Barre lost the knack in the late 1980s and had increasingly to rely on ruthless army tactics against rebel movements in the countryside and extensive use of his KGB trained security service against political opponents in the towns. This was especially true of Mogadishu. Steve, my American friend, told me that anyone visiting his house would be questioned. The watchman was undoubtedly paid to inform, and the few Somali visitors he did have would insist on sitting outside on the veranda, where the watchman could see them and vouch that nothing changed hands. If they went inside they would almost certainly be detained.

Steve's response was to make the inside of his house a slice of America, screened from the human and physical climate outside by curtains that were drawn all the time. Inside was soft lit, air conditioned luxury, like a well appointed apartment in New York. The cat had been declawed, and the only signs of Africa were a large china elephant whose tusks the cat had broken and a few carvings you might find in a New York apartment anyway. The fridge and larder groaned with American foodstuffs, tins, bottles and boxes of all descriptions that enabled you to screen your mouth and stomach from Somalia too. This was his refuge. During the day he was more prepared than most diplomats to try to mix with the local people, almost futile though the security men made his efforts.

It was pleasant walking through the vaguely Mediterranean

streets of Mogadishu, at the time fairly brightly painted and well stocked after a spell of liberalization. The government had only recently reapplied all the controls that gave its members power, privileges and opportunities for making money – and sent most goods under the counter. It was less pleasant being followed, and realizing that no ordinary Somali would want to be seen talking to you.

One day I was going to meet Steve and another American for lunch in the leafy courtyard of the Croce del Sud, the Italian hotel that offers reasonable food and telex lines in the centre of town. The rooms, like those at the Acropole in Khartoum, always seemed to be full. The same smartly dressed young man always seemed to be around when I stopped to look at anything. The other diplomat, it transpired, was called James Bond. "No jokes please," he said as he handed me his card. Soon after we sat down in a corner of the courtyard the young man came in and sat at the table next to us, though all the other tables were empty.

It is hard to prolong a meal if you are eating by yourself, and he had soon finished. He got up and left, showing a card rather than paying the waiter. Almost immediately he was replaced by another man in dark glasses. The rest of the tables were still empty as we were having an early lunch, but he still sat at the same, uncleared table next to us. James Bond asked him if he wanted to join us. "You could probably hear easier if you sat at the same table." The man spluttered something, embarrassed and pretending not to speak English.

If the surveillance in Mogadishu was irksome, in Hargeisa, the capital of the northern part of Somalia that was once British Somaliland, it was overwhelming. I flew up to Hargeisa a couple of days before Princess Anne was due to arrive, sharing a plane with a bunch of supposed Somali journalists. I think nearly all of them were security men. Before we took off at dawn the Minister of Information arrived to talk to them, getting out of his Mercedes on to the apron wrapped in a blanket and chewing qhat. This stimulant, the fresh leaves and leaf stems of an East African tree, is illegal but very popular in Somalia. I do not think I flatter myself to suggest that some of his instructions were to keep a close eye on me.

I particularly wanted to see what conditions were like in the north. Ever since independence, when British Somaliland was combined with the former Italian colony to the south, the northerners have felt ignored or cheated by the government in Mogadishu. The dominant clan in the area, the Isak, felt they were denied government posts and influence. From the early eighties a rebel group, the Somali National Movement, grew in strength and popularity, while the Ethiopians provided material support in the same way that the Somalis supported rebel movements in the Ogaden. In response the Somali army took control of the northern towns like an occupying force, attempting to stamp out resistance by increasingly ruthless treatment of a resentful northern population. The security men's cover as journalists was probably as much for their own protection as anything else.

When we arrived at Hargeisa, which sits in a valley among hundreds of square miles of low, dry, scrubby hills, we drove straight past a city of low, shabby buildings with corrugated-iron roofs to the "hotel". This used to be the British club, but was conveniently close to the Army headquarters and now appeared to be reserved for government visitors. Half the louvres in the windows in my room were missing, the mattress on the rusty bedstead had several mysterious stains and in the bathroom the water came once a day, in a plastic bucket rather than out of the taps. Downstairs my "colleagues" sat on rows of armchairs covered in cracked vinyl, conferring conspiratorially with their neighbours. I had asked for a car as soon as we arrived, having seen some taxis as we drove to the hotel. The morning wore on and nothing happened. Eventually I walked out of the door and was half way to the road before somebody caught up with me.

"Where are you going?" he asked.

"Into town," I replied.

"We'll get you a car," he said.

"You said that four hours ago."

"We have lunch now, then we get a car."

"Look, if I'm not allowed to leave this hotel why don't you bloody well say so?"

"We have lunch now."

"I don't want any lunch."

"Well, we have lunch." He indicated his colleagues.

After lunch they returned to the armchairs. I kept looking at my watch and at the man who had stopped me. Eventually a car arrived and he and another "journalist" climbed in with me. We drove at high speed through the city, one of them explaining redundantly, "There's the market. There's the post office. There's the mosque," and so on. The only place we stopped was on an uninhabited hill overlooking the city. In half an hour we were back at the hotel.

Another journalist had appeared, a Somali girl with a British passport who worked for the BBC. She said we had been invited to supper at the UNICEF director's house. There were two problems, could we get permission and could we get transport? Our minders were highly suspicious. Permission was eventually sought and received from General Morgan himself. Morgan was the nickname chosen by the ruthless and flamboyant northern army commander, Barre's effective deputy dictator in the region at the time.

Transport arrived in the form of one of the General's cars, a Toyota landcruiser with dark glass, white leather seats and a massive pair of silver bullshorns in place of a number plate. I was a little nervous that a lurking rebel might mistake us for the General, but apparently it was bulletproof. Our escort was a young Somali major. He later confided that he would rather be completing his law studies in America, but as a relative of the General he could not refuse a request to serve as an assistant. His job was mainly to look after foreign visitors. He put on the latest disco music as we drove to the UNICEF house through empty streets. When we got there he borrowed a computer to complete his draft of the General's speech of welcome to the Princess.

The visit, it was hoped, would shore up the government's claim to be in control of a stable north. The security men's dilemma was that freely roaming journalists would soon pick up the stories of ambushes, reprisal raids on villages and disappearances in the city, while obvious restrictions would lead them to suspect the same thing. The UNICEF director, a young Englishman with a network of local employees, was a gold mine of such stories. The local security chief obviously heard of our supper engagement too late. He came to the house but our host refused to let him in, citing the diplomatic sanctity of the grounds.

When the Princess arrived, shepherded by two executive aircraft carrying ITN and BBC television crews, the security men's hands were full. Competing television crews are much more aggresive than lone print journalists. They insisted on filming in the market. The people there drew the immediate conclusion from the presence of the minders that we were in some way working for the government, and started pelting us with rotten bananas. The security men looked doubly miserable.

There was nearly a punch up when the royal party arrived at the General's villa, known as the White House. Security did not want anyone to film inside the compound, but the crews had heard of the General's menagerie and were determined to get this piece of "colour". After a lot of shouting and shoving the crews won. The General kept a cheetah and a couple of eagles next to a sort of open air disco area. The President kept lions, albeit with claws and canines removed, at his villa in Mogadishu, so the General's choice of pets was nicely judged.

If further evidence of the region's insecurity was necessary, it came on the way to Boroma, a small town two miles from the Ethiopian border some eighty miles east of Hargeisa where SCF supported a clinic and school. A reconnaissance plane circled a route dotted with occasional camel trains. We stopped ahead of the royal party, to film the convoy as it passed. Leading and following the speeding line of four-wheel-drive vehicles along the dirt road were jeeps mounted with heavy machine-guns.

Unlike the muted or even hostile response at Hargeisa there was a warm welcome at Boroma. There was an obvious pro-British sentiment and the security men, far from home, looked even more nervous. They missed two of us when they took the film crews off to film the border. We walked through the town, the stone walls and sandy streets warmed by the evening sun, surrounded by a throng of smiling people. Several elderly gentlemen approached us, proudly wearing the British army campaign medals they had won in the Second World War. They seemed to be asking for help with their pensions, which were not reaching them.

An anxious security man, who had previously described himself variously as from Radio Hargeisa, the Immigration Department or the Ministry of Information, eventually found us and led us back to the inn with the news that it was time for dinner – though we did not eat for several hours. Another veteran approached us on the way back, but a few harsh words from the security man sent him scuttling away in fear. We met several more the next day and an embassy man said he would look into their complaints. It was a sensitive issue. Princess Anne had wanted to spend most of her time in the north, where most of SCF's projects were, but diplomacy dictated that she spend at least as much time in the south, to assuage the probably justified government suspicion that Britain had more sympathy for its former subjects in the north.

Aid to Somalia was a contentious issue for other, more pressing reasons. The government claimed there were eight hundred and fifty thousand refugees in the country, or nearly one in six of the population. The relief agencies estimated the real figure was half that, as many of those in the camps were ethnic Somali nomads who might live in Somalia anyway. When does a nomad become a refugee? The dispute between aid agencies and government had been acrimonious, but large sums of money were involved. The annual budget for the forty two camps was about thirty million dollars a year, equivalent to about a third of the country's export earnings. Conditions in many camps were better than in the villages outside, with surplus rations being sold on the open market.

The camp that Princess Anne visited on the way back from Boroma was unusual in that most of its thirty-three thousand inmates were not ethnic Somalis. Daawale, on a dry plain surrounded by distant hills, housed Oromos fleeing insecurity, drought and the Ethiopian villagization policy. Most had been moved from Tug Wajalle, a notorious camp on the border where overcrowding and insanitary conditions had led to lethal epidemics.

Daawale was no holiday camp. All the water had to be brought in by road tankers and rations had frequently to be reduced because of difficulties in shipping enough food. The refugees could grow no food of their own, the little arable land in the area being used by the local people, who had fought with them over the limited supplies of firewood in the area. The camps all too often accelerate the process of desertification.

There is something absurd about these official visits to refugee camps. A large group of inmates has been detailed to dance, raising clouds of choking dust, and chant some simple welcome, along the lines of "Happy, happy, Princess Anne," though this is usually barely comprehensible. There is then the walkabout in a fierce heat intensified by surrounding throngs of curious inmates, during which clinic, food store and water tank are solemnly explained, and the hut or tent of the sample refugee family visited. Further chanting and dancing accompanies the thankful return to the air conditioned vehicles, and departure in another cloud of dust.

The television crews' behaviour is also standardized. Apart from a couple of shots of the royalty facing some frenzied dancers, they concentrate on getting pictures of the camp and inmates that suggest that they are the only people there. Other journalists who happen to be in the way of a pan are likely to have rocks thrown at them. In the evenings, with competition over, they are friendly enough, their bags of equipment always providing space for a bottle of whisky or two.

When we got back to Hargeisa the Princess agreed to do an interview for each of the television crews. While the BBC crew was setting up its equipment the presenter chatted with her. She presumed she was dealing with an African specialist. He confessed that it was his first visit to Africa, and that his normal job was that of the northern England correspondent. "I see they're sending the experts," commented the Princess.

The ITN crew gave me a lift to Djibouti, the tiny French dominated country to the north, that afternoon. They and the BBC crew wanted to get to the nearest satellite transmission station. Another print journalist and I wanted to get to the nearest safe telephone, and to a comfortable hotel. The plane taxied straight to the steps of the arrivals section. We checked into the hotel fifteen minutes after we touched down, despite the fact that one of our party had lost his passport and two others had no visas. The wads of hundred dollar bills carried by the heads of the television crews have their uses.

It was wonderful to have a bath, a cold drink and be serenaded by a Polish folk trio, who eventually joined us for dinner. The prices were outrageous, but we were not paying. Room service was erratic. I was brought some drinks at two in the morning, about four hours after they were ordered and two hours after I had gone to sleep. I wrote a letter of complaint. Back in Kenya, over a thousand miles away, I received a note offering me free accommodation for two for a weekend of my choice – whenever I was next in Djibouti.

A couple of weeks after my return to Nairobi I was summoned by the Somali ambassador. Though I was not told what it was about, the content of a letter to the editor in London suggested he wanted to complain. I arrived as appointed on Wednesday morning to be told the ambassador was out. Could I come back on Friday? On Friday I was a few minutes late, because I was looking at a house and the agent had forgotten the keys. The ambassador's first words were: "Unlike you journalists, we diplomats keep our time."

"Excuse me, Mr Ambassador, but a man forgot the key for a house I was looking at this morning and there was no explanation or apology when you were out for our appointment on Wednesday."

He then pulled out copies of my articles and the letter to the editor.

"If you had travelled more and talked to more Somalis," he said, echoing the letter, "you would have known that most of what you wrote was nonsense."

"As I said in these articles," I replied, "my movements were strictly restricted and I was hardly allowed to talk to anyone. You can't have it both ways."

I scented a slim opportunity for another visa and permission for extensive travel. I told him I was willing to go back as long as I had a free hand, and that I would certainly correct any errors such a trip exposed. He agreed, but would not be drawn into dates or details. As I was leaving I told the press officer, who was once a BBC stringer in Mogadishu, about this. "You're the last person they'd let in now," he said.

The ambassador complained about my figures for refugees and the Somali foreign debt. "Where did you get this two billion dollars?" he asked.

"From the World Bank."

"Why should they know? Why not ask the Somali government? I could have given you the correct figure if you had asked."

"I did ask, but no one would tell me. Anyway, what is the government figure?"

"I can't tell you now."

He was most upset by my description of Hargeisa as an occupied city, accusing me of sympathies with "a few bandits". Everybody else, he implied, thought the royal visit a great success. Why did I have to drag this stuff up? A few weeks later the Somali and Ethiopian governments agreed to end a ten-year-old state of war, and stop supporting rebels in each other's territories. The Ethiopians were desperate to free reinforcements for the war against the Eritrean and Tigrean rebels in the north, while the fall of military assistance meant the Somalis could no longer afford a bellicose stance over the Ogaden.

Soon after the agreement the Somali National Movement launched a major offensive in northern Somalia, apparently pushed into action by the withdrawal of Ethiopian support. In late May 1988 the rebels made determined attempts to take Hargeisa and other northern towns, for a while gaining control of large parts of them. The Somali army responded by summarily executing suspected rebel supporters and bombing and shelling civilian areas. A year later visitors reported hardly a building undamaged in Hargeisa.

The UN evacuated nearly all the expatriate aid workers in the north in early June. The Somali government demanded they return or leave the country, in a desperate attempt to convince the world that the situation in the north was under control. Most of the aid workers came to Nairobi, but were reluctant to talk to the press, usually under instruction from their head offices,

Somalia

for fear of jeopardizing their jobs. A few were so shocked by what they had seen that they refused to remain silent.

A French hospital technician said he observed twenty-one summary executions of suspected rebel supporters behind his house in Hargeisa. At least a thousand army casualties had been brought into the hospital. He estimated that thousands of civilians injured from the city's population of one hundred thousand were too scared to seek treatment in case of reprisals. He described it as "a war without prisoners". Unburied bodies littered the streets.

One of the twenty-five Britons evacuated said none of them was injured "apart from one who fell off a motorbike and one who trod on a scorpion". Several were clearly distraught. They confirmed that five Indians had been killed when a shell landed on their house, and reported almost continual gunfire in and around the city. There was no doubt about the decision to leave. "We were happy to go. Most people would not want to go back," said an American evacuee. One of the Britons said, "No way would we go back, and we've got all our personal possessions, including a car, up there." An Irish evacuee said, "Give me a house in Belfast, anywhere peaceful like that."

The first official statement from an aid agency about what was going on in the north did not come until January 1989. A team of Australians from Community Aid Abroad had not left until November 1988, when Army appropriations of drugs and vehicles and continued fighting forced them to give up. Specific instances of atrocities mentioned in their statement included the execution of one hundred and three men, women and children after two soldiers were killed by a land mine, the multiple rape of a thirteen-year-old girl by six soldiers, and torture by suspending people naked with their arms and legs tied behind their backs. Both sides were arming refugees, real or otherwise.

By mid 1990 the fighting was continuing, and the SNM had been joined by several rebel movements operating in the south and centre of the country. Barre, who was believed to be in his late seventies, appeared to be on his last legs. There was little sign of who could succeed him, however. Whoever does so will have to reconcile the clans. When I was in Somalia it was illegal

99

to discuss the succession or clan rivalry. Now that Somalia is controlled by rival warring bands, it has become merely impractical.

Barre's promise of multi-party elections did not induce the rebels to lay down their arms. Nor has political freedom swept the streets of Mogadishu. A man who has ruled a country for twenty years with the help of soldiers and spies, detaining anyone who opposed him, is not the obvious choice of reformer. Perhaps he only hoped the elections – if they happened – could be arranged so as to leave him in power. Perhaps he only hoped the promise of them would encourage the Americans and other donors to maintain or increase their support. It would be surprising if the prospect of defeat had suddenly made a democrat of him, but he may have opened the door to something he and his cronies cannot stop, especially if the donors keep up the pressure.

The Price of
Onions

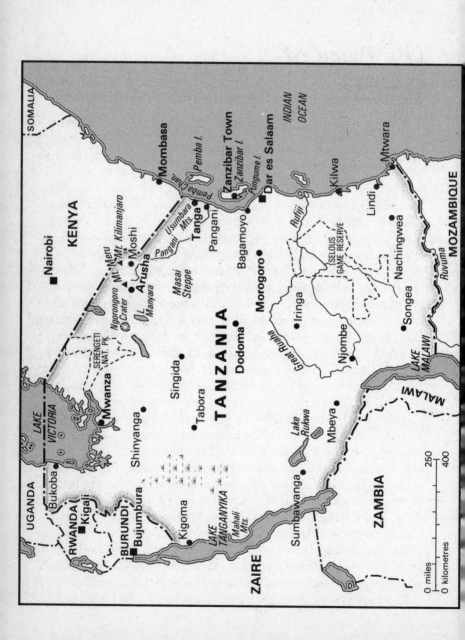

Tanzania

Sudan, Ethiopia and Somalia have been devastated by wars and famines. In Tanzania the same was achieved by one man's delusion – an extraordinary achievement given the country's enormous natural potential. Dr Julius Nyerere's delusion was that the potential could be realized if the country's uneducated peasant farmers were organized according to the socialist theories he had learned at Edinburgh University. As the evidence that this was not so mounted over the years he did not try to modify his policies to fit the world. He tried to modify the world to fit his policies. The real world would not, of course, be modified, but this did not prevent Dr Nyerere and his planners from creating an imaginary Tanzania as the real one crumbled around them.

There is a story about an attempt in the early eighties to establish a commercial prawn fishery in the Rufiji Delta. Some investors aimed to make themselves crustacean tycoons from prawns that grow the size of lobsters – there are sometimes as few as four in a kilogramme. They sent a ship down the hundred miles from Dar es Salaam, loaded with ice to store the prawns gathered by several fast lighters from the delta villages. When it was full it would take the precious cargo back to Dar es Salaam.

After several months they were collecting a lot of prawns, but needed about twice as many to meet the needs of their customers. They doubled the price. The catch halved. Twenty years of Dr Nyerere's attempt to force Tanzania into a planned, socialist economy had led to a situation so distorted that the laws of supply and demand had apparently been reversed. The villagers of the Rufiji, their natural isolation intensified by the dereliction of the roads and coastal steamers that might once have served them, had a strictly limited need for Tanzanian shillings. There was virtually nothing for them to buy with them. For the venture to have succeeded the ship should have carried down radios, medicines, soap, cooking oil and other basic goods. The trouble was that these were not available in Dar es Salaam either.

The paper money was the physical expression of Dr Nyerere's

imaginary economy. It was not surprising it had so little value. People sometimes counted large bundles of notes by their thickness. Even a few years later, in the mid 1980s, when the government was finally forced to listen to the International Monetary Fund (IMF) and other donors' demands for some approach to reality in the country's management, the lesson had not been learned. A doubling of the producer price of cotton led to a halving of production. It was only from 1985 onwards that people started talking about the need to provide "incentive goods", which meant a basic range of any goods at all, as well as paying the farmers on time instead of giving them IOUs. By then the damage was done, and it would take the country years to recover.

In the three years I lived in Tanzania, from 1983 to 1985, headlines like "Cashewnut production set to increase" appeared nearly every day in the government controlled papers. It was only when you looked at the end of the story that you discovered production had in fact fallen again. Sisal, once the country's major export, fell to a tenth of its peak production. When you flew over the country you could see hints of rectangular order where the old fields had been overtaken by the bush, the faint lines of feeder roads no longer traceable on the ground.

Coffee production held up reasonably well, but that was because the major growing areas are conveniently close to Kenya and Uganda, and a large part of the crop could be smuggled across and exchanged for money that had a real value or goods that could be smuggled back.

It is against the nature of African or any other farmers to grow crops for which the returns are enjoyed by bureaucrats sitting in the cities. Nyerere imposed ridiculously low salaries on government officials and the few professionals who stayed in the country, but that simply persuaded them to award themselves cars, houses and loans and to demand bribes for performing their duties. Nyerere retained credit for the supposed humanity of his African socialism in many quarters until the late eighties, yet the methods he employed to force Tanzania into his ideological mould meant he should be more properly described as an African Stalinist.

The basic tenets of socialism enshrined in his Arusha declaration of 1967, six years after independence in 1961, were associated with the more mystical goal of *ujamaa*, or familyhood, under which everyone would live happily in communal villages. The problem was that many people in Tanzania, as in other African countries, did not live in villages, but in family homesteads which spread them over the land more efficiently. Before ujamaa could be realized they would have to be villagized. This had to be done at gunpoint in many places, and the homesteads burned down to prevent the inhabitants returning. Like the kulaks in the Soviet Union, the more prosperous African farmers were forced into the communal mould and the successful but powerful co-operatives under which they organized disbanded.

Proponents of the villagization of the early 1970s pointed to the provision of schools, clinics and clean water, opponents to the opportunities for political domination, deforestation and erosion. By the early 1980s, when I arrived, Nyerere was still pointing to impressive numbers of clinics, schools and boreholes, but the collapse of agricultural production meant that the clinics had no medicines, the schools no books or paper and the boreholes no spare parts to keep them running. Though he could still proudly claim that Tanzania, with a handful of doctors at independence, had since trained over six hundred, he failed to mention that most had left the country. By this stage, in a desperate effort to increase production, farmers were sometimes forced to plant at gunpoint. They had no other incentive to produce more than they needed for themselves.

Most Tanzanians knew what the realities were, but were strictly denied any opportunity to express their discontent. A single party system offers no formal platform to opponents. Those who sought informal ones were usually arrested. At one stage Nyerere had about three thousand political prisoners. Meanwhile the charismatic and articulate President still managed to pull the wool over enough aid donors' – and their liberal constituents' – eyes to ensure enough money to keep the country barely afloat. To those constituents Nyerere had the engaging habit of admitting that there had been mistakes. They failed to notice that he never did anything about them, refusing to acknowledge that they stemmed from his basic and sacrosanct policies.

Unusually for Africa, he did not use his twenty-five years in power to amass a huge personal fortune, though his lifestyle was far from austere. His suits were a collarless version of those worn by Chairman Mao, his shoes, according to an Italian photographer, the most expensive Italy could produce. At functions his glass was filled from bottles other than those offered to guests, which contained the almost undrinkable Dodoma wine produced in Tanzania. These were minor luxuries for an African leader, however.

The last colonial administrators, who pointed to the dangers of entrusting the country to one they described as a professor of politics, were right. When I referred to his "stubborn pursuit of utopian goals" on his stepping down as President in late 1985, some left wing intellectuals in the United Kingdom clearly thought this was a compliment. As party chairman he remained a millstone around the neck of his successor as President, Ali Hassan Mwinyi, for five years. He could not apparently stomach presiding over the reforms that were obviously overdue when he retired. He could still hinder their implementation, however, in a continuing effort to vindicate his great and inhuman experiment. Even after his retirement from the party chairmanship his ideological allies remained entrenched in the party, ever likely to invoke the name of Mwalimu – the Teacher – in their resistance to reform.

In his last three years as president I could not help wondering if he had deluded himself as successfully as he deluded others. I had heard things were bad before I arrived in Dar es Salaam at the beginning of 1983. People often talk of bare shelves. To be strict the shelves in the stores were not completely bare. You could buy stale sweet biscuits, plastic bowls and tinned pineapples – when there were fresh ones outside. During most of that first year there was no cooking oil, soap, or sugar available at the official prices. Nyerere made a speech saying he could not accept the IMF and other donors' demands for the removal of food subsidies because it would force him to turn the Army against the people in the streets. For the previous three weeks

there had not been any sembe, the maize flour that is the
Tanzanian staple, or rice, favoured by the coastal Swahili people,
available, at official prices anyway. For those on the minimum
salary (at official rates of exchange about £50 a month but in
reality worth about £5) and unable to supplement their income
by corruption the black market prices were too high. Yet nobody
rioted, such was the fatalism inculcated by years of the dead hand
of officialdom. In fact the Army had very nearly turned against
Nyerere, who had come perilously close to disobeying the African
dictator's golden rule – keep the Army happy. Mutiny was
averted in early 1983 by the reopening of the special shops where
soldiers could buy basic goods at official prices and beer and
cigarettes, often unavailable elsewhere, duty free. The system had
become a state feudalism, but only survived because of the
black economy, by then larger than the nebulous official
version.

For an expatriate with access to foreign currency the fresh
produce available on the streets was usually reasonably priced,
the vendors easily bribing their way around restrictions on the
movement of such goods designed to bolster the official economy.
At times, however, shortages made prices absurd even for us. The
price of onions, for example, once went through the roof,
prompting an amateur cartoonist friend to draw pictures of ladies
in long dresses wearing onion necklaces and earrings and French
onion sellers in Rolls-Royces.

When Nyerere launched his campaign against economic
saboteurs in 1983, in an effort to find a scapegoat for the
shortages, some wags asked what economy there was to sabotage
anyway. Though numbers of Africans were arrested, the bulk of
those held were Asian, the old and easy target in East Africa.
They did run most of the black market, and arranging an illicit
currency deal was often referred to as going to the Bank of India.
Some of the operators offered loans and various scales of interest
for repayment schedules overseas. The only clearing bank legally
operating in Tanzania was the government-owned National Bank
of Commerce. Other euphemisms for changing money on the
black market were "mickey mouse", "chini", the Swahili for
underneath, and "doggy" fashion. There was little guilt about it,

as the official rates so clearly amounted to extortion on the part of the government. You could get up to ten times the number of shillings for your pounds or dollars on the black market than they were officially worth.

We were sitting one evening on the balcony of the Oyster Bay Hotel, a small establishment overlooking a lovely beach fronting the northern suburbs of Dar es Salaam. Unusually there was some cold beer, and it was slipping down well – as long as you removed the occasional fly. My friend pointed to the beach and said "There's the economy of Tanzania." It was one of those evenings when the Asian community gathered *en masse* in the old coconut grove behind the beach, arranging marriages and, it was generally believed, the prices of most commodities and currencies. They seemed to like the security of numbers and the hundreds of cars would all leave in one long cavalcade shortly after dark. A few policemen could rarely resist harassing some of them for bribes, however. An Asian friend told me the first thing he said when stopped by the police was "How much?" It saved time, he said.

The hardships for those without the perks of an official post had led many people to take matters into their own hands. The savagery of the instant justice dispensed if a robber was caught in the streets of Dar seemed to owe something to the fear of the crowd that they would be forced into the same position. Most of them would take the opportunity to filch something if an easy opportunity came their way. The professionals would steal from anybody, however, rich and poor, and could expect savage treatment. I saw one pickpocket beaten to death with a fence post. Even if a robber was lucky enough to be rescued by the police, they would allow the crowd a few more blows and then give him some more in the police station as long as he was not too badly injured.

One day I came across a failed bicycle thief being walked along the road at Oyster Bay. A woman with a basket on her head happened by. She carefully put down her basket, broke a dead branch off a convenient tree, administered a few vicious swipes as the policeman looked on, put the stick down, picked up her basket and continued on her way. A man passing the other way then picked up the stick for his contribution. The police station was two miles away.

The beach at Oyster Bay was a notorious place for thieves. It was impossible to leave anything on the beach when you swam, even towels and flip-flops would disappear. If you had a Walkman or something else of obvious value, there was another ploy. A man would wander up to the dozing sunbather, to people a distance away apparently offering something for sale. He would then quietly produce a knife from his bag, make a dire threat, put the desired item in the bag, and walk away. This happened to a girl I knew. She was so shocked to wake up with a knife at her throat that she let the man walk away without raising the alarm.

When I was first in Dar I lived near Oyster Bay and thought I had found the solution – walking down to the beach wearing only my swimming shorts – until somebody told me that frustrated robbers on a quiet morning had demanded his and his friend's swimming attire. They had to hitch a ride home, clutching palm fronds to their fronts. However embarrassing this might be, I decided the risk would not prevent me enjoying the Indian Ocean after a draining day in town. I finally gave up the beach after another incident. There were a couple of isolated little coves at the north end of the beach, connected by a narrow passage between two fossil coral outcrops. A European was in the first, so I walked through the gap to the second. An African passed the other way. Moments later the European yelled from the water and started rushing for the shore. Guessing what had happened I picked up a rock and ran back to the gap. There I ran straight into the African, who had a pistol in his hand. I knew what it was really like for the first time to have your heart sink. He was cornered, excited and I had a rock in my hand. He pointed the gun at me. I looked aside, so as to deny the likelihood of recognition, dropped the rock and put my hands up. He ran by, shortly to be followed by the European. As he gave pursuit I shouted: "Watch out, he's got a gun." "I know," he replied, "it's mine." The fool had left it in a bag when he went swimming. We went to the police station and filled out interminable statements, the policeman apparently unperturbed by the loss of opportunity to search for the man. When he and a colleague with a rusty AK47 finally got into our car – they did not have their own – to return to the scene it was dark. He suggested looking for footprints in the sand, but by then the tide had come in.

People arranged their own security by hiring watchmen, who might have to be extremely violent to be effective. The police did not object to this. If you or your watchmen killed a thief they suggested you put the body on the road outside, and call to say you had seen a body there. To be fair this happened but rarely, though often enough to indicate the cheapness of life. The most popular watchmen were Makonde tribesmen from the far south of the country. Usually heavily scarified on the face, they were remarkably accurate with their short, powerful bows and poisoned or barbed arrows, despite the flightless shafts. Their behaviour was also calculated to deter thieves, who would not hesitate to kill a watchman that got in their way. One Makonde was known to have woken his employer in the night to ask for some kerosene. The groggy man gave him some and went back to sleep. In the morning he found that his watchman had incinerated a thief incapacitated by his arrows.

The Makonde are also some of the finest wood carvers and sculptors in Africa. Some of their figures, particularly the shaitani, or devils, are startlingly grotesque and deformed chimeras. I got one of the carvers to make me some lures out of ebony for deep sea fishing. They were very effective.

For a while I had a watchman even more effective than a Makonde. A tree in my small garden was the nightly roost of a flock of small birds. A green mamba took up residence. Some mornings the flock must have been a bird short. The gardener was horrified when I told him to leave the snake alone, in the expectation that the word would soon get around the neighbourhood. Like most Africans his immediate and fearful response to any snake was to stone it to death. Green mambas are not aggressive to people, however, relying on immobility and their brilliant green camouflage to remain undetected and undisturbed. I would look for it every few days, and sometimes find the slender, six foot reptile curled around a branch a few feet away after staring at the tree for twenty minutes. When I returned from leave a few months later both snake and tree had gone. Ali told me it had blown down in a storm. The neighbours' trees were all intact, and nobody remembered a storm. I reflected it was unfair of me to expose him to daily fear, even though I had told him he could leave the grass near the tree uncut.

The economic lunacies, robberies and bureaucratic inanities of daily life I discussed with Abdulla Riyami, a venerable Tanzanian journalist who came from a respected coastal family with links in Tanga, Zanzibar and Mombasa. His home, also his office and my base in town, reflected the state of the country. There was no paint to freshen up the walls, and the piles of building materials at the back, acquired piecemeal here and there, had not yet reached the height which would enable the completion of an extension to his house necessary for the many members of his family who came to him for assistance.

As a result the telex which Abdulla and I used to send our stories into the outside world was in the front room used by all visitors. An elder brother, a devout Muslim, would often lay out his prayer mat next to the telex. As I tapped out a tape or fumed about the impossibility of getting a line as a deadline approached, I would often be taken aback by the large posterior sticking up beside me. The old gentleman would only speak to me in excellent Swahili, a problem for someone with only a basic grasp of the language. It was only months after I arrived, when Abdulla and I were discussing the meaning of a Latin legal term, that he suddenly explained it in perfect English. It transpired that he had been educated to a high standard, including the classics, at a Catholic mission school, but national and religious pride had since led him to eschew all but impeccable Swahili and Arabic. His pride in the former, a difficult, but expressive and musical tongue, was understandable. The version most Europeans in East Africa use omits most grammar, and would have sounded like baby talk to him. Mine was even worse.

It also took me several months to realize that it was a breach of manners to refuse to join Abdulla and the male members of the family for lunch if it was served when I was working there, despite my scruples that he already had enough mouths to feed.

The food was delicious, several dishes of spicy fish, meat and vegetables eaten with the right hand with rice, which he somehow managed to obtain most of the time. I soon discovered a way to contribute, which was to bring along fish which my friends and I caught on the weekends. Eventually I spent more time on fishing and preparing tackle and boats than on journalism. It was more fun and there was not much appetite for stories about the mess the country was in from my clients. There was also probably more money to be made out of it. I could only write the "Socialism Ruins Tanzania" story about once a year for each of my clients. Our weekend catches, sold on the ramp at the Yacht Club or hawked around the hotels, sometimes made us tens of thousands of shillings. Tanzania's fishermen were starved of the boats and other equipment that could enable them to take advantage of the rich fishing off the Tanzanian coast, and get the catch to the markets in Dar and other towns while it was still fresh. Hooks and lines were almost impossible to buy. Like most other things in Tanzania there was no incentive to produce them locally and no foreign exchange to import them. There was keen competition for these items when we discarded them because they were too worn or damaged to trust on large fish.

Few of the fishermen could find or afford nets, so many of them resorted to blowing the fish up. Their desperation had combined with the need of the quarrymen at the cement factory to supplement their official incomes to make dynamite fishing common. Late one Sunday morning we were sitting on the terrace of the Yacht Club, contemplating our first beer, when two waterspouts rose into the air across Msasani bay, right in front of the President's house, which was supposedly part of the Msasani ujamaa village. The percussions reached us a moment later. There was a gunboat moored nearby, presumably to protect the seaward approaches to Nyerere's villa, but it had not moved for months. This had not stopped the police from arresting the British High Commissioner's son when the took a photograph of the rusting hulk.

Members of the club had made attempts to discourage the dynamite fishing, especially when people were diving in the vicinity, but were forced to concede defeat. A power boater who aimed to swamp a dynamiter's canoe was put off when the man stood ready to throw a stick at his boat. It was thought highly likely that boats at the moorings might be sunk at night if such efforts continued. The authorities in Zanzibar, not at the time noted for their scruples in such matters and still in possession of some functioning gunboats, had more success in discouraging the practice. They machine-gunned several canoes caught in the act.

Some of the reefs around Dar were peppered with craters, like underwater battlegrounds. The flashes of smashed, white, dead coral would take years to recover, along with the the marine life that depended on the living reef. Not even the marine environment, it seemed, was safe from the destructive effects of the socialist dictatorship and the appalling inflexibility and pride of the man who led it.

The damage to the reefs had also, it was believed, led to the erosion that was sweeping away whole beaches near Dar. Buildings at two of the four beach hotels near the city had already fallen into the sea. Not that it mattered. They were usually empty. Any tourist who braved the absurd prices stemming from extortionate exchange rates risked restaurants without basic foodstuffs, as well as rooms without working lights, fans or air-conditioners and bathrooms without water.

It was also speculated that the damaged reefs would allow sharks in to the beaches, where they might attack swimmers. There was little substance to this. Sharks come inside the reefs regularly anyway. There are plenty of deep passages enabling them to do so. Such inshore visitors include tiger sharks and makos, large and potentially dangerous species, but their behaviour seems to offer little risk in these areas. Perhaps they are coming in to breed rather than feed. I have never heard of a confirmed case of shark attack on the Tanzanian or Kenyan coasts in recent years, despite large numbers of swimmers, particularly in tourist-ridden Kenya.

Local newspaper reports of attacks in Tanzania and Kenya in recent years appear to have been false. When I followed up the reported death of a fisherman in Dar a doctor at the hospital told me the body had its leg blown off, not severed by sharp teeth. It appears he had been attempting to retrieve a fishing charge that had not gone off. A Kenyan Navy diver working in the harbour at Mombasa was also reported to have been killed by a shark. I was told there had been a failure of communication when he was working on the propeller of a ship. A British Navy trained diver, however, helped convince me that there are places off the East African coast where it would be extremely dangerous to swim.

Our favourite fishing spot was a tiny island twenty miles off the Tanzanian coast. Its only inhabitants were thousands of sea birds, mainly the gannet-like blue footed booby and the sooty tern. We sometimes found the island by aiming for what appeared to be the smoke of a ship on the horizon, but was in fact the circling birds. What looked like a large sandbank in the middle of the ocean was actually the tip of an underwater mountain, and deep sea predators would come right up to its underwater cliffs. Reef fish, barracuda, wahoo, giant trevally, tuna of several types, sailfish, blue, black and striped marlin, and oceanic sharks all mingled together. It was a poor day if we did not get a total of over four hundred pounds of fish in about five hours' fishing, and sometimes we met individual fish of that size.

Few local boats fished the waters around the island. One reason was the distance from Dar and other markets and the shortage of fast, seaworthy boats. The other was that strong currents and the large numbers of oceanic sharks discouraged dynamite fishing, in which the stunned fish are usually collected by swimmers. We often lost fish to the sharks around the island, the appearance of a cleanly cut head presaged by a couple of savage jolts on the line.

One day we got a line tangled around one of the rudders following a multiple strike from yellowfin tuna. Our ex-navy man offered to go over the side to clear it. I said this was dangerous, but he said he had swum with sharks before, and Jimmy, the skipper and owner, seemed unconcerned. Before he went into the water I told everybody else to go up on the flying bridge, look down into the clear water and yell if they saw anything. I tied a cord to his wrist to pull to alert him, and leant over the transom as he disappeared under the boat. A few moments later I saw a flash in the water, which I immediately and almost unconsciously realized came from the fin of a white tip shark. The oceanic white tip is highly aggressive. Unlike most sharks it will grab a plastic lure, and not insist on a carefully presented fish bait. Before I had time to pull the cord our friend shot on to the back of the boat like a penguin on to an ice floe.

"There's a bloody shark down there," he spluttered.

When we asked him how big he said, "Either it wasn't very big and it was very close, or it was very big."

"What did it look like?"

"It had a knife in one hand, a fork in the other and a napkin tied under its chin."

Nobody would have wanted to clear a line if he had seen what happened a few weeks later. We had hooked a big yellowfin tuna, which kept heading for shallower water. Most go as deep as they can. After about an hour we saw the fish zigzagging behind the boat and then we saw why. A huge white tip, at least fifteen feet long, shot up, hit the fish and disappeared in a cloud of blood and foam. We got the head, which weighed thirty two pounds. The shark had taken the rest, probably over one hundred pounds of fish, in one clean bite. The thickness of the tuna at that point was at least that of a man's waist.

We were probably in less danger from sharks than the sea. It was easy to forget, when it was calm and the boat was running well, that there was no coast guard or air–sea rescue. Buoys marking reefs had disappeared and the few lighthouses often had no light. There were few safe anchorages and little likelihood of anybody finding you if you broke down in open sea. If you were far enough out you would drift all the way to India, if you survived that long. The risk was not so much that this was a wild piece of coast, however, as that it was very difficult to maintain a boat properly. The economic collapse meant that no one stocked any spare parts for engines or other gear, that the fuel and oil was often dirty or of the wrong specification, and that the mechanics' ingenious, makeshift repairs might fail at a crucial moment.

The only comfort when we broke down on my small boat was that we stayed inside the southern tip of Zanzibar, and therefore safe from the ocean currents which would carry us on the long, dry drift to India. A slight change in the wind could have put us over the invisible line, though we were only a few miles from the country's largest city.

The problem started in mid-channel, about half-way between Dar es Salaam and the southern tip of Zanzibar. Two friends and I had set off at 7 a.m. one Sunday morning, aiming to sweep out into the channel and then down to Sinda Island, a few miles south of the entrance to the port of Dar es Salaam. At about 10 a.m. we caught a fish, a large rock cod, but after we had boated it the main engine would not go back into gear. I later discovered that this was because a hardened steel pin had been replaced by an improvised, soft steel one. I could not see that it had sheared. I fiddled with the engine for some time, gave up and fixed the back-up on the transom. It would not start. The first pangs of unease began. They soon built up.

We were drifting fast, pushed by the wind and current, towards Pungume Island, which lies to the west of the southern tip of Zanzibar. The southern side of Pungume, to which we were heading, is a fossil coral cliff which drops straight into deep water. A heavy swell was raking over the jagged rock – and there is little more jagged than fossil coral eroded into serrated pinnacles and ridges by the water. I threw the anchor over and continued tinkering fruitlessly with the two engines, thinking all the while that this would not be a very good place to spend the night. A squall could blow us straight on to the cliffs. Fortunately the anchor rope was not up to the strain imposed by a boat lifting and falling some twenty feet with the swell and parted. We were headed for the cliffs. I tied together some empty jerrycans to act as a raft for a few belongings which we might swim around the cliffs if the boat was wrecked. Then I threw the spare outboard over as an anchor. Though the remaining rope was too short to reach the bottom, the engine acted as a sea anchor, and helped the current carry us around, sometimes less than a hundred yards from the cliffs.

There is a shallow lagoon on the west side of Pungume, and our luck held. We managed to paddle the boat in, somehow avoiding the waves that broke just before and after we passed in the three feet of water that covered the reef. Now, anchored in the lagoon to an outboard that would never run again, it was time to wait for a passing boat or see what the morrow would bring. We still had a few sandwiches and tins of beer. I thought I saw a seal, its head quietly rising from the still, turquoise waters. Only later did I realize it must have been a dugong. There are no seals on this coast, the only thing close to them being this rare and elusive sea mammal, along with its cousin the manatee supposedly the origin of the mermaid legend. It was a beautiful evening. It was hard to remember that we were to all intents and purposes shipwrecked on a desert island.

It was not a beautiful night. A squall blew up, making us swing wildly to our outboard anchor and drag towards some rocks. I was pelted with a cold rain as I kept watch in the open cockpit. When the wind and tide dropped I heard fish splashing around the boat. They appeared to be moray eels foraging in the open under cover of darkness. These have as false a reputation for viciousness as the barracuda, normally lurking timidly in their lairs. You are only likely to get bitten if you waggle your fingers in front of their noses. I did this once accidentally, playing with a little shoal of brilliant blue fish in a depression in the reef. A large, interested head appeared from a hole two feet from my hand. I proverbially rose in the water, but was left unscathed.

Only in the morning, with the boat heeled over and beached on the mud, did I wish we had collected some of the rain water. We had only one bottle of water and one tin of beer left to drink, and it was getting steadily hotter. We walked all round the island looking for water, but even that dripping from the cliffs was salt. We climbed to the highest point, little more than fifty feet above the water, hoping to reach the Yacht Club with our radio, but all we could hear was them calling for us. They could not hear us. We waved our lifejackets at a passing dhow, but it gave no sign of seeing us. Probably it had a smuggled cargo – watches, radios, cloves or ivory – and did not want to get involved with some stranded Europeans.

Towards the end of a long hot day, during which I attempted to cook the fish we had caught the previous day but found it had gone off, we decided to walk the boat around the island. The idea was to cast ourselves off the far end in the hope that the tide and offshore breeze from the mainland would push us on to the main island of Zanzibar. Shortly after we started we heard an aeroplane in the distance. Suddenly it appeared over the cliffs, already past us and flying away. This time frantic waving of the lifejackets attracted attention. The plane turned back, buzzed us and flew off towards Dar. It turned out to belong to the German ambassador. His secretary was one of the three of us on board the boat. An hour and a half later another boat appeared, crewed by two Italian friends. My guests immediately crossed over, Roberto threw me a tow line, and we set off.

There was another squall as we recrossed the channel. At times the tow rope went straight into the wave ahead and I could not see the boat towing me. As darkness fell so did the wind, and we were left with a long swell. I lolled at the wheel as we picked our way towards the entrance to Msasani bay. There were no power cuts that night, so we could use a radio mast and the university buildings on a hill outside Dar as marks. Suddenly something large swirled in the water right beside me, a few feet away. After a moment of fear I realized I was surrounded by a group of dolphins, playing around the boat in the darkness. I could see them clearly in the black water, their bodies shrouded in phosphorescence. When the shimmering shapes broke the surface their wake sparkled, like the wake of the boat. I was in a reverie until we reached the moorings at ten o'clock at night, and Stefano passed me a bottle of whisky. Dehydrated and hungry as I was, it went straight to my head. When I woke the next morning, all I had was a little sunburn.

The Yacht Club was the island of sanity to many of the Europeans in Dar, though to a casual observer it must have looked like something dropped from space into the city's crumbling ruin. Pleasant buildings in well-kept grounds overlooked the bay. On shore and on the moorings were rows of expensive power and sailing boats, from dinghies to ocean-going yachts. Cold beers and most of the common spirits were usually available on the quarterdeck bar, kebabs, lobster and other seafood from the charcoal grills and more basic fare from the kitchen. There were occasional threats to take the club over – it had already been forced to move from its original site in the harbour – but these were met by stout resistance from the diplomatic corps, who pointed out it would be almost impossible to entice people to Dar, especially the aid workers, without such a place to relax and keep boats. Apart from the Gymkhana club, where you could roast on a nine hole golf course with ash greens or swelter on the tennis courts, there was nowhere else to go.

Many of the members came from the Scandinavian countries, whose governments had been taken in by Nyerere for longer than most. They knew their governments or people were being deceived, but continued with their lucrative contracts. A thirty-five-year-old Finn told me that he could retire in another five years. There were various ways of supplementing the large tax-free salaries such people received. For the senior ones it was often possible to bring in the foreign currency for their projects on the black market, spend an amount equivalent to the official rate and pocket the rest. Since the black market rate was up to ten times the official, large sums were involved. Since most agencies could only contemplate using the official rate, however, it was argued that this made no difference. Government extortion was replaced by bonuses for aid workers. The end recipients of the projects, workers or peasants, would receive a tenth of the value of what the donors had provided whatever happened.

The aid workers were also allowed to bring in a duty free car. Many brought Mercedes, sold them in advance when they arrived for millions of Tanzanian shillings, left their salaries untouched at home, and handed over the car when they had finished their contract. Most of the diplomats also enjoyed this benefit. Most also changed their Tanzanian shillings back into hard currencies at the official rate at their embassies on their departure. This effectively meant they could sell things like fridges for thousands of dollars.

Some of the aid workers, often called experts or consultants for no obvious reason, tried to be honest. One of the Finns told me what had happened when he presented a report about a sawmill his agency was backing. He wrote that the staff were hopelessly inefficient and corrupt, and that it was a waste of money to continue providing assistance. His ambassador, through whom such reports normally passed to the Finnish government, called him in and told him he would not forward it in that form. He could not suggest that assistance to this plant be stopped unless he could suggest a better one to receive the money. This, as they both knew, was virtually impossible. It was also apparently impossible for the ambassador to contemplate any reduction in the Tanzanian aid budget, however badly it was used. "What about all the people whose jobs depend on this money?" my friend said he had been asked. The ambassador was not referring to Tanzanians.

There were few occasions when I heard the full details, but similar things happened in all the western aid agencies and embassies. The pulp and paper mill at Mufindi was completed while I was in Tanzania, at a cost of nearly $1bn. The railway expected to carry its products did not have the capacity to do so, and a 60 kilometre road had to be built down an escarpment to link it to the forests expected to provide the raw materials. It was calculated that the mill could not produce paper at less than three times the world price, but the contractors went away happy.

It is nearly always impossible to admit that a project was ill-conceived or to halt it prematurely. Failure cannot be confessed. All that can be done is allow the matter quietly to drop with the supposed "completion" of the project. That everybody knows the factory will grind to a halt, the road be full of potholes or the dam silted up in a few years is unimportant. Everybody has fulfilled their contracts.

Tanzania has more than its share of the resulting development archaeology. The most famous example is the British-sponsored groundnut scheme of the 1950s, but the bush has reclaimed almost every sign of the millions spent on that folly. More obvious are such things as the Nachingwea to Songea road, completed by the British company Balfour Beatty in 1985. Paid for by the British government, it was sometimes referred to as the road from nowhere to nowhere. It was built despite the obvious inability of the country to maintain its two most important roads, west to Zambia and north to Arusha and Kenya.

The Arusha road is a nightmare that adds years to the life of car and driver. Long stretches have lost their tarmac completely.

These are probably the best stretches, except in the rainy season, when mud may make them impassable. The tarmac stretches are dotted with sharp edged potholes. You are tempted to speed up, then come round a corner to an unavoidable array of holes. Crash. You go slowly for a few miles, then a good stretch tempts you to speed up again. Holes appear again. You may weave successfully for a while, but sooner or later you meet the impossible combination. Crash. There is a theory that you skate over the top if you go fast enough. This may work with company or hired cars. For those in private cars on which huge amounts of duty have been paid the possibility of meeting one of those really big holes that will take the wheels off is too much to contemplate.

The other risk of travelling these major roads was that there might be no fuel. On one trip from Dar to Arusha and on to the Serengeti National Park in north-eastern Tanzania not one petrol station had any fuel. I had started with five jerrycans, however, and managed to get back with the help of a farmer friend near Arusha, who refilled them from his private stock.

Prince Charles came to open the new British road, still almost devoid of traffic. Apart from bogging the Queen's Flight Andover on landing at Njombe airstrip, he might also have been embarrassed by the Commonwealth Development Corporation estate he toured. In the guise of development assistance the CDC was doing exactly what a well-run private estate would have done, had it been permitted by the government. Along with him we were shown the wattle plantations, the factory where wattle extract was made for the tanning industry, and quickly passed by the basic labour lines on the way to the comfortable bungalows of the English managers. At one stage in the tour two other journalists and I somehow got ahead of the cavalcade and ended up alone with the Prince, rather foolishly looking at a few Friesian cattle. "You with the agricultural press?" he joked.

At a reception that evening, to which we were condescendingly asked at the last minute because of our "good behaviour", he did not talk to us. I was cross with myself for being disappointed, at the same time as being amused to see how people manoeuvred themselves in the apparent direction he was taking, looking over their shoulders and ignoring what their partners were saying. I thought how frustrating it must be to meet so many people almost speechless with awe, and how dangerous to have such power. Towards the end of the reception he asked a young wife to dance, and swirled her away to the vigorous music of an African band. She virtually swooned, and her husband still complained of being ignored several days later.

John Sankey, the British High Commissioner, ended the reception by diverting the royal conga chain out past a blazing bonfire to the waiting cars. Before the visit he told a story about the joking advice he had given a senior Tanzanian politician on the correct method of greeting the Prince – kneel. Now he was the soul of deference, and only pretended to join the dancing to keep everything on schedule.

Some of the assistance provided for commercial fishing has been as misguided as that for new roads when the old cannot be maintained or that for new factories when the old are silent. At Bagamoyo, a sleepy little town thirty miles north of Dar that was once the Sultan of Zanzibar's slave trading port on the mainland coast, the Scandinavians have built an impressive fisheries school and development centre, the buildings attractively finished with red tiles, complete with ice making facilities, jetty and trawler. One problem is that the part of the Zanzibar channel it faces is poor in fish. Another is that none of the fishermen could afford to buy the sort of trawler they were trained to work on. It did not help that much of the road to Dar was deep sand or mud. The Danes had offered to tar it, but the Tanzanians had said they would rather spend the money on something else. "We don't think you understand," said the Danes, "we are offering to upgrade this road, nothing else." The Tanzanians did not understand, still asking that the money be spent elsewhere. The Danes put it back in the bank. The Japanese provided what at first seemed some more appropriate fisheries assistance, bringing in some small trawlers with simple equipment. It soon became apparent, however, that all they were interested in was securing access to Tanzania's fishing grounds.

Such tropical seas are in fact only sporadically productive. As far as is now known, the stocks are probably only sufficient to justify small trawlers working between the reefs and in the river mouths for the smaller fish, for local consumption, and prawns, for export. The tuna would require high speed purse seiners with highly skilled crews or indiscriminately destructive drift nets. There may not be sufficient numbers of the fish throughout the year to justify the expense.

There may be other possibilities. I spent a week on a Norwegian's trawler, a fifty-five foot fibreglass boat with which he was making a living while investigating the coast's potential. Extraordinary animals came up on our experimental trawls, things like the shovel headed mud lobster or the Indian ocean halibut. The locals rarely caught these, since they live in deep water. They were excellent to eat. Most went straight to the French embassy. There were rays weighing over one hundred pounds, strange bottom fish with huge mouths, and mantis prawns, large and savage looking with their jagged claws but inedible. There were various catfishes, suckerfishes and occasional representatives of the pelagic species we normally caught trolling with rods on the surface. Four times we picked up turtles, and spent frustrating minutes trying to release them as their clawed flippers caught in the net.

We tried trawling for prawns off a beach by the mouth of the Pangani river, and caught reasonable numbers though they were supposed to be out of season. The by-catch of small fish was sold at the port of Pangani each evening, along with the catfish the crew caught on handlines as we sat at anchor. The local fishermen seemed unequipped even for this easy catch on their doorsteps. Our anchorage was in the middle of the river where it split the sleepy little town in two. The religious implications of that partition seemed to be the cause of the only initiative or competition in the place. There was a mosque on each side. Before dawn the highly amplified call to prayer would explode on one side, to be followed a moment later by an equally distorted but deafening message from the other side. Sleep was impossible for a heathen caught in the middle.

Early one morning we headed up stream in the dinghy, passing mile after mile of coconut palms. Herons, egrets and kingfishers flew by. Occasional sullen Africans watched us from the bank.

The part-Arab owners of these plantations, it was said, provided their labour with basic food and accommodation in lieu of wages. A system very close to slavery. The only way to move was by boat up or down the river.

As we headed south from Pangani back to Dar we thought the sophisticated echo sounder had broken. There was apparently a solid band of fish about a fathom deep, approximately half-way to the bottom. It went on for about twenty miles. Our nets were not rigged for mid-water trawling. When the tape was later analysed in Norway the experts concluded that we had passed over thousands of tonnes of herring-sized fish. We had no idea what they were, where they were going or when they would come back. The answers might open up a fishery on a scale closer to the North Atlantic than most tropical waters.

When we got back to the Yacht Club the kitchen was closed, a sign informed us, "due to heavy rain and lack of water". We were having trouble getting the roof repaired and rain in Dar never guaranteed the water mains had any water in them, even if the roads were flooded. Despite the efforts of the committee and staff, the club could not be completely isolated from the surrounding country. At one stage we had a hamna board. *Hamna* means "none", or "there is none", and there were often many items chalked up. A local party official insisted the board be taken down.

I woke one morning at a friend's house to the sound of a heavy diesel engine in the drive. When I peered through the curtains I saw a fire engine, and leapt out of bed thinking my friend had forgotten I was staying as the house went up in flames. In fact it was his weekly water delivery, and the firehose was pumping water into his roof tank. Such salary enhancing morning errands may help explain why the central bank headquarters were gutted a few months later. When the fire engines did arrive, over half an hour too late, it was discovered they did not have any water anyway. The fire appeared to have been carefully set, by those who had an interest in destroying records of foreign currency transactions.

There was always too much water in the wrong places. At the time of independence malaria had almost been eradicated from

Dar es Salaam, with the help of strictly enforced by-laws that ensured that all standing water was drained. The by-laws were no longer enforced, the city authorities no longer cleared the drains and malaria was common. It was often resistant to chloroquine and other drugs and many people died every year, including several from the expatriate community. They were usually killed by cerebral malaria, which happens when the parasites thicken the blood – a process described as sludging – and so block the tiny capillaries in the brain. The resulting coma is often irreversible. A Frenchwoman complained of feeling vaguely unwell for a few days then went into a coma when she was supposed to be holding a dinner party. She died on a plane to Europe that night.

When I arrived I took the recommended prophylactics and went down with malaria a few weeks later. I woke up one morning lying on the bathroom floor, aching and shivering. The houseboy was away for the weekend, but I staggered across to the Yacht Club and got someone to get me some medicine and check on me later. After that I stopped taking the prophylactics and never got it again, though I was often bitten in the next three years. There was a wide range of susceptibility to the disease. An English woman got it every couple of months, until the doctor told her and her husband they must leave the country.

Many of the Africans had a continual low level infection, which effected a sort of continual immunization as long as they were healthy. With the food shortages and low salaries they were often unhealthy. If they contracted some other disease they would often go down with malaria as well. It was the largest cause of admissions and deaths in the hospitals, which often had insufficient medicines to treat the sufferers because of foreign exchange shortages exacerbated by the corruption and inefficiency of the underpaid and demoralized staff.

The problems with water, electricity and disease supported the expatriates who described Dar as a hardship post, and so claimed extra allowances for living there. Leading them were the Americans, who had almost all their food and drink flown in, including fruit and vegetables. I could not agree with the description as far as the expatriates were concerned. Fresh fruit

and vegetables, temperate and tropical, were on sale throughout
the year. Superb seafood was available from the beautiful ocean
at your doorstep. To us the prices were usually reasonable.
Kerosene lamps, candles and jerry cans solved the water and
power problems. "Hardship post. Hardship post," friends used
to say, shaking their heads as they lay on a beach on one of the
uninhabited islands near Dar es Salaam, cold drink in hand,
lobster grilling on the charcoal.

A fisherman used to stop at our house two or three days a
week with a tempting basket of crab, lobster, prawns, or squid.
You had to be careful with the crabs, the same size as an Atlantic
king crab, but dark green until cooked and highly agile and
aggressive. I once had one in the sink, which I was trying to push
into a pot. When the wooden spoon was about a foot above it,
the crab jumped and seized the end with a crack, breaking it into
three pieces. Tatu, our housemaid, was shocked by our
consumption of shellfish. She called them *dudu*, or insects.
However Tatu, which means three and illustrates her parents'
excitement at producing a third daughter, liked the fat bellied
termites that flew out of the nests in fluttering clouds to breed
in the rainy season. They were attracted to the streetlights and
people gathered them underneath. We used to joke that each
streetlight was a restaurant and muse about which one we would
stop at when we had visitors in the car. A friend correctly
rebuked me for using the termite eating as an illustration of
poverty in an article which I wrote. They are considered a
delicacy by many Tanzanians.

Larger game was our main source of meat. Residents could
cheaply buy licences to hunt the common antelope, the major
trophy species being reserved for people paying large quantities
of dollars. We used to drive off into the bush for the weekend,
sleeping by a fire under the stars, hunting at dawn and dusk. I
did not enjoy the blood and the death, but these animals had a
wild life, instead of facing the inescapable premeditation of a
slaughterhouse. If one is to eat meat and preserve some of
Africa's wildernesses, culling game seems infinitely preferable to
rearing cattle or goats. The quarry takes its chances, against both

human and animal hunter. And though the risk is not great unless you make it so, the human hunter takes his chances too.

One night, overwhelmed by the moonlight and scent of the bush and intrigued by the noises of animals, my girlfriend and I decided to go for a walk. As our eyes became accustomed to the absence of the fire it seemed the moonlight let us see as well as daylight. We walked for about half a mile, hearing what sounded like lions killing and seeing an occasional animal moving in the distance. Then sanity returned. Hyena, lion and leopard all hunt at night, and are easy enough to stumble on during the day. A disturbed buffalo could be even more dangerous. I carried a gun, but might have little time to use it. When we turned back the spark of the camp fire seemed a long way away. We were careful to keep it stoked through the night. In the morning there were leopard tracks over the ones we had made on our nocturnal stroll.

The beauty of the coast and interior was exaggerated by the economy's dereliction. We liked the way you could spend days outside the towns without seeing anyone else, on beaches devoid of hotels and villas or in bush unscarred by human hand. We liked the virtual absence of tourists. But this could not justify the government's incompetence. The lost opportunity and poverty were too severe. One evening we were sitting on a friend's balcony, looking over Msasani bay as the sun went down. An old man with a pot in his hand wandered up to some fruit trees in front of the neighbour's house. My friend warned him off and he slowly walked away, though he seemed either senile or deranged. He must have been hungry. After dark we heard rhythmic thuds, like somebody driving in a fence post. After a while we investigated, and found the neighbour's watchmen methodically beating the old man, who had tried to take a couple of unripe pawpaws. The only way we could stop them was by calling the police. They walked him away, but the passers-by left him alone, so old and miserable was he. With luck, he might get some food at the police station.

You can sympathize with the Tanzanians' aim to attract a small number of rich tourists. In Kenya the beaches are littered with package tourists, while in the game parks a pride of lions is likely to be surrounded by six minibuses. The gullibility and carelessness of the visitors has spawned an army of conmen and thieves. When I was in Tanzania, however, the supposedly luxurious lodges were mired by the state hotel corporation, run by fatalistic, underpaid staff and unsupplied with even basic goods.

In 1984 I took two friends out from England to the Manyara Lodge, which has a superb view over Lake Manyara National Park from the top of an escarpment. Elephants could be seen like ants far below. At dinner my friends were slightly surprised that zebra stew was one of the few items from the menu available. In the morning the guests, most of them tourists paying $70 a night, came down to breakfast to find some old pawpaw, dry toast and coffee or tea without milk or sugar. There was no jam, butter, eggs or anything else. We were on the upper level of the dining room. I looked at the lower. There were long tables, laden with fruit, bowls of boiled eggs, jugs of milk, honey, butter, jam and sugar, all awaiting the late rising party of Aboud Jumbe, at the time President of Zanzibar and Vice-President of Tanzania. (Tanzania is the name of the republic which unites the islands of Zanzibar, once an Arab sultanate, with the mainland, once known as Tanganyika.)

I got up, walked down the steps, collected all the things we needed, and walked back up with my arms full. The waiters were too shocked to do anything. Everybody else tried to follow suit. A tremendous row ensued as the waiters tried to obstruct them. Some got through, and the lower tables were thoroughly despoiled by the time we left. I would have liked to stay to see what happened when the vice-presidential party came down, but we wanted to drive on to the Ngorongoro Crater before it got too hot.

Tigerfish, Trout
and Terrs

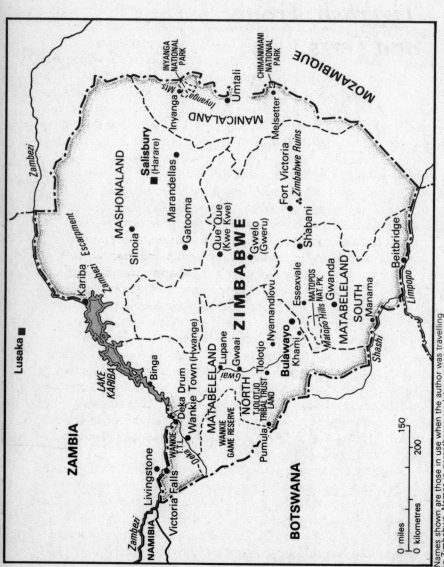

Names shown are those in use when the author was travelling in Zimbabwe. Names in parentheses are later versions.

Zimbabwe

Tanzania had reached rock bottom nearly twenty-five years after gaining independence in 1961. It was frightening that the new government in recently independent Zimbabwe appeared, according to its members' speeches, committed to the same sort of socialist goals. By 1990, ten years after independence in Zimbabwe, several ministers had been charged with corruption, but President Robert Mugabe was still saying that socialism and the single party state was the best model for Africa and made no secret of his annoyance that a handful of seats in parliament were still held by parties other than his own. The only consolation was that Mugabe had obviously taken some note of what was happening around him in the years he spent in exile in Tanzania and Mozambique. Despite his rhetoric most of the large private farms and businesses that fed the country and employed thousands of Africans were allowed to continue to operate, usually under European ownership and management.

But I am getting ahead of myself. Zimbabwe was the first place where I spent much time in Africa. When I arrived just after independence in 1980 I naïvely shared the belief that majority rule would automatically improve everybody's lot, that with good will between the different groups and their representatives in parliament Zimbabwe could be an example for all of Africa, especially South Africa. Salisbury, the capital city now known as Harare, was full of optimism, but my first trip into the country, to the northern border with Zambia, showed that the way forward was not so clearly marked. The legacy of the civil war was too strong and the new processes of democracy would take time to learn – if they survived.

Borders can be good places for fishing in Africa. Though many are arbitrary lines drawn across desert, savannah or forest, the colonial powers did notice a few rivers and use them as convenient markers for their territories. The problem is that they can be highly insecure. The Zambezi was a particular example. It had been a front line in the fight between the rebels of Joshua

Nkomo's Zimbabwe People's Revolutionary Army (ZIPRA), based north of the river in Zambia, and forces raised by Mr Ian Smith's white government of Rhodesia.

I went to the stretch of the river between Victoria Falls and Lake Kariba both to see what had been one of the most active war zones and to fish for tigerfish, one of the world's most exciting fresh-water species. The first time I was out on the river the calm of the morning was wrecked by an explosion, as some poor animal wandered into one of the land mines left along the river bank or along the sides of the road behind. Several sections had signs warning you not to leave the central track.

My travelling companion on this first trip was a South African exile called Arthur. He wanted to assess the medical problems in Wankie Tribal Trust Land, a wilderness just south of the great river. I ended up sharing his home in Bulawayo in between many other journeys into the bush in the year that followed. At the time he was the only doctor for about three hundred thousand people in the Tribal Trust Lands of northern Matabeleland. Many of them had recently returned from exile in Botswana, Zambia or other parts of Zimbabwe, to find schools and clinics burnt and rocketed and their homesteads and fields overtaken by the bush. They rapidly set about repairing the damage, with the assistance of Arthur and other dedicated, if eccentric professionals, but under the euphoria of independence lurked a real fear for the future.

Most of these people were Ndebele, descendants of the group of warlike, cattle-herding Zulu that settled in western Zimbabwe in the late nineteenth century. Until Cecil Rhodes and his associates forced the Ndebele King, Lobengula, to accept their control of the region, the Ndebele had dominated, raided and taxed all the other tribes, in particular the Shona who farmed the more fertile land in eastern Zimbabwe. Though the Ndebele liberation army, ZIPRA, had been just as strong as the Shona version, the Zimbabwe National Liberation Army (ZANLA), and the Ndebele expected, along with many observers, that they would have a major role after independence, this flew in the face of demographic reality.

The Shona and related tribes accounted for some 80 per cent of the population, and Mugabe's Zimbabwe African National

Union (ZANU), of which ZANLA was the military wing, got a proportionate share of the vote in the election that followed the agreement of a ceasefire and a new constitution in London in late 1979. This left Mugabe and his friends in charge and the people of Matabeleland in fear of retribution for their traditional role and the more recent and often bloody rivalry during the civil war.

Reconciliation was supposed to be the policy of the government but within two years much of Matabeleland was closed to visitors and a special Shona army unit, the 5th Brigade, was on the rampage, killing thousands of people. The justification for this tragedy was the activity of dissident Ndebele guerillas, small groups of which had taken to the bush rather than be integrated with the national army. This was either just because they feared such an outcome or because they had become too used to living by the gun. The Zimbabwe African People's Union (ZAPU), the Ndebele party, failed to restrain the dissidents, and was accused by the ruling party of encouraging them. Whichever was indeed the case ZAPU did a poor job of representing its constituents in Matabeleland. Its senior members ended up taking the bait of government jobs in return for merging with the ruling party.

When I was travelling in Zimbabwe the problem of the dissident guerillas had already arisen, but civilians on both sides were praying that it could be defused, that they could be left to rebuild their lives rather than face another bout of killing. Most of the material in this chapter was offered to and rejected by the *Observer* and other newspapers. Most of the journalists, and there were about seventy in Zimbabwe at the time, were sitting in Salisbury, painting by numbers, filling in their editors' convictions that all they had to do was tie up the loose ends of a successful decolonization. It was not until Donald Trelford, editor of the *Observer*, came down in defiance of the commercial interests of his owner, Tiny Rowland, to cover the atrocities in Matabeleland in person that anyone took much notice of Zimbabwe's post-independence problems.

On many occasions when I was covering Africa I was called by excited editors asking for stories I had sent them weeks if not months before. As an editor at *The Times* once said to me, "You can be too early with a story." What this essentially means, given the gutlessness of many editors, is that it is not a story until television gets there. Conversely it remains a story until television leaves, however difficult it is to say anything new or interesting about whatever the crews are filming. The television crews stayed a long time in Khartoum for the minor floods of August 1988, mainly because there was nowhere else they could easily go at the time. This was unfortunate for the thousands being slaughtered in tribal massacres in Burundi. If media attention had been focused on the country sooner thousands of lives could have been saved.

Arthur and I set off from Bulawayo on that first journey, as on many of the others that followed, with a tinge of excitement. There was five hundred kilometres of arid, sparsely populated and often lawless bush between us and the Zambezi. In the first miles of the journey from the provincial capital there were a few farmhouses, whose European owners had erected high security fences topped with barbed wire during the war. They had not taken them down. Many of these farmhouses had become fortresses. Gun positions might be built on the verandas, the fences electrified or the lawn sprinkler system connected to a petrol tank. After the first few miles there was little more than a very occasional roadside stall, group of huts or shot-up hotel. The dry bush had been cleared for about fifty yards on each side of the road, to reduce the risk of ambushes. A few weeks before people would only drive along this road in convoys.

The rivers we crossed were dry, with beds of sculpted sand and rock, but the first showers of the rainy season had pushed out a few green shoots, vivid against the greys and yellows of the dry thorn trees and grass. The monotony was only slightly relieved by a sense of danger. When we finally reached the township of Victoria Falls it was relieved by absurdity. The first thing I saw was a Wimpy Bar. I wondered what Livingstone would have thought. There were also a couple of modern hotels, one with a slot machine casino, and the Victoria Falls Hotel itself. This colonial masterpiece stayed open through the war despite the occasional rocket fired at its ornate terraces by rebels across the gorge in Zambia.

In the morning I walked up to the falls – "the smoke that thunders" is the local name. It is not until you are on the brink of the great trench of rock, along one side of which the water falls, that you see more than a cloud of spray rising from apparently flat bush. You can hear it though, and understand the traditional belief that thunder was made here. The rent torn by water in the earth could be a model for the Styx. You catch occasional glimpses through the swirling mist and spray of wet, jagged, black rock and the torrent running along the bottom.

The falls create powerful winds of their own, which force the spray high above the edges of the void. Standing on the rim opposite under a humid sun at one moment, you are drenched by a rain of spray the next. There is a thin line of tropical rain forest fed by these continual showers. The bright flowers and rich green vegetation are as refreshingly unwordly as the millions of gallons of water tumbling into the chasm beside you. A couple of hundred yards away are parched thorn trees, lifeless grass and sand.

I walked up the river above the falls, looking at the easy flowing river, which seemed unaware of its fate less than a mile away. Livingstone came down this way over a hundred years ago. He must have heard the roar and seen the spray before he came upon the falls. Even so, and even if he had heard stories from neighbouring tribesmen, it must have been a surprise. For the river above meanders in its wide and flat course, a quiet flood for puffing hippos and surreptitious crocodiles.

But the falls were living up to their reputation. Thunder clouds were piling up, and gusts of wind rattled the leaves and stirred the dust. I headed back. On the road I came across the Elephant Hills Club and Hotel. Damaged by rockets and abandoned, its adventurous modern architecture looked forlorn on its single hill. The golf course cut into the bush around was equally abandoned. The fairways were frequented by flocks of guinea fowl, impala and the occasional waterbuck.

The next morning we headed into Wankie Tribal Trust Land. The well-graded dirt road ran several miles south of the river, with wide spaces cleared each side. It had been built, like many roads in Zimbabwe, with the aim of allowing the fast and relatively secure movement of patrols and reinforcements attempting to control the guerillas' infiltration from across the river in Zambia. After the war the road proved an unexpected benefit for the inhabitants of Wankie. Like those of most Tribal Trust Lands, they had been left out of sight and out of mind, a cheap reservoir of labour, until the war developed.

Wankie had been poor enough before the war, but its position had then guaranteed the ruthless treatment of its people. Virtually every clinic, school, cattle dip or borehole was either closed or badly damaged. Our first stop was a primary school with crumbling mudbrick buildings. We dosed about a hundred children for bilharzia, but there was little point. Their open waterholes still harboured the larval cercaria that would reinfect them with the parasitic disease. In the absence of sanitation the eggs from urine and faeces would probably get back into the water, and reinfect the snails that are the alternate host.

After another few miles of bush, just stone and sand between the trees and occasional derelict huts, we reached Ndlovu (or "elephant") camp, site of one of the keeps from which the security forces had tried to control the country. There had also been a clinic, but because of the keep the villagers had decamped and it had closed. The keep was a hundred yard square earthwork, with firing points built from railway sleepers and sand at each corner and at the middle of each ten foot high rampart. Twenty yards out was a barbed wire fence which could be illuminated by floodlights. Beyond were the trees.

Now, under a peaceful sun, it seemed a symbol of the futility of a tragic attempt to stifle the aspirations of a people. We met a Scotsman there. He was in charge of a malaria field team which was supposed to spray the mosquitoes' breeding sites and the homes of their targets, an Augean task. Its African members were camping outside, but to their amusement, not untinged with sympathy, their boss was still preyed on by the war and insisted on staying alone inside the keep. He offered us a drink from his fridge. Despite the presence of two African medical assistants he told Arthur and me "you still can't trust these people". He had a gun, which he showed us. He said that all this time alone in the bush made you slightly crazy, which we believed, though we did not say so. He made us quite nervous when he said that anyone who got in his way would get it between the eyes. But his attitude was more likely to get him killed than anyone else.

We carried on, passing another clinic where a group of women sat on the ground singing, lamenting the death of a child. Arthur said this was nothing unusual. A measles epidemic was sweeping through. He estimated that one in three children died in their first year in this area, succumbing to a fatal combination of malnutrition and disease. At some of the kraals a few huts had been rethatched and their walls of poles resealed with mud, but there was no sign the returning people were starting to plough again, or clear the ground before the rains. A few children waved at the car, a few women pounded grain, a few thin cows wandered in search of a blade of grass.

At Jambezi stood another massive keep, silhouetted at the end of a ridge of naked gravel where once stood a village. We were told the people here, as in most Tribal Trust Lands, had supported the guerillas. Rather than stay under the noses of the keeps where they could be watched and interrogated they took to the hills with what they could carry or drive with them. Some crossed into Zambia as refugees, most stuck it out in kraals away from the keeps and the road, harassed by security forces who knew they gave shelter and food to the guerillas. Several whites confirmed to me that it was common practice to wipe out a kraal to which a guerilla was tracked, while a helicopter pilot told me they used to blow the roofs off huts with their downdraft out of curiosity or sheer devilry.

Several thousand people in Wankie were herded into "protected villages", not so much to protect them as to stop them supporting the guerillas and to create free fire zones in which any wandering African was liable to be shot. In all this Wankie was fairly typical, though more remote and violent than most areas. Though Smith's propagandists managed to persuade many people, and perhaps even themselves, that the guerillas intimidated the people, destroyed their means of livelihood and were as great a threat to most Africans as they were to the whites, this is not the story I heard from the rural Africans themselves. Surely there was some intimidation, and "sell outs", or people considered to be collaborators, were harassed or killed, but the majority were behind the liberation movement in their area. More problems arose when the movements overlapped. In a few places there was a three-cornered civil war.

Beyond Jambezi the land got even more desolately beautiful. Pale green leaves sprouting from stunted trees caught the evening light, giving the hills a friendly look against the dark thunder clouds building up over the river. But the green was an illusion of fertility. Look between the trees and all you saw was burnt rock and sand that had had no taste of the waters flowing a few miles away. It was a relief to reach the river after driving for so long over a jarring, stony road, trailing a plume of dust that overtook us every time we slowed down. Our destination was the Deka Drum, a fishing camp where we were to spend the night. It is a cluster of simple cottages overlooking the confluence of the Zambezi and the Deka, a small tributary.

The Zambezi was a surprise. I had expected a murky stream meandering through dried out sandbanks, a classic African scene. Instead there was something like a giant salmon river, clear water flowing swiftly down rapids connecting massive pools. We walked up the Deka a little way, disturbing geese and waders feeding in the evening shadows, and watched a group of Kudu come down to drink. It was dark when we got back, the lights beckoning. Because of the damp and oppressive heat all we could do was sit on the terrace below the bar, sweating over mercifully cold beers.

I talked with the elderly British couple who had bought the place in 1975 and stayed throughout the worst of the war. They had neither guns nor security fences, treated their staff well, and were left completely untouched. One of their boats was occasionally taken for late night river crossings, and found moored to Zambia the next morning. They even drove through the Tribal Trust Land once or twice a week for supplies, something most whites would have called suicidal, as it would have been if they had had rifles sticking out of the windows. The guerillas' approach was quite simple. If you had a weapon when stopped or ambushed, you were the enemy and they would try to kill you. Arthur and I never carried anything more lethal than a sheath knife.

Bob, the proprietor, told me they had said, "It's none of our business, we're just trying to run a fishing camp." I met several other examples of people successfully opting out of the civil war, in contrast to the general militarization of the white population. With these few exceptions there was no such thing as a white civilian, contrary to the propagandists' claims. Nearly all were armed, most able bodied men were at least part time members of the security forces and most farms were effectively rural outposts for the army, equipped with radios, fences and defensive perimeters.

Of course land mines do not discriminate. We were nervous of running into one on a little-frequented dirt track, as had happened several times as people drove more freely in the bush. Neither side could remember where they had planted all of them. Cattle and game had cleared many, an example of which I heard on the river the next morning. Poachers had taken advantage of the situation, driving herds of elephant and other game towards the minefields.

We left the camp at noon the following day. After a night breathing air like pea soup, listening to mosquitoes singing outside the net, the expected cool of the morning was missing. It was a heat-wave, and a heat-wave here meant it was 40°C by 11 a.m., and still rising, combined with about 90 per cent humidity. I could not persuade the others to stay for some more fishing. I came back by myself for a week a few months later. The rains had set in somewhere hundreds of miles upstream, and the river had been transformed into a great swollen flood. All had changed, except the often angry conversations at the bar.

One evening ended with a Rhodesian (the word reflected the attitude and was the choice of most of the whites, despite the country's official change of name) calling me chicken because I had not come to the country before, and fought for it. I had said I loved it. He assumed I wanted to own it. On another evening a man from the Wildlife Department came in after shooting a couple of elephants, so driving away a herd that had been raiding crops. He loved his life, he said, but predicted that the Africans would ruin the wildlife, indeed the whole country. "The whole thing's a disaster," he said, repeating the catchphrase of his fellow young Rhodesians. Bob exploded. "You people have got to make your choice. Either you stop complaining and try to make it work or you get out."

"I can't get out, this is my country. Where can I go?"

"Well in that case you'd better shut up and make a success of it."

Every morning, wakened by the roaring of a hippo, I crept out under the still chilly stars and took a dinghy out to fish. The dawn was sudden, the sun soon turning goosepimples into sweat as myriads of birds came to life, their wings and chatterings announcing the heat of the day. The river was too swollen to fish in the main stream, but drifting a bait along the edges of the rushes on the banks would often produce strikes. The tigerfish takes to the air in tremendous leaps as soon as it is hooked, shaking its head with mouth open to display the interlocking rows of sharp-edged wedge-shaped teeth on upper and lower jaws. The fish often come off but there are plenty around, running up to about fifteen pounds. One of these silver-bellied black-striped and green-backed bullets may explode from the water at any time, though dawn and dusk were the best times, and also the most beautiful. There was much else to watch while you waited, the animals coming down to drink, the birds and the other denizens of the river.

One day we saw a hippo and calf attempting to cross the main stream. The cow, her large head still forging ahead against the strong current, failed to notice that the calf had been swept away from its sheltered position behind her. When she finally looked round to check the shock and panic were obvious. She looked around in all directions, then charged off downstream. By evening the two were back in the sheltered eddy where the Deka joined the main river in front of the camp.

A hippo with a young calf can be very dangerous if approached too closely. A couple of days later the cow's head rose right beside the boat as I sat quietly anchored at the edge of the stream. I froze as the great eyes calmly considered me. She seemed to realize I meant no harm, and silently disappeared. On another occasion they passed right by me as I stood on a log projecting from the bank. The crocodiles were more worrying. Though you

were safe enough in a boat, standing on the bank to fish was to
emulate the behaviour of the larger reptiles' favourite targets, the
animals that came down to drink. You rarely saw the crocodiles
during the day, but at night a torch would reveal reflecting eyes
all along the bank.

A few other people were fishing from the camp, most of them
with the shorts, floppy hats and unreconstructed racialism of the
standard white. One had brought his manservant, who sometimes
baited his hook or removed a fish from it. He was hugely amused
to swing a wriggling electric eel across to the unsuspecting
African, who muttered and sulked for the rest of the week. I
fished a couple of times with an elderly tobacco farmer, originally
from Rhodesia but now living in South Africa. One evening he
was highly disturbed to discover that his guide for the next day
had been a local guerilla. No other was available and he was
torn between his principles and his desire to fish. The next evening
the guide's English and ability as a boatman were highly
complimented and his past forgotten. The tobacco farmer had
caught a very large tigerfish.

One morning when his wife and I were left alone after breakfast
she said, "You mustn't be too hard on us you know, Andrew.
We had to try to protect what we had made here, it was like
paradise."

"Yes, maybe, but why the discrimination?"

"You must see that the Africans can't run things like we can.
It was better for them too, they were better off than in the black
countries."

"Perhaps, but why couldn't you let the ones with ability move
up as far as they could? It was people like that, stuck in some
menial job while whites less qualified or intelligent than them
were promoted over them, that gave the push to the nationalist
groups. OK, the result would have been the same, but you could
have avoided a war, and be in a much better position today."

There was a long pause.

"We couldn't do that, it would have been the thin end of the
wedge, we couldn't keep what we had without keeping
control . . ."

The whites were reluctant to admit that the thousands of

physical and mental casualties of the war had achieved nothing.
It began in the form of occasional guerilla actions, some of which
could justifiably be called terrorist, not long after Smith's
Unilateral Declaration of Independence in 1965. It ended in
December 1979, after it became apparent that even the total
militarization of the white community could not contain the
increasingly aggressive guerilla armies. These ignored the
cosmetic internal settlement of 1978, in which the whites
attempted to placate the Africans by installing Bishop Abel
Muzorewa as Prime Minister after highly dubious elections.

The young whites who bore the brunt of the fighting in the
late 1970s were among the psychological casualties. It was
particularly hard for them to acknowledge that what they had
been doing at the behest of their community was a waste of life.
Anybody outside their group was subject to distrust and
aggression. Several journalists were beaten up while I was there.
They took refuge in extreme racism. They refused to believe
anything good could come of the new government. "Just wait.
This place will be like Zambia in a couple of years," they said,
ignoring the fact that the country had an immeasurably more
developed infrastructure and thousands more educated Africans
than Zambia, or indeed most African countries.

Many were "gapping it", going down to South Africa in the
belief that the struggle for white supremacy could be won there.
Their parents were much more likely to say they were prepared
to "give Mugabe a try". But they did not have to come to terms
with direct experience of the futile savagery of the war. Under
the not entirely assumed mantle of sympathy, I heard many
stories from the young white veterans.

A few days after I arrived in the country two of them gave me
a cackling introduction to the terms I would need to know.
Some, like "terr" for terrorist, were fairly obvious. Others, like
"floppy" for a dead terr, less so. Occasional signs of humanity
escaped the bravado. "Hell, man, we did some pretty bad things,
but nothing like them." It is true the guerillas' lack of training
and equipment encouraged them to go for soft targets, but the
security forces could hardly claim they did not use their superior
weaponry against equally soft targets.

I also met some young men who had been on the much publicized raid on Victory Camp in Zambia. It had been justified as a pre-emptive strike on a guerilla base – an extension of the hot pursuit policy that had allowed several military actions deep inside Rhodesia's neighbours. Air strikes were followed by attacks from helicopters and a ground column. "It was just slaughter," said one of the young men. "You should hear the tape a buddy made on one of the choppers. All you can hear is the engine, a machine-gun going like hell and the guy firing it yelling 'Christ, they're like flies down there.' There were hundreds of them running all over the place. We killed about three times the figure they released. Jesus."

"How come they didn't release the full figure?"

"You don't think they were all terrs, do you? Everybody knew there weren't that many there. Anyway they always used to minimize casualties. Try to make the whole thing look smaller."

"You mean most of them were refugees?"

"Of course. Hell, a lot of them were kids. Kids who would become guerilas, maybe, but kids all the same."

Such comments combined with the deserted kraals in the Tribal Trust Lands to suggest that the real death toll of the war, including those who died of malnutrition and disease, was at least three times the official figure of thirty thousand. Nobody will ever know for sure.

Many of the young whites from élite units like the Selous Scouts, who lived like the guerilas themselves, tracking them relentlessly through the bush, had gone straight from school into the army. Their lack of qualifications also encouraged them to go south, where the South African Defence Force would welcome them. A squad leader told me: "The thing I know is how to kill. Fighting's the only skill I have. I don't want to but I suppose I'll end up joining up in SA or becoming a mercenary. Haven't got much choice, have I?"

"Have you ever actually killed someone?"

"Only once for sure. I came round a bush and there was this Aff with a gun. For a moment nothing happened. I just stood there thinking, Christ, if I don't shoot him he'll get me. I could see he was thinking the same. I was quicker."

As many of these young men all too happily pointed out, the danger now lay in a new war between the fifty thousand unemployed guerillas from the two rebel armies awaiting demobilization or integration into the national army. On our way back from my first visit to Wankie and the Deka Drum in November 1980 we heard that guerillas in adjacent camps in Entumbane, a township in Bulawayo, had started machine-gunning and rocketing each other. With the help of the Army and Police a truce was agreed, but the threat of an all-out war between the two movements had remained.

We met a party of ZIPRA reinforcements on the road to Bulawayo, returning to their base at Gwaai River Mine after barely being prevented from joining the fray. They had stopped at a roadside store for cold beer, two Volvo trucks (originally donated by Swedish aid as humanitarian assistance) standing on the hard shoulder loaded with heavy machine-guns and mortars. These men were not really guerillas, unlike their comrades in Entumbane. The force at Gwaai River Mine was virtually a conventional army, complete with armoured cars and other sophisticated weaponry, whose imminent battle-worthiness had probably helped persuade the Rhodesians to negotiate the end of the war. The uniformed men, some of them swathed with machine-gun belts, leapt back on the trucks as soon as one of their officers blew a whistle. Moments later they departed in a cloud of dust.

A few months later, in February 1981, more serious fighting broke out in the camps at Entumbane. A column from Gwaai River Mine was again turned back, but only by the threat of aerial attack backed up by heavily armed roadblocks and patrols that prevented small groups from slipping through. A convoy of armoured cars and trucks from another ZIPRA camp at Essexvale, south of Bulawayo, reached the outskirts of the city. It was ambushed and virtually wiped out by the Hilltop Motel.

The sceptics that doubted the army, many of whose African soldiers and predominantly white officers had fought in the civil war, had the will to intervene in a battle between the rebel movements were confounded. This evidence of support for the new constitution gave Mugabe's government the confidence to disarm the remaining guerilla camps in the following weeks. The immediate risk of a large scale military confrontation had abated, but there were enough dissidents and arms hidden in the bush to continue to threaten the government's attempts to establish some sort of law and order and security. There was a slight but constant risk of being ambushed or shot at driving around the country all the time I was there

On another journey down the road from Victoria Falls to Bulawayo I had hitched a ride with three nervous people in a yellow Volkswagen. "It can't be far now," one said somewhere near Lupane, about half-way back. Soon after that we stopped ceremoniously to relieve ourselves, and another told me, "We were shot at here on the way up." The almost perfect star of broken glass in front of the driver had fascinated me since I got in. It transpired that was where a rifle grenade had glanced the screen, but it had either been a dud or the impact was too soft. A few inches further back and it would have slammed straight through the driver's side window. He had seen the muzzle flash, covered his face with his hands and ducked. They almost crashed, but he recovered and sped to the nearest police post, where they were told to keep quiet about the incident. Two weeks after we got back to Bulawayo we heard that Father Edmar Sommereisser had been killed at the Catholic mission in Lupane.

One weekend Arthur and I drove west from Bulawayo to Khami, where a couple had turned their farm into a nature reserve. They showed us a list of the birds that could be seen there. Two weeks later they were dead, shot as they drove along one of the tracks in their reserve. On several occasions we came across roadblocks, with armoured cars blocking the road and machine-guns pointing at the approaching vehicles, to discover there had been another incident. The people who perpetrated them, whether they were dissidents seeking to destabilize the government or simple bandits, bore a heavy responsibility not just for their victims but for giving the government the justification for sending in the 5th Brigade.

Most of the time our path seemed to miss that of the gunmen, if only by a few days. Not always. When I went down to Manama, site of a mission school and hospital in the remote

south-western corner of Matabeleland, near the border with
Botswana, the atmosphere was tense. The school had been robbed
by armed men, just after the fees had been collected for the new
term. The nearest tarred road and police post was at Gwanda,
over fifty miles away. The police were too nervous to establish
a permanent presence any closer.

After driving for several hours through sparsely settled, flat
bush, marked by occasional baobabs and boulder-strewn kopjes,
I saw a belltower rise in front. Complete with buttresses and
arched windows, the church would have looked at home in a
small Swedish town. This was a Swedish Lutheran mission.
Around the church were comfortable bungalows, one of them
occupied by my friends Pierre and Brigitte, a doctor and nurse
sent out by Médecins Sans Frontières, the French medical relief
agency, to run the hospital.

In the evening Pierre and I went to a bottle store, or bar, at
Manama's "Business centre". A familiar sight in the trust lands,
these consist of a few simple shops selling basic goods along a
swath of open ground beside the road. The bottle store had a
tin roof and a bar which divided the store room at the back from
the serving room at the front. You sat on empty crates and
swigged your beer from the bottle. A couple of candles provided
illumination. This place was quite advanced, however. There was
a kerosene fridge to chill the beer and a battery powered record
player with three singles.

We were chatting quietly when they came in. Their bush boots,
black trousers and T-shirts identified them as ex-guerillas. One
helped himself to my cigarettes, another to my beer, jostling me
in the process. As we ordered more the landlady warned us not
to leave, saying they had probably left a friend outside with their
guns. We must stay, whatever they did. They helped themselves
to our beer and cigarettes again. We were getting a little scared
when the woman put one of the singles on. Now I had spent a
few days with some musician friends, some of whom had been
in the guerilla movements, a few weeks before. I had learnt about
the highly politicized but rhythmical music they favoured. Only
certain singers were acceptable to each group, and, more
important, there were completely specialized dances for the

favoured songs. With huge relief I realized I had been taught this one.

Pierre thought I had gone mad when I stood up to dance. So perhaps did our friends. A few moments later, however, I was explaining where I had learnt their dance, and we were offered apologies and beers. One confessed that he had thought we might be plain-clothes police. In fact I think it would have been enough to be white and connected to the mission to be in serious danger – unless I had known that dance. The mission, like others in the country, was not generally popular. Though the missionaries had often been at loggerheads with the white government, they too often shared its paternalistic attitudes to the Africans. Though medical treatment and education was theoretically open to all, it certainly helped to be a regular church-goer.

The missionaries at Manama were furious with Pierre and Brigitte for failing to set an example by attending the church services. They were usually attending to a never-ending case load, or snatching a moment of rest. When one of the missionary nurses came to the bottle store to call Pierre to an emergency, shortly after our reconciliation with the boys from the bush, her face radiated disapproval. So did theirs. At the time Pierre and I could only laugh, but such incidents did not help Pierre introduce new treatments or overcome the racial and religious prejudices of the older staff. The government was taking over most of the missionary schools and hospitals because of such problems, but this was not immediately helping to overcome the daunting backlog of untreated patients.

The next day I went to help Brigitte and two African nurses with a mobile baby clinic at the village of Shanyawugwe, a tiny village about twenty miles away. In the last seven years of war hardly any of the children in the area had been vaccinated. We started at dawn, having set up under various trees for the shade they would later provide. We had to give each child up to five injections. Our limited supply of needles rapidly grew blunt. We did not know about AIDS then, and I can only hope that the disinfectant in the dishes in which we rotated them was effective. If the virus was already present in the district, however, I doubt it would have made much difference. On the medical cards I helped fill out, when injecting dirty bottoms or weighing screaming children became overwhelming, the mothers often listed several different fathers for their six or seven children. Some of the children's names displayed a touching faith in the politicians who arranged the ceasefire. Several were called Carrington, after the British Foreign Secretary who led the negotiations. At dusk we had dealt with about six hundred children, and were totally exhausted. I had picked up a throat infection.

Arthur had another brush with the gunmen in Tjolotjo, the sprawling Tribal Trust Land north-west of Bulawayo where he spent much of his time after the ceasefire. The police rarely ventured into its hinterlands, and Arthur quickly dispensed with the armed escort he had been given on his first visits. He reckoned it would be provocative, identifying him with the previous regime when he wanted to present himself as an apolitical doctor. He eventually became known to the people in the area as the mad doctor, his white pick-up and bearded face a passport for safe passage. Before that reputation was established he had to take a few chances.

One day he was flagged down by a man with an AK47. When he stopped a rusty bayonet came in each side window.

"Have you got a gun?" one asked. It would have been a death sentence.

"No."

"Give me your watch."

"I haven't got one.'

"Give me your money."

"I haven't got any." He often travelled without either.

"Where are you going?"

"Nkunzi." A small village in southern Tjolotjo.

"Why?"

"I'm a doctor. I'm going to the clinic."

"Aah. I've got *nongwe* (malaria). Give me some pills."

Arthur gave him some, with strict instructions as to how to take them, and was waved on.

Tjolotjo, like most of the Tribal Trust Lands, is highly infertile. It is the beginning of the Kalahari sand-veld that stretches through Botswana to the desert of that name. It is mostly sand covered with low scrub, mainly thorn and the drought resistant mopane tree. This tree, not unlike a stunted beech, is eaten only by the mopane worm (in fact a caterpillar). These larvae, which can be eaten fresh or dried for storage, are an important and prized source of protein in this area. They are a little smaller than a little finger, green when alive and black when dried.

The hunger in the impoverished Tribal Trust Lands for more and better land fuelled the guerilla movements. The war was about land. There has been some resettlement since independence and the government continues to declare its socialist intentions, but it faces a cruel dilemma. Subdivide the fertile, efficient and white owned commercial farms and you risk starving the country in return for short term political popularity. Leave them alone and risk accusations of neo-colonialism. So far the government has leant to the latter course, perhaps mindful of what happened in the countries where its members spent years of exile. In Zambia, Tanzania and Mozambique nationalization, collectivization or subdivision has contributed to a collapse in agricultural production. Zimbabwe still grows enough food to feed itself in most years.

The poverty of the Tribal Trust Lands remains great however, and was uncomfortably obvious just after the war in places like Tjolotjo. I accompanied Arthur there several times, more as an assistant than a journalist. The hospital was the focus of suffering, particularly on my first visit, when efforts to revive the rural health service had only recently begun. It had over a hundred beds, all full. The overspill slept on concrete floors. Some of the roofs still awaited repair. It was the first time I had seen the terrible inadequacy to cope that is so common in African hospitals. But I would not be so shocked again for eight years, when I saw the effects of the massacres in Burundi in 1988. The stench of unwashed bodies, the sight of deep infected sores and wounds combined with a silence broken by an occasional cough or moan. There was no resident doctor, though ZD, as the Shona clinical officer in charge was known, had an unrivalled knowledge of local diseases and could perform successful operations in circumstances that would daunt a Western surgeon.

The problem was that he and his assistants had no time to deal with all the patients individually. In the absence of obvious injury they would treat them with chloroquine, against malaria. If that did not work they would try a broad spectrum antibiotic. If that did not work they would start trying to find out what was wrong. The rehabilitation of the rural health service coincided with the return of thousands of refugees from Zambia and Botswana. Malnutrition made many prone to disease while others suffered from injuries or conditions untreated for years.

The next day we drove to Pumula, a village near the Botswanan border where relief food was being distributed. The road took us through a virtually uninhabited section of the trust land, a large area of dense bush marked by tall trees. These had disappeared elsewhere due to the demand for fire wood. They probably have not lasted here either, as a logging operation owned by Anglo-American was hauling out the valuable hardwoods. As we approached Pumula there were increasing numbers of people on the track, some in scotch carts. These are simple box carts with a single axle and two old car tyres, pulled by from two to eight donkeys. We also met several herds of scrawny, long boned cattle, dwarfing the little boys who chivvied them off the road and then waved and grinned at us. A few months before they could have been mujibas, the young scouts of the guerillas, who would have scurried off to tell their older brothers what they had seen, with the probable result of an ambush on our return.

When we reached Pumula hundreds of people had gathered round the food store. I could not see one who showed obvious signs of hunger, indeed many were quite fat. Scotch carts were departing laden with bags of maize meal. There was almost a holiday air, with the colourful clothes under the hot sun. Though there were starving people in the area, they were in a few small pockets, and this feeding programme, paid for and monitored by the United Nations High Commission for Refugees (UNHCR), was like trying to kill a housefly with a shotgun.

It was at this time that Arthur and I started thinking about putting an "aid kills" sticker in the back window of the car. Here, yet again, foolish philanthropy was leading to a dangerous

dependence. Many of these people should have been preparing
their fields for the coming rainy season, instead of walking for
up to three days to collect free food. Not all had to walk or ride
in scotch carts, however. A few, including a minister's daughter,
had arrived by car. Local party officials dominated the
committees choosing the recipients, and it seemed stalwart
supporters were first in line.

I returned to Pumula a few weeks later with Arthur and Nils
Kastberg, the UNHCR boss for Matabeleland. The rains were
beginning, and we slithered and splashed through mud and
puddles, using speed to get through the worst patches. Greenery
was sprouting from what had seemed totally barren ground a few
weeks before. Nils and Arthur explained changes in the feeding
scheme to the hundreds gathered around the food store. Only
children under five with an upper arm circumference of under
fourteen centimetres would now receive food. This was
apparently a reliable guide to malnutrition, and could easily be
assessed using a plastic tape that was red up to fourteen
centimetres, then yellow for a couple of centimetres, then green.

There was some predictable grumbling. The women asked why
older children, just as hungry, should be excluded, or if women
doing the cooking could eat themselves. In Africa it is often the
children who go short first, not the adults. This may seem
shocking to Europeans, but our morality is tempered by affluence.
In a land where drought and famine are expected every few years,
and where an adult is usually the survivor of several potentially
lethal diseases, the men and women who till the fields or herd
the cattle are far more important to the family and tribe than
young children. If the worst comes to the worst, more babies
can be born in fatter times. These were fatter times for most of
the country, and nearly every woman seemed to have a child on
her back. The population was growing by nearly 4 per cent a
year.

A few weeks later again we stopped at the village of Nkunzi,
to hear from a man on the committee entrusted with setting up
the new feeding system in the area that no feeding had started.
He asked us to come to his kraal and look at his sister, who was
having trouble giving birth. On the way he told us that his family

was getting a good harvest, and was sending food to market in Bulawayo. His jeans and sunglasses were further evidence that they were doing well. Chickens scattered in front of us as we drove into the kraal, and the women went on pounding maize. Arthur decided that we should take the girl, who was about fifteen, to Tjolotjo.

While we were clearing a rough couch among sacks of food and medical supplies in the back of the car we were showered with gifts – cobs of cooked maize, groundnuts, a bundle of fresh sugarcane and lastly a chicken with its legs tied together, clucking angrily. Arthur joked that there could not be anyone here on the feeding scheme. Oh yes, said the man who had brought us, one of his own children would be. Brought forward from the throng of children, he was indeed thin but some way from qualifying by his arm measurement. Then I noticed two that did look very thin and pointed them out to Arthur. Out came the tape and they proved under the limit. It was agreed that they should be on the scheme too. Their mother was probably a lowly relative, taken in because she was widowed or unmarried, but if an organizer could ignore her children for such reasons, what hope was there for the scheme as a whole? Few of the children at the feeding points we visited later qualified.

The journey back to Tjolotjo Hospital was chaotic. The girl went into the advanced stages of labour. The car's fuel system started to play up, so that we had a top speed of about 30 m.p.h., our progress marked by unpredictable lurches. I was sitting in front, between Arthur and a young man with a serious case of trachoma, his eyes red and raw. In the back was the girl, panting, as Musa, an ex-guerilla paramedic now training to be a medical assistant, tried to stop her pushing. Towards the end Musa said she could see the head, but managed to prevent further movement by holding the girl's legs together. The girl's mother looked on impassively, chewing a piece of sugarcane, while our hen and an unruly dog staggered about on the pile of food sacks, which occasionally came adrift when we hit a bump. A boy was born shortly after we arrived at the hospital.

My last journey in Zimbabwe was a long one to the opposite end of the country, to the mountains along the eastern border with Mozambique. The objectives on that border would be trout and a closer look at the war zones where the Shona guerillas of ZANLA had challenged white supremacy. Nobody in Matabeleland could tell me how accessible the rivers were, or if there were many fish left in them. Our first target was the Chimanimani Mountains, near the farming and logging town of Melsetter. The cool air was welcome as we rose into the hills. For the last twenty miles we passed through the Charter Estate, a huge forestry enterprise that has covered the hills in unnatural conifers. Some people say it looks like Scotland. If they mean the areas blighted by the Forestry Commission they are right.

The craggy, dark bulk of the Chimanimanis lowered mysteriously and invitingly across the valley as we arrived at the hotel in Melsetter. In happier years it would have been full of visitors come to walk, climb and fish in the mountains. Now it was nearly empty. The bar was the gathering place of the remnants of an embittered local European community. Melsetter was a bad place during the war, the guerillas coming from Mozambique through the gaps in the mountains. Nearly every farm was attacked, nearly every family lost a member. That this was also true of the Africans in the area was of little concern to the whites.

I had met a farmer from Melsetter in Salisbury. The first thing he said to me was: "I didn't fight for eight years to see the bloody British come and sell us down the river." He was leaving for South Africa, despite having been one of the handful of white farmers to stay on their farms in the Melsetter district throughout the war. About fifteen of the sixty-five there at the beginning had been killed, and most of the rest had given up.

He was attached to another farmer, a lady who had also stayed on her Melsetter farm. One evening in Salisbury they announced they were celebrating their anniversary. They were not married, and it turned out to be the date of their ambush. They had been driving along, the lady in front in a borrowed Land-rover, when the guerillas opened up. They reckoned from the cases picked up afterwards that over a thousand rounds were fired, but only six hit her car. A similar number hit his. Neither was injured. She got a note of apology from the local guerilla commander.

Presumably as a single woman who had good relations with her workers she was not a target, and was only attacked because she was in a borrowed car.

The man they had happily attacked because he was a highly enthusiastic part-time soldier. He seemed to have treated the war as a tremendous adventure. His favourite story, frequently interrupted by chuckles, was of the time he and a group of African soldiers were pinned down by a machine-gun. They were trying to spot where the shots were coming from. His African NCO raised a hand to point, apparently saying "There it is boss," and was hit in the wrist. The NCO then pointed with the other hand, and was hit again. He then stood up and started to walk away, mumbling, "I've had enough of this bloody war. You can fight it yourself." He was then hit again, and lay still. I was glad to hear he recovered, and surprised to hear the narrator agree with him. "He was right, you know, it wasn't his war."

It was the farmers' war, and what they could not seem to take at Melsetter was that they had lost it. The atmosphere in the bar was savage. The first thing a woman said to us was: "You're not journalists are you? We don't like them around here." Arthur said we were doctors. The conversation revealed that these people regarded the African as subhuman. I noticed the totally withdrawn expression of the African barman as his kind were referred to as "munts", "kaffirs" and the rest. He had to listen dumbly when the woman who had spoken to us first told us this story, why I don't know.

A local lad and two other Europeans, one of them a German mercenary, were waiting by a forest track to ambush a group of "terrs". The German was apparently so keen to "kill some gooks" that he opened fire too early. One of the guerillas, a sixteen-year-old-boy, got behind them and killed all three. She said that they found out later that he only had three shots in his magazine. Usually the guerillas were credited with a total inability to hit anything. He was wounded and captured by the reaction group, and taken to a hospital. The woman's last comment, and the smug satisfaction with which she said it, left us stunned. "They kept him there for a week and then they finished him off." I didn't ask for details. A captured guerilla could expect to hang anyway.

The park encompassing the Chimanimanis was still officially closed, but we asked if anyone would stop us going there. "I will," said a young man. He was a local policeman, and told us that there were still land mines and booby traps in the park, and that he and his mates would not be very happy to have to come and pick up the bits if we ran into one. Some "affs" had recently done just that, and he promised to arrest us if we went anywhere near the park.

The next day we took the Cashel road north. First running along the valley that separates Melsetter from the Chimanimanis, it passes the gap at their northern end and then climbs into another, lower range. For most of its course it is within a few miles of the Mozambique border. The dirt track soon broke out of the pine forests around Melsetter into an open green valley rising up to crags and virgin woodland. A breath-taking landscape in which to fight a guerilla war. The loneliness, and some of the fear, seemed to hang there yet. We passed several abandoned and burnt-out farm houses. By a brook there was a group of soldiers relaxing and doing their washing, but with their rifles propped nearby.

They were taking no chances. Mozambican rebels could easily cross the border a few miles away, either to raid or to escape the Mozambican army. The Resistencia National Moçambicana, known as RENAMO, was set up in 1976 with Rhodesian assistance in an effort to disrupt the new Mozambican government's support for ZANLA. A socialist liberation movement, the Frente de Libertacao de Moçambique, or FRELIMO, had taken power there in 1975 on the departure of the Portuguese. With the new government in Zimbabwe now closely allied to Mozambique, RENAMO had become reliant on South Africa for supplies.

Once Zimbabwean troops started helping the government side in the Mozambican civil war RENAMO struck back with occasional attacks on police or army posts inside Zimbabwe. Refugees from the fighting or intimidation inside Mozambique were also likely to cross. Shortly before our visit to the border area a group of Mozambican government supporters had fled into Zimbabwe, a couple of village officials minus their ears.

The loneliness increased as we climbed into the mountains, only mitigated by an occasional cluster of huts and maize fields. The former labourers were now working some of the land for themselves, in the absence of their European masters. We stopped at a derelict farmhouse. The mud bricks of the main walls, now disintegrating under an open sky, showed that it must have been the homestead of some early settlers. This was proved by the little graveyard where the generations of Steyns – they must have come from Afrikaaner stock – went back to the turn of the century. Now it was all over, and the evidence left by these pioneers, victims of a future they could not see or change, would soon disappear.

I climbed up a hillside nearby, through waist-deep grass and ferns. A distant rumble brought my eyes to two army trucks creeping like toys up the hairpins below. I sat hidden by the grass and imagined what it must have been like for a guerilla waiting in ambush, or for the African soldiers in their so obvious, crawling vehicles. I also thought that if there were mines in the Chimanimanis there were just as likely to be mines near where I was sitting. I was relieved to get back to the road. Arthur told me a story about a colleague who had worked among the Africans in the eastern highlands. Not long after the ceasefire he met the local ZANLA commander. "Ah, Doctor. You've got a little yellow Renault, haven't you." The Doctor asked how he knew. "We often watched you go by when we were waiting by the road." Sometimes the guerillas even turned people like this back, and they might hear later that a military vehicle had hit a land mine further along the road they were travelling.

After passing the summit of the range, where dense, cool mossy forest clung to the plunging hillsides, the track wound down to the valley of the Umvumvumvu river, and followed its tumbling course out of the mountains into the heat of the rolling hills below, where we joined the main road north to Umtali. Umtali, now known as Mutare, is a large town that grew up on the border where the main road and railway enter Mozambique on their way to the Indian Ocean port of Beira. The town had

declined in the war years, with the road and railway closed and
rockets coming over the border, but was now recovering. We
stocked up at one of its supermarkets and then headed north
again, towards the Inyanga National Park.

In one of the Tribal Trust Lands we passed, the valley floors
were peppered with the conical thatched roofs of huts, in some
places almost crowding out the little fields. It seemed impossible
that the land could support so many people. It probably was. As
we gained height we entered the commercial forests again, in
marked contrast to the trust lands, where the trees were
disappearing under the demand for fire wood. When we reached
the park the hilltops were shrouded by mist, the side road we
had taken hemmed in by a seemingly endless procession of cold
and dripping trees. Eventually we came to a bluff overlooking
the Pungwe Falls, clear water plunging down into the mysterious
wooded depths of a great U-shaped valley that led into
Mozambique. It was too windy and wet to admire the view for
long, so we drove on to the park headquarters, where an artificial
trout lake nestles among mature pines, overlooked by a hotel.

The hotel was made by extending the solid stone cottage Cecil
Rhodes had built when he carved this area out as his personal
estate. Inyanga, like the Matopos hills in Matabeleland, was his
gift to the country. These two parks demonstrate his appreciation
of natural beauty. Neither can have been a very profitable estate.
The simple house at Inyanga stands in stark contrast to his grand
visions of an Africa dominated by the Britons.

The next day we went to a rural hospital serving the Trust
Lands near the park to visit a friend of Arthur's, an African
medical officer. He showed us round. The hangover of the war
was evident in three patients. An elderly man was recovering
from the removal of several pieces of shrapnel from his body.
Like many African wounded, whether directly involved or not,
he had not come for treatment before for fear of the authorities.
There was a legless orphan, staying at the hospital because he
had nowhere else to go despite the fact he had been blown up
long ago. Finally there was a recent casualty, a boy of ten
recovering from the amputation of both legs just above the knee.
He had being playing on a heap of earth with his younger sister

when a land mine someone had hidden there had gone off, tearing his lower legs to pieces and killing his sister. I hoped that Arthur's friend was not right when he said that maybe she was the lucky one.

He told us where I might be able to borrow some fly fishing tackle. I had always considered fly fishing to be a peculiarly European obsession, a view which I suppose reflected fundamental doubts about the compatibility of African and European. I was chastened and happy to discover that the local expert to whom I was directed was also an African. He lent me some good equipment, recommending a fine leader and several flies with which he had caught fish.

In the afternoon we returned to the Pungwe river, walking upstream from the falls. I waded into the cool, clear pools, the sun shining hot on the grassy slopes above as I cast into the deeper holes. Small, silvery trout darted for the fly, and I soon had enough for us to eat that night. There was no sign of any other people, not even any tracks along the river. I could only presume I was one of the first people to fish it since the end of the war. Perhaps others were still nervous of the proximity of the Mozambican border.

In the evening we grilled the fish on the embers of a fire and camped on the river bank. Pungwe, according to some Shona friends, is hard to translate directly. Loosely speaking it means "something that runs on continuously, perhaps inexorably". Thus it is an apt name for the rapids and cascades of a mountain river. It can also be used to describe the guerilla war, the years of struggle. More happily, it could cover an all-night drinking session. The next morning the trout were still rising freely.

Ten years later this border was still potentially dangerous. Like Malawi, one hundred miles away across lawless Mozambique, Zimbabwe was still subject to the occasional overspills of the Mozambican civil war. Even more serious was the disruption of trade and transport through Mozambique. RENAMO may be supported by South Africa and have a reputation for barbarity, but its successes and longevity speak for themselves, as does the record of the South African supported rebels in Angola. Such movements cannot survive without at least some popular support.

Such conflicts can only be ended by governments that enjoy wide and real popular support. This means that the people drawn into RENAMO and other rebel movements throughout Africa must be given the opportunity either to participate in government or to oppose it through means other than the gun.

By August 1990 there were signs that this might happen in Mozambique. The FRELIMO leadership announced that Mozambique was ready for multi-party democracy. If and when it is implemented one of RENAMO's major demands for an end to the war will have been fulfilled. Perhaps both sides have finally realized that their claims to righteousness have not been worth fifteen years of bloodshed.

The Cold Heart
of Africa

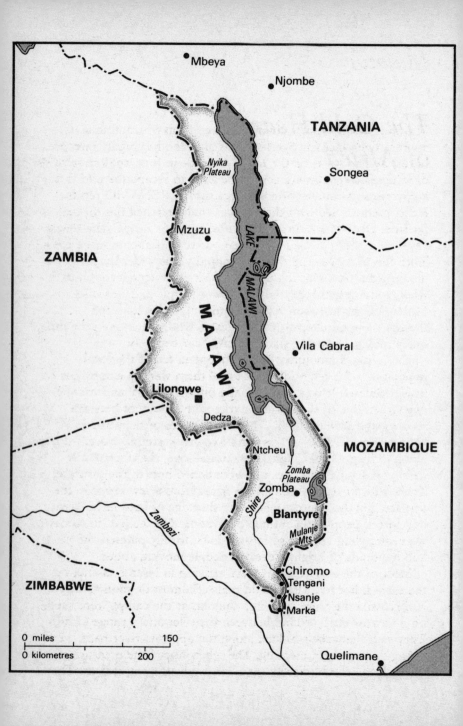

Malawi

The Shire River, which divides Malawi from Mozambique, is
another fine place for tigerfish. It is also another highly insecure
border. When I was on the Malawian side in June 1988 thousands
of refugees were coming across the river to escape the effects of
a government counter-offensive against the RENAMO rebels.
Helicopters circled over the swamps that stretched out on the
far side. Occasional bursts of gunfire could be heard. The rebels,
I was told, were in the reeds a few yards from the opposite bank.
Since the river was less than a hundred yards wide, I was
discouraged from putting up the rod. It also seemed frivolous
when you knew that seventy thousand people had fled into
Malawi in the last month alone, bringing to six hundred
thousand the number of Mozambicans who had entered the little,
overpopulated country since the civil war began in 1976.

The refugees amounted to nearly one in ten of the local
population of seven million. Most of them were in camps just
inside Malawi. It was odd how the often arbitrary and usually
unguarded line of the border marked the difference between
security and violent death. The twenty miles of main road
between Dedza and Ntcheu is part of the western border. I drove
along it once. On the right, in Mozambique, there were only
derelict roadside buildings and abandoned huts in the distance.
There was no sign of human life apart from a few crops in the
first few hundred yards, which the shortage of land in Malawi
had forced people to continue cultivating. On the left, in Malawi,
were sprawling villages of refugee huts, freshly painted shops
and hundreds of brightly dressed people moving about.

Most of the new refugees were arriving in Nsanje district on
the eastern border. They could register almost as soon as they
had crossed the Shire river in a dugout, as the camps were sited
on a narrow strip of land between the river and a range of hills.
They said that rebels hidden along the opposite river bank were
trying to stop them crossing. The rebels hoped the presence of
the civilians would discourage further government attacks. They

were also appealing for support. We met one man as he unloaded his family and a few pots from a canoe. He told us that he had been asked: "Why don't you want to stay and die with us?" Like most of the refugees he was equally unimpressed by the rebels and the Army. It was just a question of avoiding provocation, and hoping the nearest man with a gun did not steal too many of his paltry possessions.

Like most of the refugees, he looked well fed by the bountiful land across the river. But years of war, particularly the last four in which the rebels had controlled the area, had cut him off from the vestiges of civilization. The absence of manufactured goods, medicines or virtually anything that he could not make himself had pulled him back to the subsistence lifestyle of the previous century. He had held on to one remnant of better days. He still wore a tailored shirt, even though all that was left was the collar, the line of buttons down the front and the cuffs. His shorts were a complicated patchwork.

In the camp at Tengani, to which he was headed, most people were equally poorly dressed. Some wore only the blanket they had been issued from camp stores, and slept in it in the open at night. Most of the new arrivals had not had time to build pole and thatch huts and there were not enough tents for the twenty thousand people who had come here alone. The first evening I was there was cheerful enough, however. A thirty-a-side football game went on with a ball donated by the British High Commission next to a food store where maize flour and a few dried fish were being given to several hundred people who had arrived that day. It was good humoured, except when an old lady in a ragged loincloth proved too weak to carry away her ration, weeping with rage and shame. One of the overseers angrily demanded that someone from her village or district help her.

As the sun set its golden light was tempered by the smoke of hundreds of fires. Children laughed, and many of the parents permitted themselves an occasional smile. As I have written before, heavy rain and the news of five cholera cases transformed the atmosphere overnight. In the morning people stood wrapped in damp blankets, staring into smouldering fires. There were no smiles.

Another Mozambican arrived a week later in very different clothes and to a very different welcome. President Joaquim Chissano flew into Blantyre, Malawi's largest city, in an impeccable pin-striped suit to join the thirtieth anniversary celebrations of Dr Hastings Kamuzu Banda's return to the country to lead it into independence. Placards everywhere proclaimed "Long live Kamuzu" and thousands of dancers, mainly the women who were his greatest supporters, raised the dust in homage to the old autocrat. The President for Life was believed to be in his late eighties, but still occasionally came down in his hallmark frock coat and top hat to take a few steps with the dancers. He may have looked a little frail, but diplomats I spoke to said he was still in firm control of the country, retaining the ministerial posts of Agriculture, Justice, External Affairs and Works and Supplies as well as being the Commander-in-Chief of the Armed Forces.

To discuss the succession, or being perceived as a potential successor, remained unwise, or even dangerous. Politicians seen as too ambitious had been dismissed, detained and assassinated. A leading contender called Dick Matenje and two other ministers died in a car crash in 1983 in suspicious circumstances. In the same year Attati Maakati, the leader of an exiled opposition movement was killed in Harare, and Orton Chirwa, the leader of another, was brought back from Zambia, some say kidnapped, and sentenced to death along with his wife. The sentences were commuted, but Banda has threatened to reinstate them in the face of dissident activity.

Any private discussion of the succession centred on Cecilia Tamanda Kadzamira, the close confidante of the President known as the Official Hostess, and her uncle John Tembo, treasurer of the sole ruling Malawi Congress Party (MCP) and a close business associate of the President. To fall foul of these people was nearly as bad as falling foul of the President. A relative unknown had however recently been appointed Administrative Secretary of the MCP, a post theoretically senior to the Treasurership. Educationalist Maxwell Pashane's apparent lack of ambition may have been his leading qualification. He had only been appointed to the cabinet, as Minister of Education, a year before.

No Secretary-General, the top party post after the President, had been appointed for years, a telling omission since under the constitution the Secretary-General was supposed to chair a Presidential Council in the event of the President's death. Ever since his return to the then British colony of Nyasaland to lead the MCP's precursor in 1958, following, among other things, a spell as a GP in Harlesden, he had appeared less and less willing to contemplate a Malawi without him.

So far Dr Banda had retained a reputation for the sound management of the economy from right-wingers and institutions like the World Bank, for paying the country's debts on time, and a reputation for unreconstructed fascism from left-wingers and other black African countries, for maintaining diplomatic relations with South Africa, Israel and Taiwan. The Soviets and East Germans were unwelcome. He had also accumulated a massive personal fortune, which he used on such things as his palace and Kamuzu Academy, the African Eton in the bush where classics were compulsory and most of the staff were recruited from English public schools.

Those in favour of paternal authority, or totalitarianism if you prefer, also approved of his codes for personal appearance. He banned long hair on men – the unwary were likely to be cropped on arrival – and trousers that were wider at the ankle than the knee – so prohibiting the dreaded flares. Trousers were forbidden on women, who had to wear skirts that came well below the knee. I seemed to run into a party of female South African rock climbers wherever I went. Their long skirts almost touched the ground, and would have made precarious the use of the ropes and pitons on their rucksacks. Presumably they could dispense with the skirts in the privacy of the rock-face.

Much to my surprise I had been allowed into Malawi but probably only because of the celebrations and the government's desire to publicize the influx of refugees in order to receive assistance in looking after them. International agencies were providing over $50m a year for this purpose but more was needed. For many years Dr Banda forbade the entrance of foreign journalists as a matter of principle, and mine was one of the first visits to be officially sanctioned.

A limited experience of dealing with journalists was exposed once I got there. When I arrived at Lilongwe, the new capital, the immigration official did not have my name on a list of expected visitors. He was especially worried because I was a journalist. I was detained for a hour while he called the Department of Information in Blantyre to confirm I was expected. I thought I would have to wait for a minder, but was allowed to spend a few days in Lilongwe by myself, travel down to Blantyre however I chose and get in touch when I got there. I was then assigned a minder, a cheerful and rather eccentric man who neither drank nor smoked but was very fond of the girls, despite his religious beliefs. It would be God's judgement, he thought, if he caught AIDS, so why take any precautions? He did not seem to mind who I talked to and was prepared to let me go off on my own again for several days. I hope he did not get into trouble over what I wrote.

I decided I would rather see more of the country than watch four days of mass dancing, so a friend from Kenya and I hired a car to go to the Zomba Plateau, a table-land over ten miles in diameter surrounded by cliffs up to three thousand feet high. The car broke down almost immediately, the gear box falling to pieces, and we had to leave the car and return to Blantyre. It was probably my fault. Waiters and other people who serve tourists and officials have obsequiousness bred into them in Malawi, the demand for respectful service reinforced by their desire to keep their tiny but precious salaries. I had asked for a car from the man at the hotel counter. He could not say no, though he did hint that there was a shortage of serviceable vehicles.

Blantyre looks on the surface a bit like a British country town. The streets are clean and well kept, the buildings unexciting but well painted. There are banks, building societies and stores well stocked with necessities. Most of the people are black, of course, but they dress in a similar way to people in an English country town. The illusion is shattered by the ragged hawkers who pester you, one offering carrots, another oranges, another cabbages, mats or woodcarvings. The prices are ridiculously low, but they are obviously desperate to sell something, to make a profit that will allow them to eat.

We set off again by taxi, eventually reaching the town of Zomba, once the colonial capital, with a clear sun warming the red tiled roofs of the old administrative buildings. We passed a factory that made fishing flies. Most of the world's flies are now made in places like Malawi, Kenya, Zimbabwe, Guatemala and India, places where dextrous fingers are cheap. Zomba is mostly an agricultural town, a trading centre and way-station on one of the country's main roads where produce can be bought and sold or shipped on. Malawi's seven and a half million people, squeezed into one of Africa's smallest countries, depend on agriculture. Almost all its export earnings of about $250m a year come from tobacco, tea and sugar.

From Zomba we climbed the narrow road winding up a gully that cuts through the ramparts of the plateau. At the top is the Kuchawe Inn, where our room looked out over Africa, thousands of feet below. There was a log fire in the evening, and an excellent dinner washed down by South African wine. The service, as usual, was a little too good. When we went for a walk the next day, however, we saw something that made the country's tourist slogan – "Malawi, the warm heart of Africa" – start to seem slightly sickening.

We climbed a steep, winding path through a pine forest to a lake where I would cast my flies. On the way we met lines of shuffling men with great bundles of logs balanced on their heads, their feet slapping the hard earth between the rocks. One hand balanced the front of the load, which must have been well over a hundred pounds, the other held a stick that went over the shoulder to control the rear. They could only move their eyes to acknowledge our presence as they went by. A slip could result in serious injury. This was how Zomba, four thousand feet down and ten miles away, got its firewood.

Apart from its willingness to pay its debts – Malawi must be one of the few countries ever to refuse an offer by the International Monetary Fund to arrange to reschedule them – Malawi has received praise for feeding its people. This is

presented by Dr Banda's apologists as their trump card. After all,
how many African countries can do so? The claim is, however,
based on a false premise. That a country sometimes exports food
does not mean its people are well fed. In Malawi many are so
poor they cannot afford to buy enough food. Agricultural workers
like the wood carriers of Zomba receive a minimum wage of
25p a day, against 30p for a loaf of bread. In practice it is a
maximum wage, because few local or foreign employers pay
more.

The veneer of development – the good roads, the occasional
light industry, the well-kept hotels, the well-dressed urban middle
class, the well-stocked markets, the new capital at Lilongwe – is
all based on the hidden poverty of most of the population. Most
of them are smallholders who are forced to seek work on
plantations or in factories to supplement the income from their
tiny, overworked plots. Appropriately enough, these are called
gardens. True, cheap labour is one of overpopulated Malawi's
only resources. But can such a system be justified if the labour
force is half-starved?

A friend working for the BBC in Nairobi had suggested I talk
to a man with UNICEF in Malawi. I went to his smart office in
Lilongwe, expecting the usual noncommittal mediocrity of most
UN representatives. He proved to be feisty and unusually frank.
I had to ask three times to check if I had heard him right when
I asked him about child mortality in the country. I had heard
him right. It was, he said, 320 per thousand in the first five years
of life. This compared to the mortality in Ethiopia during the
great famine, yet here it was the underlying, normal rate.

A number of donors and concerned Malawians were debating
how to translate the country's relative macroeconomic success
into food for its children, as most of the mortality is the direct
result of malnutrition. There was little hope of achieving
anything other than temporary alleviation with aid. You could
not tamper with the system as long as the old man was still
there. And the fear was that the long years of autocracy would
lead to chaos on his death, as everyone scrambled for power and
influence.

Though Dr Banda's state feudalism increased the wealth of a

country with relatively few natural resources, as opposed to reducing the wealth of a country with huge natural resources, it was much the same for the peasants as the state feudalism of Dr Nyerere, his ideological opponent in Tanzania. The common element is autocracy, justified by the spurious democracy of the one party state, and the consequent parasitic élite. If ideology or natural endowment is not the cause, perhaps this autocracy explains such countries' woes.

Both could point to external problems, particularly Malawi. Because its logical trade routes to the Mozambican ports of Nacala and Beira were closed, it had to use the much longer routes south through Zambia, Zimbabwe and South Africa, or north through Tanzania. The inefficiency of these routes absorbed over 30 per cent of the value of its exports, and accounted for nearly 40 per cent of the cost of its imports.

I visited the border post at Marka, at the southern tip of Malawi near the Shire River. It used to be a bustling trading centre on the road and rail routes to Beira. It was now a ghost town, nearly as devastated by the loss of business as the Mozambican post across the border had been by war. Roofs sagged, wood rotted and brick walls crumbled. There was hardly anybody around. Even the chickens seemed depressed. The barrier was rusting and irrelevant. There was no fence on either side and no customs or immigration officials to be seen. The dirt road disappeared, unmarked by tracks, into the Mozambican bush. I took a few steps into Mozambique, and then retreated, mindful of RENAMO's occasional kidnapping of Europeans.

Tanzania, like Malawi, can also point to the fall in price of its agricultural exports, and the increase in price of essential imports like oil. Governments have to deal with the world that confronts them, however, not imagine some paradise where everything is in their favour and then go to the aid agencies when reality intrudes on their dreams. Accountable governments, rather than autocrats surrounded by sycophants, might be more likely to follow the former course.

Malawi could be the "warm heart of Africa" especially for fishermen. There are trout in the Zomba plateau and other highland areas, the Shire has tigerfish and Lake Malawi, where you can see the bottom in twenty feet of water, has species of game fish found nowhere else in the world. But I could not go back with a rod to enjoy the streams, lakes and rivers, while I knew that away from the lodges or campsites, away from the excellent roads were hamlets where children paid with their lives for the country's good credit rating. Tourism is no less obscene than palaces, new capitals and grandiose schools when this is happening.

It is strange that many of Africa's smallest countries have its most unpleasant or eccentric governments. One might have expected some form of consensus, even democracy, to be reached more easily in a small country. In practice it appears to make it easier for a despot to take over and channel the country's resources to his own purposes. There are several examples other than Malawi. In Liberia in 1990 there was a salutary lesson in what is liable to happen at the end of such a despot's rule. By September over three hundred thousand of its two and half million population were reported to have sought refuge abroad. President Doe was dead but a seven month long civil war and tribal bloodbath continued. As with previous attempts to unseat him during his ten years of capricious leadership the possible successors were expected to do little more than replace his hand in the till and the executioner's glove.

No Bananas

Liberia

"That man you see up there is a rock, and you Allison, the way I look at you, you are a chicken egg. If you fall on the man, you will burst, and when he falls on you, you will still burst." An unusual sales pitch, but then these were unusual circumstances. This apparently was what the heartman, Mr Sekou Sachko, said to General Gray Allison, the Minister of Defence and second most powerful man in Liberia, when he asked for assistance in gaining the extra strength necessary to topple the man up there, President Samuel Doe. The heartman could assist in such matters through his expertise in the theory and practice of ritual murder, or human sacrifice.

The words of the heartman were reported at the murder trial of General Allison in August 1989. It was of course really a treason trial, because the General's recourse to a heartman amounted to planning a coup. Most of the witnesses were his accomplices, and described the end of Patrolman Melvin Pyne in very similar terms. One of them got the thirty-two-year-old policeman drunk and lured him to a government clinic nearby. There several people pinned the man down to a table under the General's supervision, and a male nurse cut his throat. The blood was collected in a plastic container, which the General took back in his Pajero, a luxury four-wheel-drive vehicle, to Monrovia, the capital, for the heartman to perform his rituals.

The patrolman's body was found headless on a railway track, after an apparent attempt to suggest he had been run over by a train. Usually the victims of ritual murder are all too clearly recognizable. Small boys are usually preferred, and the hearts and other organs are excised. Somebody appears to have given the tale of Melvin Pyne away, and at the end of the trial General Allison was sentenced to death by firing squad. The Army press office delayed issuing the verdict until a laborious statement had been typed up, apparently believing this supported their claim of due legal process. Eyewitnesses said the General was kicked and slapped out of the court as soon as the verdict was announced. It was uncertain if the sentence had been carried out.

Samuel Doe, who now preferred the title of Doctor, had resisted several other plots to overthrow him since he took over in 1980 as Master Sergeant Doe, an NCO whose age was uncertain and whose literacy was in doubt. He and sixteen other soldiers had gone to the Executive Mansion, with some rather unspecified goal in mind. To their surprise the Presidential guard was absent. They barged in, killed President William Tolbert and assumed power themselves. Others, it seemed, believed the route to power could be as easy. Many of them met a similar fate to thirteen of Tolbert's ministers and other officials, who were shot on a beach outside Monrovia after perfunctory trials, to international outrage.

At first Doe was popular with the indigenous people, as a fellow "country man". Such people accounted for a large majority of the population of two and a half million, but Liberia had been dominated since its birth by the Americo-Liberians, descendants of the ex-slaves from America who founded what was essentially a black colony in 1847. One justified the absence of his wife from several social functions by explaining to me that she was a "country woman". By the time Doe attempted to legitimize his position through elections in 1985, however, they had to be so obviously rigged that the result was greeted with embarrassment rather than outrage.

Doe ruled Liberia with a many-ringed hand. The accumulation of wealth appeared to be the only policy of his administration. Many Liberians took little notice of the Allison trial. To them it was just a squabble between soldiers about who would enjoy the spoils of power. As one said to me, "If they blow his brains out, or he had blown Doe's out doesn't make much difference to us."

One day President Doe went out to get the people's views, in jewellery, casual clothes, beret and open sports car more suited to a stylized Harlem drug peddler than a head of state, except for the armoured cars in front and behind. Indeed it was generally believed that the gleaming banks opening in downtown Monrovia owed much to the proceeds of drug trafficking in the States. They rose in marble and bronzed glass in sharp contrast to the mould streaked walls and rusting corrugated iron of most of the city, with street signs, traffic lights and police uniforms disconcertingly identical to main street America.

The President spotted a woman passing, who happened to be working for some people I met in Monrovia, and jumped out to ask her what she thought of Liberia. She was so terrified she was nearly speechless, repeating that everything was fine "for true" and trying to extricate her hand from the President's grasp. He, on the other hand, was apparently nervous of the impression that might be given by a loyal citizen running away from the President. By the time he let go his rings had made indentations on her fingers.

As a businessman said to me, "The problem with Liberia is not so much bad management, it's the absence of management." When a Liberian ambassador tells you that his is "one of the most backward countries in Africa" you know something is wrong. "Nobody wants to work in Liberia," he went on. "They all want to sit on their bums with a white-collar job."

A cab driver gave the expected pithy judgement, delivered in Liberia's mid-Atlantic English – midway, that is, between the United States and Africa. "First it's one thing, then it's another. First it's no rice. Now it's no gas. This place is sick."

Finally an embittered journalist and teacher at the university, who had been detained several times for his articles and political activities, almost repeated the businessman's comment. "When it comes to management," he said – and then the lights went out. "Well, you see what I mean."

The banks, the shipping authority that issues flags of convenience to vessels from all over the world, and many of the other businesses in the country operate in the absence of regulation. Competition is corrupt and capricious. If an enterprise reaches any size it will require the protection of a minister or the President, and may suffer sudden shifts in approval.

Probably the most profitable business in the country, the export of timber from the country's massive but rapidly dwindling rain forests, was under the control of the President's office, through the misleadingly named Forestry Development Authority. Flying into the country you could see the great bites taken out of the dark green bank of the forest, the great trees lying like twigs on the cleared ground.

I had lunch one day with Michael Gore, the British Ambassador. He told me that he had recently and urgently commissioned a video extolling the beauties and importance of the Sapo National Park, and sent it to the President. This, he believed, had narrowly averted the granting of a concession to log in the park to an Italian company. Michael was an expert ornithologist, who said he had just recorded a new species for Liberia – the house sparrow. A couple of times he jumped up from the table to a telescope on the balcony, to check the identity of a bird in the garden or above the sea beyond. His boat was out of the water, so we could not go fishing.

Up to half the timber leaving the country was undocumented by either customs or the Finance Ministry. The country's total exports, including timber, were officially about $400m. The real total was believed to be about $600m. The impossibility of tracing the movement of such funds led a US team sent out to help establish control of the country's budget, as a condition for further aid, to give up and go home. They could not find out where 40 per cent of government revenue was going.

The lack of control was eloquently illustrated by one's ability to get the black market rate, double the official one under which the Doe dollar was pegged to the US dollar, using a credit card at the reception desk of the Hotel Africa, Monrovia's finest. The same applied at the cheaper, more central and fraudulently named Hilton, run by Lebanese businessmen attracted, along with various international syndicates, by the absence of the rule of law.

The Hotel Africa, an ugly slab overlooking a fast-eroding beach outside Monrovia, was built for an Organization of African Unity summit ten years before I stayed there. But signs at the airport, another anachronism placed an hour away from the city in the interests of the US Air Force during the war, still advertised a fixed $25 cab fare to what was then called the OAU village.

History seems to stand still in Liberia. President Tolbert was killed a year after the summit, to some extent the victim of his extravagance in hosting it. It cost an estimated $100m. Yet on the long road from the airport my cab driver, who had explained that the fixed rate was a little out of date and that he must now charge $45, pointed out the house of one of Tolbert's relatives, burnt out during the coup and still unrepaired. Shortly afterwards we passed a crashed car, still wrapped around a lamppost, a tree growing through the roof. Presumably nobody had repaired the house for fear of appearing disloyal to Doe. A colleague met a woman who had been offered the finger of a conspirator in one of the plots against Doe. She was worried that her failure to accept and consume it would have been reported back as evidence of disloyalty.

The purportedly Christian Americo-Liberians were not immune from superstition. If most of the experts in witchcraft came from the "country people", the Americo-Liberians had made the Masonic Lodge the glue of their society and the bastion of their economic and political dominance. The Temple was the most imposing building in Monrovia, a battered neo-classical oblong on top of a hill. After Doe's coup it had been ransacked and damaged, as a symbol of Americo-Liberian hegemony. The windows had been boarded up, but plans were afoot to restore it. It was common knowledge that President Doe had joined the Masons a few months before, an action symbolizing the rapprochement between him and the Americo–Liberian élite.

His first years had proved to be a brief aberration from Liberia's normal regard for tradition. Though most people I talked to chuckled at the cults and rites when they were exposed to public view, in private many hedged their bets. Judging by the success of its members the Masonic rite was the most powerful. It was the obvious one to join if you could. But that would not stop you going to a heartman if you were desperate, or at least being wary of their powers.

There was official sanction of occult practices. A "witch" died and forty-nine others were badly beaten in the Gbao clan area of Nimba County, according to the local papers while I was in Monrovia. They said an occultist from the Ministry of Internal Affairs had been asked by local chiefs to identify those responsible for the deaths of several young people by performing a trial by ordeal. These were accepted as an aspect of tribal law. The one that died, it seemed, must have been guilty.

Such a regard for witchcraft and its practitioners is common in Africa, amongst politicians as well as villagers, though it rarely has such official recognition. Educated people in Dar es Salaam would mention the general belief that Nyerere was protected by his mother's powers, and that he would be immune to opposition until she died, or that his carved swagger stick was a magical device. While I was in Tanzania there was a more concrete demonstration of the politician's nervousness of the witch doctors, following the death of one hundred and fifty children around the southern town of Lindi.

The children had all had their uvulas cut out, as the local witch doctors had decided this would prevent fevers. Dirty knives had been used and lethal infections set in. The first medical team to investigate concluded that the witch doctors were responsible for the children's deaths, and it was expected they would be charged with manslaughter. After several days of inaction another medical team was sent down. This concluded that the children's deaths could not definitely be ascribed to the uvulectomies, as malaria and other diseases were endemic in the area and the children were poorly nourished. The implication was that the children would not have died of "complications after surgery" if they had been healthy to start with. Obviously somebody wanted a medically plausible excuse for not charging witch doctors. And equally obviously nobody in the government was going to complain.

The world of the witch doctor or medicine man in Africa includes a multitude of sins and virtues. The range runs from unrelieved superstition and manipulation, via confidence trickery to effective herbalism. The Madagascan periwinkle, now the source of a proven medicine for several cancers, was discovered by Madagascan herbalists. A friend in Zimbabwe cured a case of ringworm with a preparation given to him by a local herbalist. Such remedies are now being investigated by medical research institutes in several African countries, but the rivalry between traditional and Western medicine does not encourage herbalists to come forward with their favourite recipes.

In contrast there was the the case of the witch doctor on the Zambezi in Zimbabwe. He sold little pouches of dried herbs which were supposed to keep crocodiles away for the fishermen to tie around their waists or necks. For a few months they would all buy them, but then they tired of the expense. A few months more and one of them would be taken by a crocodile, whereupon the witch doctor would say "You see what happens," and the rest would all start buying again. A few months later they would tire of the expense, and so the cycle continued. If somebody was taken while he was carrying the medicine, he had obviously either done something bad or another witchdoctor had put a spell on him.

This was a relatively harmless confidence trick, but some of the effects of the witch doctors' prescriptions are horrifying. As we were driving through the bush in Zimbabwe one day we were flagged down by a man at the side of the road. His son was sick, he said. He led us up a small hill nearby, at the top of which stood his family's group of conical huts. The boy had oozing sores that exposed his spine. His limbs were twisted and nearly useless, so that he could only move with a long pole as a crutch. He was terribly emaciated. Arthur guessed that advanced tuberculosis was eating into his bones. All this was gruesome enough, without the deeply infected rows of cuts on each side of his chest and on his cheeks. These had been made by the witch doctor, who had rubbed herbs into the wounds.

Arthur sent the boy, who his father said had been perfectly healthy a few months before, to the nearest hospital, forty-five miles away. Such people often went to the witch doctor rather than walk such distances, and then the patient had to be carried to a hospital when it was too late. Arthur was fairly sure the boy would die within a few days, if not hours. It might have been better to leave him to die at home. The witch doctor would surely claim that he had died because he went to the hospital.

Arthur did not try to stop people going to the witch doctor. He condoned the surreptitious use of herbal remedies in conjunction with the prescriptions handed out at clinics and hospitals, as long as they were taken by mouth and not dangerously powerful. In one case we saw a fertility preparation was so corrosive that urine was leaking directly from the bladder into the vagina. The main battle was to get people to seek treatment at the clinics soon enough to deal with potentially serious but easily treatable complaints, such as infections for which the witch doctors' herbs were usually useless.

We heard that one mission doctor had become so exasperated by people bringing in patients too late for him to do anything that he refused to treat them. This may have been a breach of the Hippocratic oath, and Arthur balked at such extremes, but it is quite possible that this approach saved more lives than treating probably hopeless cases. The more irresponsible witch doctors could no longer claim the white doctor killed many of the people who came to him. And people certainly came more promptly to the hospital where he worked than to most.

I wrote this chapter at a house on the creek at Kilifi, on Kenya's Indian Ocean coast. A few minutes up the creek by boat are two active witchcraft shrines. The caves, into which you must wade at high tide, are screened by mangrove trees, the roots covered with razor edged oysters. The mouths of the caves are festooned with strips of red and white cloth, as are the altars in a dry cave a few miles south of here, hidden in a patch of forest at Vipingo. The strips each record a visit to the shrine, when sacrifice was made to the resident spirits in pursuit of some goal, benign or malign.

The polished rock of the altars at Vipingo points to centuries of use. Little piles of ashes, coconut husks and empty bottles point to continued activity. The friend who showed me the caves strongly urged that I touch nothing. His nervousness transmitted itself to me. In the past human sacrifice, usually of twins or albino children, was not uncommon. The removal of the heart reflected the practice in West Africa. Indeed adepts from the two sides of the continent are still believed to travel, by jet, to consult each other.

The witchcraft has co-existed uneasily with Islam on the East African coast from the time of the first incursions of Arab slavers and traders, which may have been before the tenth century. It remains strong, though Islam probably has more serious adherents. The boathouse in front of my writing window at Kilifi was believed to be haunted. The *m'ganga* (the Swahili word for "witch doctor") apparently failed to exorcize the place, so the Imam was called in, with apparent success.

More often, however, it is a case of rendering unto Caesar what is Caesar's due. A friend in Dar es Salaam arrived at his small factory to find the workers sitting outside. On the gate were fetishes and splashes of blood, probably from a chicken or goat supplied for sacrifice by a rival. The workers refused to enter until he had found, and paid, another m'ganga to perform a cleansing rite.

Spells and fetishes hung in the garden by a m'ganga were better than watchmen for keeping out thieves, so general was the belief in their power. You had to be very careful, however. According to Shabir, a friendly engineer who meticulously observed the fasting of Ramadan, even to the extent of giving up beer, the spells were very literal. A typical one would say that anyone stealing from this ground would die a lingering death. If a guest unthinkingly picked up a box of matches and left with it in his pocket, it would still apply.

Jimmy, a Greek businessman in Dar es Salaam, had a beautiful motor yacht, on which we regularly went fishing. It was full of valuable equipment, radar, echo sounder, radio, not to mention the expensive rods and reels necessary for the big fish, yet the robbers never touched it. At night an elderly man with a clubfoot slept on board, a m'ganga well known in the area. We treated him with respect, and only smiled about the mysteries of his craft in private. Yet when we were fishing we were not strictly rational ourselves.

The improbability of your course crossing that of a hungry marlin in hundreds of square miles of open ocean lends itself to superstition, like pouring a splash of each bottle of beer over the side for the sea gods. Deep sea fishermen worldwide have another belief. If you carry bananas on board you will not catch anything. The taboo has survived the efforts of a team in a marlin fishing competition in Hawaii, who took a steadily more rotten bunch on board every day, and won.

The banana taboo is particularly strong in East Africa. One day several of us were out on Jimmy's boat. To our disappointment a spot usually guaranteed to produce fish appeared empty. The birds were there, wheeling over the baitfish, but there was no strike for nearly two hours. "Right, who's got the bananas," Jimmy asked in jest. A newcomer thought this was a simple request, and produced a fruit salad which contained the forbidden fruit. He looked a bit surprised when it was tipped over the side. He still looked a bit surprised when the laughter subsided and it was explained to him.

Five minutes later the first fish struck, and for the rest of the day the action was continuous. Even with the benefit of a Western education, which included the study of the philosophy of science, I have to be strict with myself to say this was pure coincidence. To people still living in the midst of unpredictable nature, such events may give taboos and the spirits invoked by the witch doctors an irresistible force. The system may not have the predictive ability of Western science, but at least it provides some sort of explanation for what is going on.

It will of course tend to have a lot to do with politics when there is no electoral reason for one leader's success and he manages to resist several attempts by those jealous of him to take the same violent route to power, like President Doe. He gave himself a spurious electoral legitimacy through a rigged poll, but people plotted rather than campaigned against him, and General Allison was probably not the only one to seek supernatural assistance. In the end, as in the following chapter about Burundi, the dictatorship which enabled him to pack the government and army with members of his own tribe and its allies led to an explosion of intertribal violence.

The insurgency against Doe's rule began in early 1990 with the relatively harmless incursion of a few rebels from the Ivory Coast into the eastern part of the country. When the army was sent to deal with them, however, its Krahn and Mandingo soldiers started raiding villages, indiscriminately killing the Manos and Gios in the area. They, of course, began to join the rebels in large numbers, and by July 1990 they had penetrated the centre of Monrovia, killing as many Krahns and Mandingos as they could on the way. Thousands were believed to have died.

The rebel movement split when it got to Monrovia, delaying

Doe's downfall and extending the chaos and killing. Charles Taylor, the leader of the main faction, was not everybody's choice of a successor. Once an official in Doe's government, he had fled the country to escape arrest for embezzlement. Another rebel leader, Prince Yormie Johnson, suggested Liberia did not want a criminal as President and appealed for American intervention. There were two thousand Marines standing offshore and just as much reason to intervene as in Grenada or Panama. Almost everybody would have preferred a policing action by the Marines followed by an imposed election to continued bloodshed and anarchy.

Here was a great opportunity for a Western government to take the responsibility for ending a situation that it had helped bring about by giving aid to a dictatorship. To allow the killing to go on under the guise of respect for sovereignty would be in line with previous Western policy towards Africa, the sort of policy that had allowed the civil wars, famines and massacres of the previous three decades to continue unabated. America did not act. After the Marines had watched the killing in Monrovia for several weeks a joint force from other West African states, most, including some of its neighbours, with far less to do with Liberia than America, moved in to try to restore order. There was little sign of early success. Doe was killed near the headquarters of the peacekeeping force, and it was reported that Prince Johnson's group had kidnapped sixty of its members to encourage more decisive action on its part.

Too Many Bodies
in the River

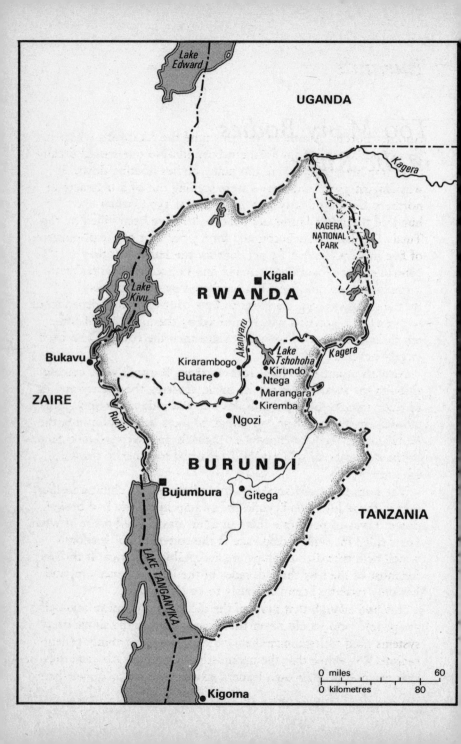

Burundi

Another border. Another river, this time the Akanyaru where it separates Rwanda from northern Burundi. No one would dream of fishing here. There were too many bodies floating down. It was August 1988 and stories were seeping out of a massacre in northern Burundi nearly as bad as that of 1972, when one hundred thousand Hutus are believed to have been killed by the Tutsi. The Tutsi only accounted for 15 per cent of the population of five million, against 85 per cent for the Hutu, but they controlled the Government, Army and Police. In Rwanda, with a similar ethnic mix, elections organized by the departing Belgians had enabled the Hutu to take control since independence in 1962. This position was reinforced by the massacre of some ten thousand Tutsi in 1963, but since then the country had been largely peaceful.

Now thousands of Hutu from northern Burundi were coming through the swamps on the far bank, crossing the twenty metres of river and climbing the hillsides into Rwanda and safety. Not all of them made it. The Burundian soldiers were ambushing the Hutus as they fled, catching them right up to the river bank. Some of the bodies floating down had been tied together to drown together.

The tales the many survivors told gave you the chilling feeling that in those low hills beyond the swamp humanity had broken down. I was to penetrate there in a few days. The horror of what I saw filled me with a cold rage at the conventional wisdom which held that dictatorships are acceptable in Africa. It thrived for most of the first three decades of the independence era, and has only recently begun seriously to be challenged.

It is bad enough that most of the dictators' European apologists are people who would never themselves tolerate the single party systems used to legitimize them, so exposing their thinly veiled racism. It is worse that the justification for telling Africans they cannot vote for their own leaders, except in the occasional sham of the single party election, is that a multi-party system allowing a choice would exacerbate tribal rivalries.

The massacres in Burundi provided an extreme example of what the one party system in fact allows, the tyranny of one group over another and the suppression of tribal rivalries until they explode in mindless violence. At the time of the August massacre Burundi was in effect a no-party state, as Major Pierre Buyoya had suspended the Union pour le Progres National (UPRONA), in the palace coup that brought him to power eleven months before, but for most of the previous two decades UPRONA had provided a façade of respectability to Tutsi governments, and denied the Hutu any political voice.

There will, of course, be intertribal violence in multi-party elections in Africa. But do we advocate a one party dictatorship in India because of the ethnic violence there? One has to believe that the Africans, like the Eastern Europeans and South Americans, can learn to operate a genuine democracy, even if it takes time. If not we face the endless repetition of events like those of August 1988, and indeed their increasing frequency as Africa's high birth rates make more and more countries as densely populated as little Burundi.

For too long the West has timidly bowed to the African dictators' argument that the multi-party system derives from Western culture and history, and would be an unwanted imposition in Africa. It has got nothing to do with culture or history. The multi-party system is obviously, both in theory and practice, that most likely to allow individual freedom and prosperity, in Africa as elsewhere. It has also proved itself that least likely to promote the welfare of despots.

To accept the one party state is the counsel of absolute pessimism. Yet that is exactly what nearly every Western government and aid agency does, despite occasional recent statements that more democratic countries will be favoured. They only withhold the money on which the dictatorships depend when their behaviour becomes obviously rather than surreptitiously inhumane, as it did in Burundi.

I had just returned to Nairobi from covering the floods in Khartoum, feeling pretty disillusioned with my profession, when we started to hear about the situation in Burundi and Rwanda. Rwanda gave me a visa first, so I flew down to see the refugees, hoping to get into Burundi by land or air from there.

In Kigali, the Rwandan capital, some other journalists and I hired a car to drive down to the border. We stayed the night at the Ibis Hotel in the small town of Butare, since there was little we could see at the border in the dark except the fires of burning huts in the distance. The Belgian proprietor handled our requests for phone lines to Europe and America, calmly accepting the sudden attention and profit.

The next morning our departure for the border was slightly delayed by the start of a bicycle race, for which the main street in front of the hotel was temporarily closed to other traffic. Then the Préfet, M. Frederique Karangwa, gave the journalists a brief address in French, saying that his government would do everything to help the refugees, but would need outside assistance. He hoped circumstances would soon allow their return. His criticism of the Burundian government was restrained, presumably in the hope that this return could be arranged as soon as possible. Rwanda is as heavily populated as Burundi, and no Préfet would want an extra forty thousand people in his district.

Then we drove on narrow dirt tracks through well-tended fields, heading through the hills towards the Akanyaru. People had already started to call the sites where the refugees were gathering camps, but there were no tents. Shelter could only be found for the wounded, sick and the very old and very young in the occasional school or clinic. The rest slept in the open under the rain at night and stood about wrapped in blankets during the day.

Nearly all reported the killing of family members. One old man said all his sons, their wives and children had been slaughtered, thirty-five people in all. To start with, the refugees said, the army was shooting every one they saw. Later on, they said, the soldiers started using bayonets, so that the sound of gunfire would not frighten people in neighbouring valleys.

There were many babies in the clinics who had been stabbed or slashed, and then left alive after their parents were killed. "It's as if they're deliberately left alive to terrify the rest," said a missionary who had volunteered to help in one of the clinics. At the village of Kirarambogo we saw a five-year-old boy, Immaculata Nsengimani, whose side was peppered with infected wounds. He had only survived because he was buried under a pile of bodies when the army herded fifteen people from his home village of Jihome into a house, and then started shooting and throwing grenades into it. His mother and father were killed along with five hundred others in Jihome alone, according to his uncle, Reverian Ndururutse. Mr Ndururutse went back to collect him when he heard the boy was in hiding with his grandmother.

Some of the refugees admitted the killing had begun with an attack by the Hutu on the Tutsi in the northern province of Kirundo. Soon after that, however, the Army arrived and it was automatic weapons and helicopters against spears and machetes. The government was talking about "sporadic resistance on the part of the rebels" and claiming that the trouble had been stirred up by infiltrators, presumably from Rwanda. How could peasant farmers resist a well-equipped army?

One villager reported his fellows being slaughtered when the Army opened up after they were called to a meeting. Those that escaped the initial firing were hunted down by helicopters. Though the government was saying that the Army only "reacted" if people did not submit, it looked as if the fear in every Tutsi of a Hutu uprising had unleashed a brutal campaign of elimination by the Army. The refugees treated the government's request that they return, because peace had been restored, with scorn.

But nobody outside knew at this time what was really happening in Kirundo or what had caused the violence in the first place. The Burundians had sealed the area off. An official at the Burundian embassy in Kigali was very helpful over our visa requests, when we finally got to see him, until we said we would like to drive directly over the border into Kirundo. He doubted it would be possible. "Even a Burundian needs a permit to go from commune to commune," he said. When pressed for reasons he cited our personal security, in apparent contradiction of the government claim that the area was peaceful. "We wouldn't want you to get a spear in your leg," he said.

I took advantage of his offer of a visa to fly to Bujumbura, the capital, where several of our colleagues had been stuck for several days, waiting for permission to travel north to Kirundo. Somewhat to their annoyance it was granted the morning after I arrived. We hired a minibus, amazed that no minder was being sent with us. The Ministry of Information had simply given us a piece of paper saying we were journalists and had permission to travel to Kirundo and the communes of Ntega and Marangara, where the worst of the violence had taken place.

When we set out I was glad to have the front seat from which to admire the mountainous scenery. Then the frequent roadblocks, where I had to wave the piece of paper out of the window and answer questions, became irritating. Later on, when pick-ups roared past, screeched to a halt and disgorged excited soldiers to point their guns at us, the others were still less keen to swap places with me, to take over the role of gingerly handing out that piece of paper. One of our party, Ray Bonner of the *New Yorker*, was particularly surprised at its effectiveness after some unpleasant experiences in Central America. Several times, when some particularly wild-looking soldiers stopped us, he exclaimed "God, we've had it now." But they continued to let us pass.

We were expected to proceed straight to the town of Kirundo, where an escort had been arranged. However Massimo Nava of the *Corrière del Serra* had discovered that a short detour would take us to a hospital at Kiremba, just south of Marangara. It had been founded by Italians and still had a couple of European doctors. We might see or hear something revealing there. We did.

It was very quiet when we walked into the courtyard. People with open, infected wounds sat or lay around, waiting for attention. More were still arriving, several carried on pallets by their relatives. Dr Ralph Dupre came forward, his green surgical apron covered in blood, after a young woman who had just had her leg amputated was wheeled out of the operating room. "Why have you taken so long?" he asked. "Why didn't you get here before?" His face was exhausted and angry. It was almost as if he was in shock.

The killing had started nearly ten days before and had only

just stopped, he thought. The wounded, many of whom had been hiding in swamps, had only recently started coming to the hospital in numbers. "Before," he explained "they were afraid they would be killed on the way." As a result many of the wounds were so badly infected that he had done more than twenty amputations in less than a week. He showed us the bullet-shattered foot of another young woman. A gesture of his hand indicated it would have to come off.

Almost all the patients were Hutu, though there was one eight-year-old Tutsi boy whose face had been slashed with a machete. His mother said his father had been killed in the initial attack on the Tutsi in the area. Fifty of the eighty patients at the hospital were Hutu women and children with up to twenty bayonet wounds each. "They are very strong," said Dr Dupre. "It takes a lot of things to kill them."

They were lucky to have Dr Dupre. He had left Germany to get away from the terrible autobahn crash injuries with which he used to deal, to concentrate on preventive medicine in Africa. Now his surgical skills were proving invaluable, even as he shook his head about his unrealized intentions. He left us to walk around the wards and went back to the new cases.

Several of us had to go outside to be sick or at least get some fresh air. We then plunged back in, pale faced, to force ourselves to ask more questions or even take photographs. I did not carry a camera, partly because I did not want to be forced to take such photographs, but also because I believe you cannot watch and write about things well at the same time as taking good photographs. The impression of those wounds on my mind is still as strong as a photograph would be.

One man sitting in the courtyard had a six-inch long, inch-wide gash in the back of his neck which exposed the spine. Another had his mouth shot away, exposing his teeth like those of a skull. One woman had a pus-filled, infected hole in her breast, left by a bullet that entered her back. There was a seventeen-month-old baby with a bullet wound through her jaw. Her mother had also been shot in the face, the father killed.

A two-and-a-half-year-old boy sat up in bed, his right arm being held by his father. His left had been amputated at the shoulder, after being shattered by a bullet. His mother, brother and sister had been killed. In another bed were two eight-year-old girls. One had been bayoneted while lying on the ground, the other had machete wounds to the hands and neck. "It was the soldiers," she said.

Eventually we drove on to Kirundo, where we arrived in the early evening to find a group of anxious policemen and soldiers who had been waiting for us all afternoon. Like the soldiers and peasants we had seen on the road, they radiated a barely suppressed hysteria. They told us to return to Ngozi, a town two hours back down the road, and return the following morning. We said we would, but had no intention of doing so. We could not have made it before the curfew at sunset. The little hotel was full, but we had heard of a Catholic mission a few miles to the north, where there was supposed to be a resthouse for visitors who wanted to pray, fish or simply contemplate the lake in front.

When we arrived, just as it was getting dark, we decided we would sleep on the wide terrace overlooking the lake or in the car if the mosquitoes were too bad. The doors of the resthouse were locked and there was nobody about. It would be crazy to drive at night. But eventually a nun appeared, opened the doors and hoped we did not mind that two of us would have to share a room. The generator would be turned on shortly for the lights and there would be hot water in the bathrooms in half an hour. The beds would be made up. When she came back again and asked if anybody wanted a beer a colleague facetiously asked what brands she had. She replied with the names of three. All cold of course.

When she came back with the beers she told us that with the recent problems getting food was a bit difficult but asked if we would like some pasta. We said anything would do but that she should not plunder the mission supplies for us. Who knew when things would return to normal? An hour later we were summoned to the dining table. There was pasta, it was true, but after a delicious carrot soup and before kebabs, salad and potatoes. There was no wine, so we had to make do with more beer.

In the morning, when my hope for croissants as the crowning achievement of this extraordinary hospitality was dashed, we were told that visitors normally left a small sum to cover the costs of maintaining the resthouse. We left large donations. I hope I can go back in more peaceful times to fish that beautiful lake. We had to hurry on, for we had decided to go straight into Ntega commune by ourselves. The officials in Kirundo would not expect to see us until around midday. By then we should have seen all we wanted.

The government's claim that peace had returned to the area had a certain grisly truth. For thousands it was the peace of the grave. As we drove the first ten miles into the commune there was not a person to be seen. We passed hundreds of empty huts, some burnt, most with the door swinging open to reveal a few scattered belongings, clothes, cooking pots, the odd shoe. All that could be seen in the normally intensely cultivated gardens and fields were a few goats.

Our driver broke the silence. "But where are the people?" There had been one hundred and fifty thousand in Ntega and Marangara, a few miles to the south. Of the seventy thousand in Ntega three thousand five hundred had been gathered by the army into the main town, also called Ntega. A similar number was believed to be left in Marangara. Around fifty thousand had fled to Rwanda, thousands more into other parts of Burundi. The government said five thousand had been killed, but appeared only to count the Tutsi killed in the initial attack on them by the Hutu. They never did increase the count, as if only the Tutsi mattered to them. The sheer absence of people, the damage and bloodstains around many of the huts supported Dr Dupre's reckoning. "If the government says five thousand, I'd estimate twenty thousand," was his conclusion.

The Catholic mission at Ntega town was a sharp contrast to the one by the lake. The African nun we met there could offer no hospitality. At first Sister Liberatrice seemed too nervous or shocked to talk to us. Then she agreed to tell us what she had seen and heard, but once only, and then we should leave. On the night of 14 August she woke up and heard screams all around. "We had no idea what was happening." The next day some Tutsis came to hide at the mission. She heard more screams and saw burning houses and people throwing stones in the town below all that day and the following night. At 4 a.m. on the morning of 16 August a mob of Hutus arrived at her house. She showed us the windows they had broken.

"Listen. We're ready. Give us the people you have hidden," they shouted. They came back several times, threatening to burn the house and kill the sisters unless they told them where they had hidden them. The sisters said they had hidden nobody, but thought that someone from the mission was forced to give them away. At about 11 a.m. a crowd of about one thousand people with spears, stones and machetes surrounded the building opposite hers, at the side of the church.

There were piles of stones round the windows and doors, which had been battered down. The people inside had bolted out of the back door. The sister led us across the sunny little grassy area where five men had been killed as they ran to a tiny outhouse at the back of the church. Another nine people were killed there. I stared at the smashed door and gaping hole where the window had been. Inside, the blood-splashed floor was covered with more stones thrown by the crowd. Splatters of dried brown blood reached up the walls. Some blood-soaked dresses and a shovel whose blade was caked with blood completed the memorial. The sister said she had rescued three wounded children from among the bodies. "A normal person would not do things like that. I'm sure they were drugged."

The army arrived a couple of hours later, their progress slowed by trees felled across the road. The sister had heard a lot of shooting, but could not be sure what had happened. She had stayed in the mission. The area was sealed off until ten days later and there were still armoured cars and trucks full of soldiers with automatic weapons and fixed bayonets all around the town. The first people we saw in Ntega, packing up on the steps of the mission, were a squad of soldiers led by Lieutenant Anatole Bavugiruhoze. When asked where all the people were his first response was a chuckle. He later said it was "very difficult for us, we had to restore order". He agreed that there were "many, many people dead".

From the mission we drove into the town, spread along each side of a main street. People stood sullenly around, watched by the soldiers. The windows and doors of the smarter houses were battered by stones, attesting to the initial attack on the Tutsi. Most of the poorer huts had patches of blood, sprinkled with disinfectant outside their doors. We all suddenly decided it was time to go.

A few miles back we ran into an angry Major Dr Jean-Bosco Daradangwe, along with a couple of journalists who had been waiting with him for us to arrive in Kirundo. After controlling himself he insisted on explaining the official position. He showed us some bulldozer marks beside the road where he said five hundred Tutsi had been buried. He said they were collected in groups and then killed by machete blows to the back of the neck. He told us many of the Hutu did not want to take part, but those that refused had an ear cut off as a warning and if they still refused were killed. The grave may have contained the Tutsi dead and his story may have been true, but we saw or heard nothing to confirm it. The few houses near the grave all had smashed or burnt doors. The only thing alive was a terrified white rabbit I found in one.

When asked about the injuries to Hutu men, women and children we had seen at Kiremba, the Major replied: "Some were wounded when we were fighting the rebels, that's natural." When asked about the multiple bayonet wounds he suggested that they were in fact caused by spears. When asked whether it was possible to confuse wounds caused by bullets with those caused by machetes or spears he said "it's possible," but he was looking away. He then said the "rebels" had guns, the first time this had been suggested. There had been no confirmed reports of soldiers being killed or wounded, though two of the hundreds of bodies seen floating down the Akanyaru were said to be in uniform.

Dr Anselm Niyongabo, in charge of another government hospital to which the Major sent us, had obviously not been briefed by the Major. He said it was possible to distinguish bayonet and spear wounds, and that there were no injuries caused by bayonets among the fifty-two injured he had treated. Most of them were Tutsi, however, who had reached the hospital quickly. There were few serious infections and no amputees.

We could not really understand why the bloodbath had begun.

The Hutu in the camps in Rwanda said it was because they had
heard another massacre of their people was planned, and decided
that this time they would strike the first blow rather than be
killed like sheep. The Tutsi concentrated on the educated Hutu
in 1972, calmly searching for and killing them on the basis of
such criteria as literacy or the possession of a tie. That took place
throughout the country. The killing was confined to a small area
of the north this time, an area where rumour may have got out
of hand as a result of an unannounced army exercise. There were
also stories of pamphlets inciting violence against the Hutu. We
did not see one.

We felt fairly proud when we got back to phones and telexes.
For once our stories would have a real impact, supporting the
donors' decision to suspend aid programmes to the country until
there was firm evidence the killing had stopped. Since the
government depended on those programmes, and had to react to
the publicity that forced their suspension, the killing stopped
much sooner than in 1972, when it went on for at least two
months.

But those terrible wounds, those previously inconceivable
brutalities had left their mark. I began to feel guilty at my pride
in covering them. I began to wonder whether my careful record
of the horrors, designed to make people react as if they were
confronted by them in person, was not just feeding a desire for
sensation. The suspicion was confirmed shortly afterwards when
I visited the editors at the foreign desk at *The Times*. "Good
story," said one. "Graphic description," said another. I was
numbed. Not one ever asked how it felt to see such things.

My mother had called to ask if I was all right. I was not. One
of the things that most distressed me was that my editors could
read such things and be totally unmoved. That I had become
merely a proxy voyeur of titillating tribal warfare. In the
following months it became increasingly obvious that balance
and an understanding of Africa were of no concern to my editors.
The first comment of one, concerning the Burundi trip, was that
I had appeared unkeen to go. I realized this must be because I
laughed when one of them had rung me in Nairobi and asked
me to get on the next flight that afternoon, as if he were talking

about the shuttle from London to Edinburgh. A map of Africa does make Nairobi look rather close to Bujumbura, until you remember the scale, the irregularity of flights and the likelihood you will be detained or sent straight back if you arrive without a visa.

Of course such editors have usually taken on large mortgages, and are confronted by owners and managers with even less desire to listen or understand. I believe the readers of papers like *The Times* would like to be better served. Those I know say they would, though many have given up. Most were as disgusted as I with the blanket coverage given to the Julie Ward murder. The inquest into the death of one young British woman was given more space than any other story out of black Africa in 1989. It had, as the Hollywood producers fighting to buy the rights from the father would say, everything. Sex, wild animals, a pretty blonde, rampaging Africans, extreme violence and grisly remains for the investigators.

There was a clumsy attempt at a cover-up by suggesting that she had been killed by wild animals, probably with the misguided intention of protecting Kenya's tourist industry. The perpetrators or perpetrator undoubtedly took advantage of the opportunity to cover their tracks. But was it fair to give the coverage of the case such prominence that it may have helped form an image of black Africa that people unfamiliar with it may hold for several years, that it is full of wild animals and corrupt Africans who rape and murder white girls?

Until the late 1980s I thought journalism was a healthy profession, one which could point out injustices rather than perpetrate them. The Julie Ward coverage moved from the first to the second when it was kept on the front page, almost daily, for several weeks. It was Kierkegaard who said he would disown his son if he spent more than five years in journalism. I had spent more than ten to discover that Evelyn Waugh's vicious comedies about journalists and proprietors were in fact brilliant portraits.

Sister Liberatrice's last words to us were: "If you are Christians, pray for this country." We can do better than that, if we want countries like Burundi to provide more than an occasional dose of bloody sensationalism. We can try to persuade newspaper editors to take Africa seriously, and we can try to persuade governments to cancel, not suspend, their aid programmes to dictatorships prepared to send their well-equipped armies out to butcher their citizens. Only then can we call ourselves sufficiently civilized to comment on the civilization of others.

I returned from Burundi to Kenya with a great sense of relief. But in Kenya too tribal rivalries may burst into bloodshed, especially if President Daniel arap Moi continues to keep the lid clamped down by arresting people who advocate a multi-party system and using the police and army to bloody the heads of those who dare demonstrate in its favour. The personality cult developed around him threatens to leave a dangerous vacuum on his departure, and death is the most likely way he will relinquish the presidency. Both the Kikuyu and the Luo, large and politically active tribes, believe they should provide the successor to Moi, from the small Kalenjin tribe. In the absence of more legitimate competition between politicians of all origins and the public development of possible successors violent combat between the two groups becomes more probable. In February 1990 there was strong evidence that under the current climate it was highly dangerous to be considered a possible successor. Robert Ouko, the articulate Luo Foreign Minister, was found murdered near his home.

Beware of Lions
While Walking

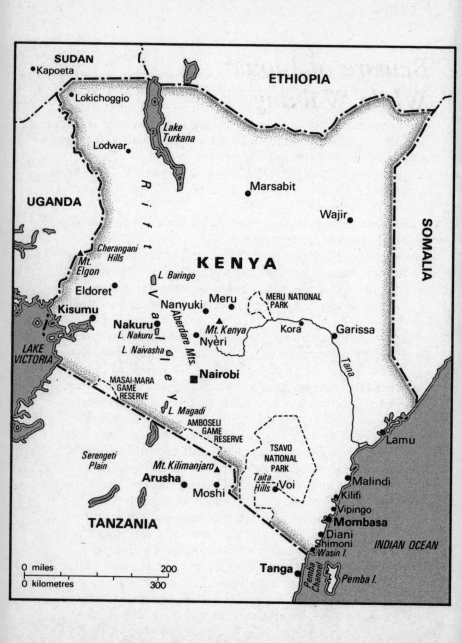

Kenya

These are the words painted on a stone where a dirt road crosses
the Chania river in the Aberdare Mountains National Park in
Kenya. It does not tell you how. The Chania and other streams
in the Aberdares offer good trout fishing in the unusual settings
of tropical rainforest and moorland, but the animals add a certain
spice. It is not an empty warning. A few years ago a Danish
woman was badly mauled. The lion was only scared away by her
husband in a car. I was advised to carry an aerosol fog horn as
a possible deterrent.

The lions in the Aberdares were particularly dangerous because
they were supposedly rehabilitated animals that had been
released there. They had insufficient fear of humans and there
was insufficient easy prey for them. They were forced to hunt
the wily, mean and powerful buffalo, another hazard for
fishermen. The elephants were the only other thing you had to
worry about.

We never worried about the elephant and buffalo as much as
the lions. Though they could kill you they would not try to eat
you, and this was their natural habitat. The lions had been
introduced by some misguided conservationist. Perhaps their
only beneficial effect was to discourage the sort of wholesale
poaching that had nearly wiped out the fish in many of the
streams lower down the mountains, where farmland and the
forest fringes were heavily populated. But then the trout were
even less natural. They were descendants of fish brought to the
country in 1912 by Colonel Ewart Grogan, a settler who is reputed
to have walked from the Cape to Cairo in order to secure the
hand of a lady but then to have decided he did not want her.

The trout, like the parks and the animals in the rest of the
country, are predominantly an attraction for the Europeans,
whether resident or tourist. Though they may generate a large
income, few Africans see any of this. Few Africans give a damn
about trout. If they give a damn about elephants it is because
they contain a large amount of meat and ivory, and destroy

crops. If they care about lions it is because they kill their livestock. There is little uninhabited wilderness in Africa where the animals can wander freely. There probably has not been for centuries. The completely depopulated parks are artificial, though they are necessary to preserve the flora and fauna that can no longer survive the population pressures outside. They will only continue to do this if visitors pay for them. But they are very beautiful.

I drove up into the Aberdares one weekend, to stay with some friends in a cottage on the open moorlands above the forest. When the sun shines up there the air is so clear that distance is difficult to judge. What looks like a little hill nearby may be a mountain which will take you hours to climb. The streams are cool and clear and achingly cold when you wade. But you can always let the equatorial sun dry your clothes later. We stopped at the Honi first. We had no rises, but the sun may have been too high and the water too clear for the trout to ignore our lines. There should have been plenty of fish this high up.

I had fished the Honi, or Amboni, lower down, outside the park, once before. A herdsman came up to talk, speaking very good English. After watching me cast my flies for a fruitless hour he said, "Of course there are not many fish here, the locals catch them as soon as they're put in." I asked if they had licences and was told "We don't believe in that, we live here." The fellow angler you are most likely to see on most of these streams is a brazen poacher who will flick in a bait in front of you. When I asked one if he was worried about the fish scout he replied, "Oh no, he's my brother."

The herdsman offered to find me some illegal worms and show me the best places to use them. I turned the offer down and went on talking. He asked if I could find him a job in Nairobi. It transpired he was an unemployed university graduate, looking after his father's cows. Kenya simply cannot provide enough land or jobs for its rapidly growing population. Though the mountainous areas through which the trout streams flow are highly fertile they are reaching saturation. Crops are planted everywhere. Steep slopes of red earth are bared to the rain and sun. Tea will hold this ground, but is rooted out if the tea price falls. The streams below are increasingly silted, the red torrents taking the land's fertility down to the Indian Ocean in the rainy season.

There is ever more encroachment on the forest reserves, those preservers of ancient hardwoods and guarantors of rainfall. Though you may still find patches of flattened undergrowth or waters muddied by elephants upstream, you are more likely to find the droppings of cattle or the stumps left by illegal woodcutters. In the fields and villages below there are children with runny noses everywhere.

Up on the top of the Aberdares there is nobody. We drove on from the Honi. I was alone in the first of two cars. After a few minutes I saw two lions run from the road into a thicket at its side. When I drove up I found a dead buffalo from which they had been feeding. I thought they might break out of the thicket, only about fifty yards in diameter, into the open ground beyond, so I drove on for about five hundred yards. The other car then arrived by the dead buffalo, and a friend got out to look at it. I yelled that there were lions and he got back in.

I went on, crossing a bad mud hole about half a mile away. I stopped to wait for the others, in case they had trouble getting through. I switched off the engine and wandered a short distance from the car, reasoning that it would be unlikely to run into some more lions so close to the others. Then I thought I heard something and looked back along the road, straining to hear the engine of the other car. I heard breathing behind me. When I turned round there was a lone elephant looking at me. I backed slowly to the car, and he ambled slowly up the hill.

We soon reached the Chania. There were some other people fishing near the road, so I went off into the overgrown area upstream. As I came back down the others mistook the noise in the undergrowth for a wild animal coming their way. When I emerged I found they had retreated to the cars.

The next morning two of us went to fish the Gura river, meandering through a piece of moorland a mile from the cottage. There was a herd of about fifteen elephants feeding in some giant heather upstream, where the best fishing was. We worked slowly towards them. It was a strange and wonderful experience. "Here I am," I said to myself, "standing in front of a herd of elephants under an equatorial sun, casting a fly to shy brown trout in a river as clear, cold and weedy as an English chalk stream." We even caught some, fish with huge, brilliantly coloured spots that we returned to the water in deference to the occasion. We finally gave up when the elephants were about two hundred yards away. They showed no sign of disturbance but our nerve gave out. It was a long way back to the car.

I thought about writing a book about Africa without mentioning the animals at all. Sensible conservation cannot be achieved in Africa before sensible politics addresses the people's needs. It often seems that most conservationists and Western visitors would rather there were no people, except perhaps a few Masai or Pygmies. I have infuriated conservationist friends who asked why I had not written more about the threats to Africa's wildlife, by saying people came first.

Media coverage of Africa often accentuates the idea that the animals come first. The only cover story on black Africa carried by an American news magazine in recent years other than the one previously mentioned, which concerned a famine in Ethiopia in 1987–8 that never happened, gave the impression that the only people in Africa were the Masai, and even they were only mentioned in passing. All the rest was purple prose and glossy photographs of animals and wilderness.

A falconer friend helped the BBC with a wildlife programme. The viewers will not have realized that the hawks and eagles they saw were trained birds. The crew kept aborting shots when a vehicle passed on a distant track, throwing up a dust cloud. My friend asked why they did not leave it in. There are few places in black Africa where there is not some evidence of human habitation. It was not the sort of Africa the viewers expected, said the cameraman. In many of the African wildlife films the pan stops just short of the tourist lodge or telephone line, and starts again just after the road or group of huts. Nor will the viewer see the group of minibuses behind the camera. Many of the drivers in the parks find game by looking for other vehicles that have stopped. The resulting gangs of cars have seriously disrupted the behaviour of animals like cheetahs. Some now hunt in the middle of the day, when the tourists too are having lunch.

Despite the efforts of the wildlife photographers the people will not go away and no wildlife will be preserved without their understanding and support. That support will only be achieved if they see the benefits of the exploitation of wildlife, whether this is through tourism or through culling. In most countries the benefits are reserved for the politicians and their business associates.

A question the conservationists do not like to be asked is: "How many elephants is a good number?" If elephants are properly protected their numbers will grow and you will have to shoot them or allow them to invade and destroy people's crops. The alternative to killing elephants is, eventually, killing people. There is no social security in Africa. If people's crops are destroyed by elephants they may well starve. If you have to shoot elephants what do you do with the tusks? I do not want to buy ivory, but it seems terrible to waste it if the animal has to be or has been killed.

When Kenya proposed an ivory trade ban and burnt its stocks of confiscated ivory in 1989 it gained huge publicity for the African elephant's plight, an estimated halving of the total population in the previous decade to about seven hundred thousand. But what it was really doing was advertising the incompetence of Kenya and other countries to manage their own wildlife. That is why an international trade ban had to take the place of internal control, to the detriment of the elephants and the economy in countries like Zimbabwe, which can manage its herds.

There has been a widespread failure to understand this outside Africa, with tales of the depredations of poachers hitting the headlines, unfettered by any understanding or explanation of the context. It is true that in Kenya numbers have fallen from about one hundred thousand to twenty thousand in the last fifteen years largely as a result of poaching. But the poaching was encouraged both by the greed, corruption and general inefficiency in government departments responsible for wildlife and by a ban on licensed hunting since 1975. The hunters no longer had an interest in supporting stocks and deterring poachers. The officials sat behind their desks, drew their salaries and not infrequently took bribes from the poachers. Why not? Almost everyone else in a single party government takes advantage of his position. There is no opposition with an interest in exposing corruption.

In Zimbabwe controlled hunting has remained legal and the elephant population has held up to the extent that the animals must be shot to prevent them encroaching on agricultural areas or degrading their own habitat. A large portion of the fees the hunter pays there must go to the area where he hunts. This gives the people there a direct return for sustaining local wildlife and compensates them for any crop losses. Poachers will not be popular under these circumstances. They thrive when a distant wildlife department takes no notice of complaints about crop damage, the sole impact of the animals on a poor rural population.

When journalists lambast an individual, legal hunter in Zimbabwe for killing an endangered animal, as they have done, they expose and spread their own ignorance. If we allow licensed hunters to kill selected surplus elephants we may prevent poachers from butchering whole herds. I suppose there will be those who suggest we dart and sterilize the elephants – a solution as practical as cutting the horns off live rhinos to protect them from poachers. Slightly more practical would be a scheme whereby conservationists paid Africans to live somewhere other than the elephants, in other words rented land to extend the parks. In this case the question "How many elephants are a good number?" has a purely pecuniary answer, "As many as we can pay for." There are a lot of Africans in search of land, so the price would be high. Elephants are expensive. We cannot expect African peasant farmers to pay for them.

Dr Richard Leakey, the anthropologist, was appointed as head of Kenya's wildlife department shortly before the burning of Kenya's stocks and the ivory trade ban. Apparently only a European could be trusted to be uncorruptible and raise the money for park equipment and salaries that years of tourist income should have paid for, but didn't. Dr Leakey said he would be a poacher himself if he was paid what the rangers were when he took over. As skilled a publicist as any in his family – his parents Louis and Mary were also famous anthropologists, he had urgently to raise support and money to save Kenya's parks. He agrees the wildlife outside the parks may best be served by a reversal of the hunting ban, but that will have to wait.

It was not so much the decline in elephant numbers that forced the Kenyan government to act, as the extension of the poachers' activities to new fields. First elephants were shot in front of tourist lodges. Then tourists started getting shot and robbed themselves. Things had gone too far. In the long term the decline of the elephants and other wildlife threatened the tourist industry, the country's biggest foreign exchange earner, but dead tourists could bring the bonanza to an abrupt halt.

The anti-poaching units were strengthened and told to shoot to kill. For a while the resulting desperation of the poachers led to an increase in violent incidents, but after a few months of the patient leadership of Dr Leakey, the authorities seemed to regain control of the parks. One of the fatalities in the interim period was George Adamson, the world famous lover of lions. I flew up to Kora, his home in the remote, arid, flat and dull bush of north-eastern Kenya, shortly after his death.

When you arrive at Kora, which almost everybody does by light aircraft, you buzz the camp before landing at the airstrip a couple of miles away, so that a car is sent to pick you up. When this had happened two days before the visitors had waited in vain for one to turn up. The pilot eventually took off with his passengers and raised the alarm after seeing a car stopped on the track with a body on the ground next to it. He may have unwittingly disturbed the killers.

We soon pieced together what had happened. Three gunmen had stopped the car sent to the strip. A German girl staying with George watched as they broke the African driver's legs with an iron bar. George and some of the people working for him at the camp had heard the shots fired when the first car was stopped and set out in another vehicle. He and two of his African staff were killed when they came across the gunmen. Though early reports said they died in a hail of bullets as George drove towards the gunmen, he was shot in the side and back as he passed them or after his car hit a tree. The windscreen on his side of his well-known old Land-rover – which had "All aboard the Nightingale" painted on the side – was intact. There were two bullet holes going out through the dashboard near the steering wheel, which must have been fired from behind.

It looked very much as though George and his staff were killed by shots fired at close range through the windows. There were fewer than ten bullet holes in the bodywork, despite the use of three automatic rifles. One of his staff obviously bled to death. The floor at the back of the car was covered in coagulated blood. George died in the arms of the German girl.

It was argued whether the gunmen were a poaching party who had come across an opportunity for robbery or were planning to kill George from the start, in the hope that the reserve he founded at Kora would then be forgotten. The apparently deliberate way in which he was killed was not the only thing pointing to the latter. George's were almost certainly the only two cars in the area at the time. Very few people drove there. A poacher would know exactly whose they were, and would be unlikely to hunt so near the camp.

One of the gunmen was recognized by the driver of the first vehicle attacked, who had his legs broken, and had been picked up in a small town thirty miles away. "What we are doing now is investigating further to find out who his friends are," said a senior officer at the camp. This sounded ominous for Abdi Osman Sheuri, who was being interrogated at the time. Though a couple of helicopters flew by, there was little sign of further investigative activity at Kora.

Over a hundred of the seven hundred men supposedly involved in the search were lounging around the camp. They had been told not to talk to us. Their officers were sitting at the table in the open sided mess hut, surrounded by old photographs of George, his friends and his lions. They told us to refer to the previous day's press release when we asked questions. Of all the soldiers and policemen present only the senior Army officer talked to us about the case.

All the policemen and soldiers seemed rudely out of place. The key to the whole place had gone. The three half-grown lions in an enclosure, the hornbills and guinea fowl waiting to be fed, and the twenty-odd free lions that lived in the vicinity of the camp were only there because of George. Here he could escape from questions about the value of rehabilitating and releasing lions, and live with them as he chose. The camp was very basic, almost bleak, and eloquent of his obsession. It was surrounded by a high wire fence to keep the lions out. Mr Adamson lived here for eighteen years, but the few thatched huts inside would probably disappear after a couple of rainy seasons if they were abandoned.

I went up to Kora again for the funeral. We had to wait for three aircraft to land before us. A pilot on the ground was running an improvised air traffic control service. After each plane landed another took off to park at another strip twenty miles away, as there was not enough room for all of them at Kora's tiny dirt runway. The flock of aircraft was carrying nearly one hundred old friends, journalists and celebrities to see George buried a few hundred yards from his camp.

Three volleys were fired by an honour guard of rangers over his grave, near that of Boy, a favourite lion he had to shoot after it attacked someone. The "dust to dust" of the funeral service seemed unusually appropriate as the dry earth was thrown on to his coffin and the cameras rolled. Armed men patrolled the surrounding bush. As Mr Adrian House, a publisher who saw George and Joy's books about lions into print, said in his address, the funeral was "slightly more formal than George would have expected".

Another colourful character had temporarily taken over the camp, and, it appeared, George's style of dress. When we arrived Major Douglas Collins was dressed only in shorts. A septuagenarian ex-professional hunter and friend of George, the ex-Game Warden, he also spent ten years with the Somaliland Camel Corps. His knowledge of Somalis would probably be more useful than his relatively limited knowledge of lions.

The three men eventually arrested in connection with the murder of George and his assistants were ethnic Somalis, as are most of the people in north-eastern Kenya. Though banditry and poaching are traditional activities for some of them, known generally as Shifta, the more serious threat to Kora and other north-eastern reserves is that they are part of the vast area the Somalis regard as their ancestral grazing lands.

The three cubs on whose rehabilitation George was working when he was killed were to be sent to Botswana. Even if Major Collins could have duplicated George's skills, there was insufficient game in Kora to support the twenty-odd lions already released there. Some of the money from the fortune made by the Adamsons, all of which was left to wildlife conservation trusts, would have to be used to continue to feed them. The meat would be bought from Somali herdsmen who resented the enclosure of Kora. So much for rehabilitation.

With all the planes and rangers, and probably the biggest influx of visitors Kora had ever seen, it was sometimes hard to remember what everybody was supposed to be there for. Funerals should be for people close to the dead. I had come unwillingly on the instructions of my paper. One of my colleagues asked a genuine mourner why he was there. "To say goodbye to George," said Mr Bill Travers, who played George to his wife, Virginia McKenna's Joy in the film Born Free. They had become good friends, and his reply had an element of rebuke.

Though the publicists of the conservation world used it to their advantage, the saddest thing about George's death was its futility. Kora had been made a National Reserve for George. The five hundred square mile area was so designated three years after he moved there. He had picked Kora because it was so remote, having been forced to leave Meru National Park after a released lion mauled a tourist. Following his death it was to be made a full National Park. Unfortunately this had no more point in terms of conservation than the rehabilitation of lions. On my two visits to Kora we scanned the bush carefully for game. All we saw was a single jackal. Apart from George's lions there were virtually no animals of note, and there was little need to conserve the lions anyway. The lion is not an endangered species. You can become bored by them in the major parks.

George's personal love for Kora and the power of his name had prevented the government from taking a more sensible decision. Kora could have been given back to the pastoralists, so relieving the pressure on and freeing funds for other, more important parks and reserves. But at least George was trying to do something about Africa's future. Most of the Europeans are fiddling while Rome burns.

In Kenya there is still a round of polo, racing and riding, reinforced by tennis, squash, golf and snooker at various clubs. On holiday it's the coast or a safari in the bush. The question "Are you married, or do you live in Kenya?' still has a certain relevance. The parties are as wild as ever. I went to a mad hatter's lunch at an old farmhouse near Nakuru. A couple of hundred people lolled on hay bales or played croquet, glasses of Pimms in hand, all in outlandish costumes. A helicopter arrived with a couple of people who were already so drunk they fell out and went to sleep on the grass. The pilot left without them.

As things warmed up people started betting on swimming races in the muddy lake at the end of the lawn. On the far side several hundred local Africans watched in silence. Many of the guests stayed the night and danced for most of it. People started drinking Bloody Marys soon after they got up, and then a convoy drove off to a trout farm nearby to eat fresh trout. Several of the cars were open and we were caught in a cloud burst on the way, so there was ample excuse, if any were needed, for copious brandies. As Evelyn Waugh was told after a similar few days, "You'll love Kenya, it's always like this."

The weekends often seem to be, but during the week some of these people run successful businesses which employ thousands of Africans. If they were given a freer hand they could employ many more, and offer some hope of providing incomes for the millions of new Kenyans produced by a 4 per cent population growth rate. Less than 20 per cent of Kenya is arable and little of that is left unexploited, so new businesses offer the only hope of absorbing the growth.

Kenya has a capitalist economy which has so far functioned far better than most in sub-Saharan Africa. When Nyerere criticized it as a "man eat man" society, according to a probably apocryphal exchange, Charles Njonjo, at the time a powerful Kenyan politician, is said to have replied that Tanzania was a "man eat nothing" society. The problem is that the greed of those in government negates the official policy, which is to encourage foreign and local investment. A friend spent months and thousands of pounds in bribes to get the half-dozen permits and licences needed to open a business. If he had known how bad it would be, he said, he would never have tried – and fifty people would be unemployed.

If you eventually become successful you face another threat. This applies as much to Kenyan citizens of European or Indian origin as to expatriates, and even to African businessmen without good connections. A senior politician will probably try to take over your business. An offer will be made, often in the foreign currency to which such people have access and usually specifying that the management stays. Some offers have been resisted by the management threatening to pull out, but usually the entrepreneur is forced to comply. Otherwise trading licences and the like can suddenly become very hard to renew. This even applies to subsidiaries of major overseas investors. Several have sold up in the last decade. No major new investors have arrived.

Contractors tendering for civil engineering or building projects have another problem. Unless they offer between 10 and 20 per cent of the contract value at the highest levels they stand little chance of winning. Their response is to build this cost into the bid, so that those financing the project, usually the Kenyan government in conjunction with an aid donor – in other words Kenyan and Western taxpayers – are robbed. Another unofficial tax is collected, some would say extorted, from businesses in the form of regular "donations" to KANU (the sole ruling party, the Kenya African National Union). To refuse is again to court the withdrawal of some crucial trading licence or the discovery of some petty infraction.

It is for such reasons that many people welcomed suggestions from Church leaders and out of favour politicians that a multi-party system be introduced in Kenya. Accountability might discourage such damaging abuses. The incumbents trotted out the old argument about tribalism. It is unlikely they will easily be dislodged from their lucrative positions. But this may be the only way Kenya can avert the fate it currently faces – the ugly growth of lawless urban sprawls packed with the unemployed, the destructive settlement of marginal land that guarantees famine in the inevitable dry years.

An American ambassador was so depressed by this prospect, and his belief that it was too late to avert, that he said he wished Kenya had a Marxist regime. If Kenya, supposedly a model for capitalist development in Africa, fell apart what hope would there be to encourage countries like Tanzania to open up their economies? As Eastern Europe showed, however, it is a mistake to dismiss the possibility of rapid and radical political reform. It is probably the only way disaster can be averted.

The sheer number of people the economy must cater for is the biggest problem. For most Kenyans a large family – eight is still the norm – remains desirable for cheap labour, security in old age and male pride. Politicians are afraid to comment on birth control, leaving the field to a handful of aid workers. One I know has spent several years trying to popularize vasectomies. In her first year she achieved one. She has since, she jokes, had a huge increase in productivity. She was hoping to achieve double figures in 1990.

Another friend took me with a mobile family planning clinic to a Masai *manyatta* or homestead. We were towing a water bowser. This kept the women in the homestead for our visit. Normally they had to walk long distances to collect water. The dry season was also the family planning season. Before emptying the bowser they had to listen to a Masai nurse extolling the benefits of various types of contraceptive.

Twenty of them sat on rocks under a thorn tree, their woven bead necklaces and ear-rings and red and blue robes setting off the fine features of their cropped heads. They laughed and joked at the nurse's words. The men, in shorter robes, some with hair dyed red, sat in silence on the other side of the tree.

Perhaps it was not surprising that only one woman asked for an injection of depoprovera, which lasts for about three months. The others believed that contraceptives might prevent them from ever having another child and warned her they would tell her husband, one of the few men not present. One of them asked why the first time any medical team came to see them it was to tell them not to have children. What about the health of the existing ones?

The manyatta was only an hour's drive from Nairobi's modern office blocks, but was untouched by the technology so close to it. It was surrounded by the classic thorn *boma*, or fence, that protected the cattle at night. Livestock, decorative clothing and ornaments were the only possessions in which these people had much interest. You had to crouch to enter the oblong huts, made of sticks and plastered with cow dung for a roof, that remained the standard dwelling. Inside there were rough couches covered with hides, and gourds for milking the cattle. Like most of the Masai these people had stuck to their traditional way of life, with what one suspected was a polite contempt for outsiders behind the dignity with which they greeted them.

In the evening we saw large herds of cattle and goats returning to many similar manyattas in this part of the rift valley near Lake Magadi. Flourishing and inedible weeds proclaim it is being overgrazed. In some of the manyattas more women are beginning at least to space their families. Joel Sayianka, a local chief, had one wife and two children, and is encouraging his people to follow the example. His father and his several wives had fifty-one children.

Throughout Kenya, whether among the Luo in the west, the Kikuyu in the fertile central highlands, the various tribes of the crowded coastal villages or the mixed populations of the towns, you hear similar stories. A sixty-nine-year-old man in western Kenya said he had married one hundred and twenty six times and fathered four hundred and ninety-seven children. He was known as Mr Denja – a phonetic spelling for danger.

An estimated eight hundred thousand school leavers a year compete for one hundred and twenty thousand formal jobs. The city streets are full of hustlers, hawkers and shoe shine boys. There are the parking boys too, who keep an eye on your car for a small fee, a mild form of protection. But the message about contraception is not getting through fast enough. Fifty thousand of the school leavers are girls who drop out because of pregnancy. Over 20 per cent of the admissions to the gynaecological department at the main hospital in Nairobi are women and girls requiring treatment after back-street abortions.

Parents say it's up to their children to cut down their families to two or three. With over half the estimated population of twenty-five million under fifteen, this still means a massive continued expansion. Even if today's under-fifteens do cut family size the population is expected to reach thirty-six million by the end of the century, and fifty million within the following two decades. Similar rates of population growth are expected throughout sub-Saharan Africa, and most countries are far worse equipped than Kenya to offer the new people even the basic necessities of life.

It has been suggested that AIDS will prevent this population growth from occurring. It may only slow it slightly. Note that the projections are based on the optimistic assumption that today's under-fifteens only have two children each. Compare that with the current rich human fertility. Even if a large percentage of women catch and eventually succumb to the AIDS virus, they will probably have had several healthy children already or others will have made up for them.

A much higher incidence of the virus than in Kenya has been reported in some other African countries. But statistics are notoriously unreliable in sub-Saharan Africa, which makes for good newspaper scare stories but means it is too early to predict the final impact on the population. Those tested are often sexually active urban dwellers who could be expected to have a higher than normal proportion of positives.

Another factor that people unfamiliar with Africa may find hard to understand is the existing high rate of mortality from other diseases. People who die of AIDS might otherwise have died from malaria, tuberculosis, measles, gastro-intestinal infections or simply starvation. By reducing the size of families they may make the others healthier and more resistant to other diseases. Even the loss of parents may not be particularly serious in this context. The extended family remains the norm in Africa. It is unlikely that AIDS or any other disease will relieve the growing pressure on Africa's resources.

Will my favourite river, a little over an hour's drive from

Nairobi, be the same in a few years? For the moment the squatters have not reached this secret, forested ravine. As you climb down all you can see are the tall, pale trunks of the hardwoods highlighted against the dark green canopies and the paler green, feathery fronds of the tree ferns. Colobus monkeys may bark a warning at your presence, and swish off through the branches with their black and white manes flying. You may notice that an elephant has rubbed itself against a tree you lean on.

At the bottom is the river, clear and inviting as it winds past cliff faces half-concealed by the foliage. Streams of butterflies pass along it and occasional bushbuck come nervously down to drink. There are leopards here, but I have not seen one yet. Will I ever see one? Will these pools fill up with silt, the rain and trees stripped away irretrievably for a couple of harvests? Will the whole continent be despoiled by ravening millions and left a desert of misery? I don't know, but I cannot give up hope.

Conclusion

Hope needs to be supported by action. The West must stop giving money to corrupt and dictatorial governments in Africa. To talk about favouring the more democratic countries is not enough. There is no time for delay, but racism is alive and well in Western capitals. We are treated to the extraordinary sight of Western governments that welcomed the developments in Eastern Europe continuing to support some of the most repressive dictatorships in Africa. Meanwhile the independent aid agencies' indirect support of these dictatorships also continues, as they go on persuading people to give money for what are supposed to be purely apolitical, humanitarian purposes.

Many agencies still had large programmes in northern Sudan at the famine-free end of the eighties, unconcerned by the arrival of General Omer el-Bashir's military junta, which was prepared to countenance the hanging of black-marketeers, the crucifixion of armed robbers, and the torture of political and religious opponents by a fanatical islamic group known as the Shabab el-Bina, or Youth for Reconstruction. Governments in Sudan had fallen to popular protest before, usually precipitated by shortages of bread or other necessities. "Humanitarian assistance" helped prevent this from happening again, as it has elsewhere in the continent. It is often a very costly indulgence for Western guilt about African poverty.

People may say it is paternalist to advocate the determined use of aid, humanitarian and otherwise, to encourage political and economic freedoms in Africa. Yet aid is never neutral. We are not afraid of using our influence elsewhere. Why this exaggerated respect for the most absurd and unpleasant regimes? One wonders if the West wants any more in Africa than the maintenance of dictatorships just sufficiently powerful to guarantee a fairly constant supply of cheap agricultural and mineral commodities that cannot be found elsewhere.

It is usually only such dictatorships that can implement the Structural Adjustment Programmes drawn up by the IMF and

World Bank, the West's only serious contribution to economic recovery in Africa. That these make further economic assistance conditional on realistic exchange rates and fair payments to producers is all to the good. That they also require the end of food subsidies and the opening of markets to imports is questionable. There is no reciprocal opening of Western markets to Africa's agricultural potential. Parts of Africa could grow more food more cheaply than almost anywhere else on the globe, if it could be sold.

The West, particularly the European Community, pays huge subsidies to its farmers, a small percentage of the population, to produce more food than it requires. The surpluses depress world prices to the point where farmers in Africa have little incentive to grow their own surpluses for export markets. When famine comes around again, the West congratulates itself on giving some of the food mountain which helped cause the problem in the first place. Then the farmers' enterprise is further sapped as poorly targeted food aid undermines the local markets. A question has to be answered. Does the cosseting of hundreds of thousands of Western farmers justify condemning hundreds of millions of farmers in Africa and other parts of the third world to the margin of survival?

At Naivasha, in Kenya's rift valley, is an example of what can be done when the protected farmers in Europe are not threatened by African products. From September to May flowers, fruit and vegetables are grown with water pumped from a lake full of hippos and pelicans. They are flown to European markets starved of fresh produce by the winter. So far at least, the farmers of southern Europe cannot meet the demand, and so have not started to demonstrate against cheap imports. The two largest farms at Naivasha employ nearly five thousand people and export $20m worth of flowers a year.

American growers have accused the Kenyan producers of dumping flowers, however. You can be sure that the Europeans will do the same if they start growing large quantities of similar items at the same time of year. The startling success of the Naivasha horticulturalists depends on the absence of protection in Europe. To forego the protection of Western producers in other areas would be far more beneficial to Africa and probably far cheaper than current aid programmes, let alone future ones.

Western policy should reflect that a more prosperous Africa, capable of feeding itself and others, buying our goods and supporting its forests and animals, is undoubtedly to our advantage. The alternative is a human and environmental disaster on an unprecedented scale. Africa must be allowed to take advantage of its natural resources and cheap labour by using both efficiently. This will only happen if economic liberalization is supported by political liberalization. It is in the West's gift to hasten this process.

There are those who do not think we need bother with such initiatives. They trust that AIDS will avert Africa's environmental disaster, if not the human one. Even if this was not unlikely it would be monstrously inhumane to sit back while the population growth rate was slowed in such a way. Population growth, like AIDS, will only be restrained by economic growth that enables people to see and plan for a future. An African working for me explained the prostitution, promiscuity, venereal disease and high birth rates of the crowded slums of Nairobi in one short sentence. "What else is there to do?"

An aggressive campaign to support political reform could be started immediately. The results will take time to emerge. But patience is more of an African virtue than a European. A herdsman came up to us once under an extinct volcano in the Kedong Valley. We were watching the cars from the Kenyan Safari Rally hurtle by, trailing great plumes of dust. We told him they would only take an hour and a half to reach Nairobi. He told us it would take him three days. After a moment's thought he asked, "But what do they do with the extra three days?"

As I have written before, one must be highly sceptical of some countries' claims to be moving towards pluralism. In many countries it is still being actively resisted. I was accused of a colonialist hangover on Ugandan Radio for writing that elections organized by President Yoweri Museveni in 1989 were designed to legitimize his dictatorship. No parties were allowed to campaign. Museveni's National Resistance Movement was not deemed to be a party.

In Nigeria the military government of General Ibrahim Babangida has promised a return to civilian government under an imposed two party system. The process has been delayed by the inability of the government to find any parties acceptable to it. It has decided to create a couple of its own design. Wags said they should be called the "Yes party" and the "Yessir party". The Sudanese military government has organized seminars to give a spurious intellectual credibility to the idea that a no party state echoing Libya's popular democracy is the ideal.

After two decades of a political philosophy defined as Mobutisme in Zaire, one must doubt the sincerity of President Mobutu in establishing a multi-party system. A group of other West African nations finally decided to intervene in the Liberian civil war in August 1990, in order to try to install an interim government committed to organizing elections. Neither of the two countries taking a leading role, Nigeria and Ghana, had any obvious qualifications. Both had military governments with little experience of elections at home.

In Kenya, as we have seen, President Moi ordered a Police and Army crackdown on supporters of multi-party democracy in July 1990. The American ambassador was lambasted for having spoken in its favour. The British Ambassador was resolutely silent on the subject. President Moi had been a moderate black African ally for Mrs Thatcher at international summits. The price for this was abstinence from public criticism of his government. Yet the leverage that could be exerted by the aid donors had been conclusively demonstrated only a few months before.

The media offshoot of Kenya's ruling party, which runs one of the country's three English language newspapers in conjunction with Robert Maxwell, proposed building a sixty-storey skyscraper, with a four-storey statue of Moi in front of it, in a park in the middle of Nairobi. The building would have been taller than anything in Europe, let alone Africa. There was no shortage of existing office space. The leader of a small but vociferous movement protesting against the building was described as having "insects in her head" by the President, and it became a matter of national or rather party pride to complete it. The estimated cost of close to $200m was equivalent to a third of the annual aid budget. The IMF, World Bank and other donors quietly let it be known that Kenya obviously did not need further assistance from them if it could afford such follies. The skyscraper was cancelled.

The donors could be a lot tougher. The IMF identified over $1bn in overseas assets held by Kenyans by the mid-eighties, contrary to the country's strict but regularly flouted foreign exchange laws. Many people believe the true figure could now be as high as $4bn, or roughly equivalent to the country's foreign debt. Despite the obvious lack of accountability that enables such money to be channelled outside Kenya and prevents it from being invested within the country, the donors keep pouring good money after bad. A similar situation applies in many African countries. The Western taxpayers who provide the money will only get value for it if reforms are forced on African governments.

When people like President Robert Mugabe of Zimbabwe go on saying that the one party system is the most appropriate for Africa, it is hard to avoid the conclusion that their personal power is more important to them than the end of the civil wars and economic inefficiency the system spawns. Would Mugabe himself not have preferred to seek power through elections without having to force the previous government to hold them by war? The fact that the government was controlled by a white minority does not alter the principle. Though the single parties are supposed to reflect grassroots opinion, I have yet to see or hear of one in which the power does not flow downwards from the top, so preventing the emergence of any alternatives to the dictates of the leadership.

The road to real democracy in Africa will be long. I remember struggling from my office to lunch with a colleague one day in Nairobi, and fuming: "How can we expect democracy when people don't even know how to walk on the pavements?" The lack of awareness of others is such that pedestrians stop, turn into your path or step into the roads without thought. The drivers' regard for traffic regulations — indeed observance of any law not strictly enforced — is equally scanty. There is little sense of community or civic duty. But why regard laws made by a government imposed upon you? The sooner the first steps to democracy are taken the better.

In places like Zambia there are signs the people can force their leaders to take those steps. Riots forced Dr Kenneth Kaunda to propose a referendum on the one party state. He then postponed it for a year, presumably to give him time to arrange a result in his favour. Finally he cancelled the referendum altogether, and promised multi-party elections by October 1991.

The rioters in Zambia and Kenya may know little about operating multi-party systems, but they do know that the old systems have failed them. The politicians who have proposed or accepted pluralism may know little more about it. Often their main motivation is that they have fallen from favour, and so have been excluded from a single party gravy train. Both Kenneth Matiba and Charles Rubia, advocates of the multi-party system in Kenya, were previously ministers. But they may help to open doors which cannot later be closed.

An obstacle to the use of aid as a weapon for political reform will be the accusations of callousness from aid workers worried about their jobs and pleading for support from the Western public. Media coverage of Africa is so poor that most people in the West see only the pictures of hungry children designed to pull at their heart and purse strings. Most of the media just portray the misery, not the context and underlying causes, so people think all that is required is money for an occasional appeal to top up government assistance. The appeals concentrate on the real or supposed natural causes of a disaster or famine rather than the political ones, reinforcing the belief that a few million dollars will put everything right. It is surprising that more contributors have not drawn any conclusions to the contrary from the appeals' growing frequency.

The low level of public awareness means that Western governments can safely work on the assumption that their constituents will not complain about their treatment of Africa and the Africans. It allows the current, genuinely callous policies to remain in place. This will only change if the media stops seeing

Africa as a source of entertainment, usually ghoulish. A colleague had lunch with the foreign news editor of what is supposed to be a quality newspaper before leaving to take up a post in Nairobi. He asked the man what he thought would be the perfect story out of Africa. "Pygmies with AIDS," came the prompt reply.

Another great obstacle to the use of aid to encourage pluralism has disappeared with the end of the cold war. Though donor countries may be reluctant to withdraw support from old client dictatorships because of short term advantages in concessions, contracts and trade, strategic importance is no longer an overriding concern. The days when the Americans and Soviets competed for influence in Africa as if the countries were pieces in some gigantic board game are over.

Some unpleasant regimes may look to the Chinese, Iraqis or other pariahs of the day for support. Several refrained from criticizing the killing in Tiananmen Square, or even supported the Chinese government, so warning their own student agitators. But in general the prospects for isolating and toppling dictatorships in Africa are better now than at any time since the beginning of the independence era. For the first time our interests happily coincide with those of the Africans.

There are Africans willing to take up the challenge. There are politicians who desire more than a Mercedes and luxurious mansions. I once sat on the floor in a simple house in Gaborone, the capital of Botswana, the vast but sparsely populated southern African democracy, discussing Africa's problems with my host as we ate chicken barbecued by his own hand. The other guests had taken all the chairs. My host was a young technocrat, Peter Mmusi, the Finance Minister and subsequently also the Vice-President of Botswana. There are others throughout the continent who would follow a similar path, but most of them are bemused by the way the rest of the world treats Africa, despair of getting their views heard and eschew politics in favour of business or exile. They need a little encouragement. Is it beyond a supposedly civilized world to foster good government, peace and prosperity in one of its largest continents?

London, September 1990

Epilogue

Since I finished this book eighteen months ago, the changes in sub-saharan Africa have been more dramatic than anybody expected. All but a handful of countries have promised or even started to implement some form of multi-party system. The end of the wars and famines that the old single-party dictatorships spawned seemed to be in sight. But as some of these wars have grumbled to an end and some of the old dictators have fallen, further chaos and misery has been unleashed. Would some countries, perhaps the whole region, collapse entirely and irrevocably into lawlessness? Did the old despots at least have the virtue of maintaining some sort of order?

When we come back from a deep-sea fishing competition off Malindi, on Kenya's northern coast, in February 1991, we found a dhow covered with people pitching and rolling in the unprotected harbour. We passed it in the dinghy on the way to the jetty, looking at the rows of grey-faced Somali refugees sitting all over the deck, and even on the roof of the deckhouse. There was no room to lie down.

We were glad to get ashore, our eyes and bodies worn down by a day-long procession of white-crested deep blue waves under an inescapable sun, but the Kenyan authorities weren't letting the Somalis ashore. They would rock in misery all night. It was as if the Kenyans thought the anarchy in their northern neighbour was a contagious disease. A bunch of them, including a few policemen, eyed the Somalis from the jetty a mere hundred yards away. The Somalis could see the fish and coolboxes we brought ashore from our well-equipped fishing cruisers, but the Kenyans would allow no food or water to reach them.

That evening we watched from the sea-front as the dhow bounced relentlessly up and down. The Somalis are not a nautical people. A shiver passed down our backs as we considered, drink in hand and a delicious dinner being cooked, the sort of things that had made these people flee their homes. When Siad Barre's government in Somalia collapsed under the onslaught of several rebel groups a few weeks before, merely to be a member of the wrong Somali clan could be a death warrant. The mutilated bodies of Barre's soldiers lay on the streets of Mogadishu, left unburied by long-suppressed rebel clansmen. For the civilians who survived the shooting there was no water or food. A year later, at the beginning of 1992, the killing continued in Mogadishu, as the victorious rebel clans turned their guns on each other.

Somebody bought another round. "It's just because it's the sort of country where we can do things like this," I justified, "that they have come here." But we were wondering how far Kenya really was from such a collapse into brutality, where the only hope of security lay in the might of the nearest tribal warlord. In some ways Somalia was very close. Not far inland from Malindi you had to have a police escort to drive some of the roads because of Shifta, ethnic Somali bandits and poachers. A few of the routes in north-eastern Kenya were permanently closed to the public. The tourists in the parks and coastal resorts didn't usually know this. The refugees will have made the situation worse. For every one on a boat there may have been ten crossing a mostly unmarked border on foot or camel, probably armed.

The Somali boat people were obviously desperate. They came in all sorts of craft, undeterred by frequent shipwrecks. An estimated four hundred and fifty died in one incident alone, when a dhow hit a reef. None of them could swim. There were several small Somali fishing boats in Kilifi, the little port south of Malindi, in early 1991. Their skippers said the refugees would come to the harbours in Somalia with grenades, prepared to blow themselves and the boats up if they did not take them to Kenya.

Plenty of people said that Africa was falling apart, that the collapse of government and order in places like Somalia and Liberia showed that Africa was regressing to a precolonial situation where the only thing that mattered was how many men with spears the local chief had – except that now it was AK47s. But the brutal governments in these countries were kept in place for years by aid from the West and the Soviet Union. That came to an end with the Cold War. The long-awaited opportunity for revenge had arrived, not terminal lawlessness.

Ethiopia was another place that the pessimists cited as an example of the descent into anarchy and barbarism. Mengistu's last days were chaotic enough, but suddenly, in May 1991, he had gone. Within a few weeks the last cities in Eritrea had fallen to its secessionist rebels and Addis Ababa itself was overrun by the internal rebel movement the Eritreans had encouraged. But far from plunging the Ethiopian capital, and indeed the whole region, into a further bout of killing, they managed to establish interim governments for Ethiopia and Eritrea, both promising open elections within a couple of years. Imperfect as they are, these new governments have given the people they govern a prospect of peace and security unheard of for decades. In Eritrea in particular *de facto* independence has brought thirty years of violence to an end.

In other countries, most notably in Angola and Mozambique, totalitarian governments have proven willing to relinquish their monopoly of power, abandon Marxism in favour of pluralism and so offer an end to long-running civil wars. If peace unleashes the exploitation of their huge natural resources Africa's currently grim economic statistics could read very differently in a few years.

There is a down side, of course. It may be years before Somalia and Liberia are again controlled by single, reasonably stable governments. Apart from the internecine fighting in Mogadishu, the rebel movement controlling northern Somalia has announced secession, but Somali nationalism is too strong indefinitely to allow a divided country. In Liberia too, people are tiring of the blood feuds, and it should be remembered that these two blackspots have two of Africa's smallest populations.

Places like Ethiopia and Sudan may never be the same single entities again, but all to the good. Eritrea and southern Sudan have very good cases for independence. Nor is it a coincidence that the countries facing famine – Ethiopia, Sudan, Somalia, Liberia, Mozambique, and Angola – are those where there have been major civil wars. The periodic droughts are only the trigger of famines made inevitable by war and misgovernment. In at least half of these countries the end of war and misgovernment, and so of famine, is in sight. This is a huge improvement over the last two decades.

All the agony we are seeing is not evidence of a continent-wide descent into anarchy and misery, it is part of the death throes of the post-independence convention of Africa, where dictators gave themselves spurious credibility through their single parties, despoiled their countries, and forced their opponent into violence, financed all the while by craven foreign governments. Though post-colonial guilt played a part, it should be a source of shame that most of the finance came from Western democracies.

In the early nineties it began to dawn on governments in these Western democracies that instead of throwing a little money at the famines, they should be aiming to shorten the death throes by supporting those countries genuinely moving towards pluralism, and cutting off all aid, except the most essential and directly targeted emergency relief, to those where dictators were stubbornly clinging to power. For a long time the foreign ministries dithered, tempted by the short-term stability the old autocrats seemed to offer, unwilling to act on the conclusions they had so slowly reached about the disastrous long-term results of supporting African dictators. They finally realized that without more responsible and responsive government, in other words more democracy, even countries like Kenya could indeed go the way of Somalia or Liberia.

The dramatic changes of the last two years have not been limited to the war zones. The old autocrats who merely exposed their subjects to economic ruin have also proved more vulnerable than previously supposed. Kenneth Kaunda was voted out in Zambia, and went peacefully. President Moi was eventually forced to concede multi-party democracy in Kenya. He had ruthlessly resisted internal protests for over two years, but when Britain finally joined with other donors to freeze the massive aid programme on which he depended, pending economic and political reforms, he capitulated within a few weeks.

Reforms in Kenya may allow the already relatively sophisticated economy to throw off the fetters imposed by the greed and corruption of the politicians who controlled it. It is likely that some parties, in Kenya and elsewhere, will organize on tribal lines, but the single-party system does not suppress tribalism, it entrenches it, leaving those left out of government to build up resentment and a desire for revenge, while those in charge treat the nation's resources as their own.

Of course we cannot expect the immediate development of paragons of democracy in Africa. President Moi, for example, was widely expected to call a snap election early in 1992 in the hope of securing a further term before the opposition parties could organize. All too often the new African "democrat" will be the old dictator, awarding himself 70 per cent of the vote instead of the old 98 per cent. It is important that Western foreign ministries and other aid donors do not slip back into old habits, and renew support to such leaders after cosmetic electoral exercises.

A show of democracy is unlikely to satisfy many Africans for long. The principle of peaceful opposition has been widely accepted and even unsuccessful oppositions can influence government. The most important aspect of democracy is in sight in much of Africa, that people may soon be able to say no to their governments without having to pick up a gun. Economic growth should follow this political growth, but only if the rest of the world opens its markets to African products. Agricultural protection in Europe, America, and Japan has become the biggest threat to African prosperity.

One wonders why the old dictators think they still have something to offer. Think of an old man living in a once-resplendent mansion. He does not see the cracks, the rot, the unspeakable items hidden in disused rooms. They have developed slowly and he has been able to put each out of mind in succession. He still sees the pristine paintwork and well-furnished rooms of his youth. So it was with the dictators and their apologists in the state houses across Africa. They grew used to explaining away the dilapidation, the corruption, and the unspeakable tortures and deaths. They still saw the beautiful countries they had the amazing luck to take over. They still have not realized that the important thing was not just to take them over, but to make them work. It is a lesson the new democracies must not forget.

February 1992